GW01036251

THE CHILDREN OF DRANCY

FOR PEGGY

By the same author

ESSAYS
Escape from the Anthill (Mullingar: The Lilliput Press, 1985,
    paperback 1986)

HISTORY
Ten Thousand Saints: A Study in Irish and
    European Origins (Kilkenny: Wellbrook Press, 1972)

TRANSLATION
The Thief by Leonid Leonov (London: Martin
    Secker, 1931)
The Cherry Orchard by Chekhov (London: H. W. Dean, 1934)

THE CHILDREN
OF DRANCY

HUBERT BUTLER

With a Foreword by
R. F. FOSTER

THE LILLIPUT PRESS
MULLINGAR
1988

Copyright © Hubert Butler 1988

All rights reserved. No part of this publication
may be reproduced in any form or by any means
without the prior permission of the publisher.

First published in 1988 by
THE LILLIPUT PRESS LTD
Gigginstown, Mullingar
Co. Westmeath, Ireland

British Library Cataloguing in Publication Data

Butler, Hubert, 1900–
The children of Drancy
I. Title
082

ISBN 0-946640-19-X

Jacket design by Jarlath Hayes
Set in 10 on 12 Palatino by
Koinonia Ltd of Manchester
and printed in England by
Billings & Sons Ltd of Worcester

CONTENTS

ACKNOWLEDGMENTS

Thanks and acknowledgments are due to the editors and publishers of the following periodicals, newspapers and radio programmes in which various parts of this volume first appeared.

'In the Adriatic': Section III, BBC Third Programme, 17 October 1957, under title 'A Journey to Split'.

'In Russia':Sections I and II,*The Irish Times*, 6 November 1956 and 7-8 January 1957.

'In China': Sections I-IV, *The Irish Times*, 16, 19-21 November 1956; Section V, *Peace News*, 30 August 1957.

'Maria Edgeworth': A Radio Éireann Thomas Davis Lecture, January 1954.

'Boucher de Perthes: The Father of Prehistory': *Social Biology and Human Affairs*, 1986.

'Ernest Renan: The Statue and the Calvary': *The Listener*, 31 August 1950, now expanded.

'I. . . I Suppose So: *Maria Cross* Reconsidered': *The Bell*, January 1954.

'Reflections on Royalty': Conflation of 'A King's Story' and 'British Royalty and Ireland', *The Bell*, March and June 1952.

'Nurseries of Writing': *The Bell*, August 1951.

'Saints, Scholars and Civil Servants': *The Bell*, November 1954.

'Zhivago's Creator': Sections I and II, *The Irish Times*, 18 July 1959 and 27 September 1958.

'On Loving Bulls': *The Irish Times*, 2 March 1964.

'Thalburg Revisited': *The Kilkenny Magazine*, Summer 1967.

'Carl von Ossietzky': *The Irish Times*, 6 June 1954.

'The Children of Drancy': *The Irish Review*, No. 4, Spring 1988.

FOREWORD

The chord struck by Hubert Butler's first collection of essays reverberated in the world at large with a resonance that may have surprised him. Or it may not. Writing beautifully crafted pieces, often on unpopular subjects, for a variety of short-lived or obscure journals, may not seem an obvious way to make one's voice carry. But in Butler's credo, truth echoes all the more clearly when it avoids a metropolitan forum; and the reception of *Escape from the Anthill* in Ireland, Britain and America vindicated the priorities firmly based on Kilkenny and Gigginstown. It was also a vindication of a lifetime's resolute intellectual combat in defence of that secular, libertarian ethic which can be discerned as a thin but continuous tributary stream into the main flow of Irish cultural history.

Why does Hubert Butler's voice speak so clearly and authoritatively – not only to those who lived, like himself, through the era of fascism, war and the 1950s ice-age, but also to a generation like my own, intellectually conditioned (and often disillusioned) by the various false dawns of the 1960s? Perhaps because the detachment, scepticism and tough-mindedness of the eighteenth century is nowadays more comprehensible to us than the confident certitudes of the nineteenth; and Butler as an essayist is firmly in an eighteenth-century tradition. The vehemence of his attack on C. P. Snow's innocent faith in 'science' is just one illustration to be found in the pages that follow. What he calls that 'terrible disease' of a hatred of reason identifies the enemy. Religious 'enthusiasm' (in the Enlightenment sense) is mercilessly skewered and unpicked, whether in the form of Graham Greene's intellectual evasions (as Butler conceives them) or the hilarious self-delusions of Thomas Merton. He has an acute eye for vanity masquerading as self-disgust; I should like to read a dissection by him of Westerners who folk v

Eastern charlatans like Bhagwan Shree Rajneesh. And yet his essays are pervaded by a sympathy for that helpless hope for a better world on earth which identifies so many characters in Chekhov. Attempts to realize this, in experiments such as the Oneida community in New York State, or at New Geneva in County Waterford, provide a recurring theme in Butler's essays, and it lies behind a lifelong fascination with Russia.

But solipsistic 'ideal' communities are not the way to a better world, and often go rancidly wrong. Individualism (again, in an Enlightenment sense) and awkwardness are to be treasured. In Butler's view, as expressed here, the only real believers that 'all men are equal' are the champions of class distinctions, who rely on arbitrarily partitioning people into horizontally divided shelves. Identities, relationships and perceptions are far more complicated than that. There is a characteristically subtle and penetrating passage in the haunting essay 'Peter's Window', which concludes *Escape from the Anthill*. It is a reflection inspired by participating with his friends in a Leningrad march celebrating the Fifteenth Anniversary of Socialist Construction in 1932:

I have thought that just as half our physical lives passes in sleep, it is perhaps intended that our mental life should be equally distributed between the assertion of our uniqueness and its renunciation. If that trance-like state of submersion in a public or collective mood bears an analogy to sleep, it would reflect our individual and self-centred lives by very simple images and phrases in dream-like sequences. In such a way, the caricatures and slogans that floated above them would complement, like dreams, the intricate, logical natures of Kolya and the baroness. The slogans were the shadows of human thinking in which their thoughts merged restfully, just as their footsteps concurred in the broad, beaten track upon the snow, and we do not expect faithfulness in tone or form or colour from shadows.

Butler's sympathy goes with those prepared, when necessary, to shake themselves out of the trance-like public mood. Very often they are writers. Ernest Renan and Carl von Ossietzky are two such lives celebrated in this book. 'It is the business of men of education to keep words flexible and rich in significance', Butler writes in his essay on the Croatian poet Nazor, 'and to keep them free of crude antitheses.' Elsewhere he remarks on the diminishing space in modern intellectual life between the pundit and the puppet. It is this mediating role which he himself occupies with a certain ironic flourish.

In so doing, Butler habitually pursues uncomfortable subjects to their conclusions. In this collection, the fate of the Jews of Europe recurs as an inescapable *leitmotif*: observed on Riga Strand in 1930, before the deluge; forced into 'retraining' schemes in Nazi Vienna in 1938-9; finally and unbearably, the fate of the four thousand children of Drancy. Butler begins by telling us there are 'three versions of the story of the Children of Drancy': the language deceptively indicates a folktale or a myth. The terrible point is made that the very scale and organization of the atrocity muffles its horror; the banality of evil is asserted once more. And though Butler tells us the Vichy Commissioner for Jewish Affairs 'changed his name' from Darquier to d'Arquier de Pellepoix for his long postwar life as a respectable citizen in Spain, Max Ophuls's documentary *Le Chagrin et La Pitié* shows him in 1940 proudly greeting Streicher under his full name. He did not even have to do that much. Yet against this background, Butler opens his essay on 'The Kagran Gruppe' with an arresting claim: 'I believe one of the happiest times of my life was when I was working for the Austrian Jews in Vienna in 1938-9.' Finishing the essay, one understands why. The individual effort, cast in the scale against huge forces of evil and inertia, carries its own validation.

En écrasant l'infâme, many must go to the wall. Butler may give less than their due, for instance, to the many individual German Catholic priests who opposed Nazism (and their own hierarchy); this is the picture presented by accumulating local studies like that of Thalburg, dealt with here. Nor, perhaps, would we automatically agree with the assertion in 'A Fragment of Autobiography' that Lennox Robinson was wrong to risk the County Library movement for the sake of his supposedly blasphemous short story. I do not think that Butler, put in the same position, would have followed such an emollient line; nor do I think he should. Not that it is easy to make such inferences; because where autobiography comes into these essays, it is kept resolutely in its place, to point a general argument or illustrate a theme. At the same time, the child who ignored the selection of cattle for the Kilkenny Fair because he was 'always thinking of something else' is discernible in the mature essayist; and the arguments in 'Little K', starting from the basis of a personal tragedy, span out to encapsulate all the major themes of this book, and to confront, once again, the terrible image of children flung by their parents from the trains bound for Auschwitz. This collection would be read, and argued about, for that piece alone. But every essay carries the same unadorned clarity and unique distinction.

Equally characteristic is the humour of the pieces dealing with the remnants of formidable Anglo-Irishry: Sir Hercules Langrishe sending up Edward VII, or Aunt Harriet with her Christian Science and her coveted handful of Cork ground-rents, inhabit the same ironic universe as the 'gay, self-confident and outrageous' White Russians on Riga Strand. The tone austerely avoids sentimentality or condescension. 'Neither sadness nor malice nor anything very bad can stand long in his presence.'

An Irish Protestant friend recently recalled to me the atmosphere of that curious subculture, complacent and insecure all at once, in the Republic of the 1950s. Any expressed ambition to criticize aspects of Irish life, he remembered, caused your co-religionists to round on you with one over-riding injunction: 'Don't rock the boat!' Hubert Butler has made a lifetime's habit of administering graceful but vigorous rocks, sending ripples far beyond his own shore. The boat's course is altered by the vibration of pieces like those collected in this book: imperceptibly at first, but immeasurably for the better.

R. F. Foster
Dublin, May 1988

PART ONE
TRAVEL

1

RIGA STRAND IN 1930

Once a week in the summer months, a pleasure steamer berths in Reval harbour and for a few hours troops of excited English tourists swoop down on the town, swarm up the hill, and penetrate in charabancs as far as Pirita and St Brigid's abbey. It is a charming spot; the views, the churches, the crooked narrow streets, compact, accessible and picturesque, are just what is required. Though they straggle off unshepherded in fifty different directions, they meet each other in a few minutes with glad cries in antique shops and cathedrals where everybody speaks English. When the hooter calls them back to the ship they have seen everything and yet are not exhausted.

The same ship wisely seldom stops at Riga. Riga is big and sprawling and new looking; it has clean, cosmopolitan boulevards, public parks, and large exhausting museums; the few tourists have a harried look and the hours pass in catching trams, changing money and haggling with droshky drivers. There are, it is true, a great many English people in Riga, but they are a serious, residential tribe, the complete reverse of the sightseers of Reval or Helsingfors. The Riga Britons are homesick and resentful business-men who have come to buy timber and find that the Letts don't want to sell it, or bored and studious soldiers who have come to learn Russian and find that the Letts don't want to teach it. Their subsequent stories of Riga and Latvia are naturally coloured by their experiences. The timber merchants are confronted with the petty officialdom of a young nation, proud of its new independence and snatching at all opportunities of asserting it. The officers are met with blank surprise; their shy, stumbling sentences get no encouraging response from the Letts, for Russian is out of favour and they find their society restricted to the English Club and a few embit-

3

tered Russian aristocrats to whom Latvia is only a rebellious province, governed by the lower orders. No wonder then that officers and merchants have no rosy memories of Riga; grudgingly perhaps they repeat the legend that the Riga air is very good and that Schwarz's is the best café between Berlin and Tokyo, though they've never been to Tokyo and Schwarz's is very much like other cafés; they bring home amber necklaces and caviare and polished birchwood cigarette cases, but they don't conceal that they are thankful to be out of Riga and would gladly never return.

All the same Riga Strand must have a fascination for more leisured visitors, who have time to be interested in the past and the future of the small republics which rose from the ruins of the Russian Empire. It is the holiday ground not only for Letts but for all the newly liberated peoples of the Baltic. There one may meet Estonians and Finns, Lithuanians and Poles, bathing side by side with Germans, Russians and Swedes, who were once their masters.

Of all the Baltic nations perhaps the Letts have suffered the most, yet their story is typical. Their nationality and their language have survived a double conquest and many centuries of foreign rule. From the west came the Teutonic knights bearing with them a German culture and occupying the ancient territories of Lett and Lithuanian and Estonian, as far as the Finnish marshes and the empire of the Tsars. Russia too was expanding. Peter the Great was casting covetous eyes upon the Baltic and at last the 'Baltic Barons' in their turn, and all their possessions, passed under the Russian eagles. The Letts now found that they had not one master but two, for the Russians respected the Barons for their solidity and thrift and good husbandry, and confirmed them in their possessions, giving them in return for their loyalty high places at court and in the army. Ever since Peter the Great had first turned the eye of Russia westward, German culture and methods had been admired and imitated. Catherine the Great was a German, and she and her successors often chose advisers from their German subjects. The Baltic Barons found that they lost nothing by their incorporation in the Russian Empire.

If the Barons were the most privileged of the Tsar's subjects, the Letts whom they oppressed were the most wretched. . .

4

their very existence was denied, the name of Latvia was abandoned, and the Baltic lands divided into Russian provinces in which the racial differences were carefully ignored. The Letts had no appeal from the caprice of their masters; an early law limited flogging to thirty-six strokes, but humane legislation did not go much further and the Letts remained all but serfs till late on in the last century. Lettish schools were closed and Lettish newspapers prohibited, even old songs and customs that might remind them of their national past were suppressed. Every year in the old days there had been a great festival of song, the rallying point of national feeling, and every town and village had its band of singers. But the rulers recognized that a song can be more dangerous than a sword and the festival was rigorously proclaimed.

Many Letts joined revolutionary organizations and, when the Revolution of 1905 broke out, the great rehearsal for the Revolution of 1917, there was an abortive revolt in Riga. A Lettish Republic was declared and for a few days maintained. The Tsar was alarmed, concessions were promised, and, when all danger was averted, forgotten: the Barons, momentarily panic-stricken, recovered their composure. But the Letts persevered, their time had not yet come, and the Great War found them still trusting in the clemency of the Tsar. It was an occasion when all the subject races must be rallied to the Russian cause, and the Baltic peoples, who were disaffected and lived upon the frontiers of the enemy, must at all costs be conciliated. The German emperor had promised to establish a Lettish Republic, and the Barons, who took this with a grain of salt, were many of them ready to welcome a German invasion. The moment was propitious for a generous gesture from Nicolas II. He agreed to grant a request hitherto persistently refused; henceforward the Letts might serve under their own officers as a separate Lettish unit. Lettish regiments were formed and graciously permitted to defend their fatherland and promised that when they had beaten the enemy they would enjoy equal rights with the Barons. There were rejoicings in Riga, and the credulous Letts believed that at last the day of their deliverance was at hand; but those who were more discerning guessed that whoever won, the Letts would be the losers, the Barons would not be shifted and the emperors would find good reasons for forgetting their solemn pledges. But as often occurs the most discerning were wrong. The unexpected, the impossible happened: both sides were defeated, Kaiser Wilhelm lost his throne and the line of Peter the Great came to a tragic end at Ekaterinburg. Yet at first it seemed as if Latvia would merely be smothered in the collapse of the two empires. By the Treaty of Brest-Litovsk Russia treacherously abandoned Latvia to Germany and after the Armistice the Allies allowed the Germans to remain in Riga to keep the country safe from Bolsheviks.

Then followed eighteen months of terrible suffering for Latvia. The Letts drove out the Bolsheviks in the east only to find the Germans in their rear, and a third enemy appeared suddenly, for an army of White Russian exiles, mobilized in Berlin, tried to conquer Latvia as a base for an attack on Russia. White and Red and Balt and German alternately ravaged the land, for their landlord barons made common cause against the Letts. But the Letts fought like tigers. At last, after foreign intervention and unheard of struggles, peace was restored, boundaries were traced by English colonels and professors, and the Latvian Republic was proclaimed.

Now at last the Letts are masters of Riga Strand, and on a June morning the sands are alive with holiday-makers. Where do they all come from? Outside Riga the pinewoods and the wastelands stretch empty and interminable, dotted here and there only with a few ramshackle wooden huts, and Riga itself does not suggest an unlimited supply of pleasure-seekers. Granted that some of them come from abroad the answer is that a seaside holiday is not so much a luxury in Latvia as a necessity. There is scarely a clerk or artisan in Riga too humble to have a rickety wooden dacha for his family during the summer months, and from there he commutes daily.

A great broad shore fringed with pinewoods sweeps round the gulf of Riga as far as eye can see: the sea is almost tideless and yet the beach is always deep and soft and clean, for the wind blows away the bus tickets and the paper bags and buries orange peel and match boxes deep in the sand. Then during the long winters the snow and the frost scavenge round the shuttered dachas, there are mountains of ice and the whole Gulf is frozen over, so that a year or two ago two men skated forty miles across the sea to the small island of Runo, but when they got there they did not recognize it for it too was covered with ice.

6

June when it comes finds the scene completely changed: the syringas are in blossom, the railway is opened and the post office and the post mistress are established; there are bands and cinemas and charabancs, and people run about the shady streets in dressing-gowns. Riga Strand is awake again. It is an annual metamorphosis, a conspiracy between man and nature that has started afresh every season since the first dacha went up in the pinewoods. There is a story that it belonged to a Scottish merchant and that he called it Edinburga thus giving its name to one of the seven villages of Riga Strand. Another of the villages is called Dubbelin though the Irish merchant who founded it is only a legend. In any case the villages bear little resemblance to their namesakes. Behind them, parallel to the shore, flows the broad river Aar; in front of them stretches the coastline. There is nothing to interrupt the long monotonous shore; one may walk and walk and still the landmarks keep the same place upon the horizon. There are no rock-pools nor seaweeds nor shells nor birds; sea and land meet each other with a minimum of detail and complication. One might walk to Lithuania and meet scarcely anything but water and sand and trees and sky.

There are three sandbanks that stretch round the whole of the Latvian coast as if to grade the depths for bathers; children can splash about in front of the first, while their parents sleep contentedly on the shore, but only the most intrepid swimmers venture beyond the third. In general, though, the Letts are very well used to the sea and the attendants have placed the long line of basket chairs with their backs to the waves, so that the occupants can watch the stream of people passing by under the restaurants in striped Turkish dressing-gowns and bathing-dresses far too modish to bathe in. The serious bathers do not wear bathing-dresses at all, for the beach belongs to the men till eight o'clock in the morning, when they must give place to the women, who have it to themselves till midday.

The villages themselves are scattered among the trees, long grassy tracks run parallel to each other, criss-crossed by others and fringed with wooden dachas. Here and there is an outcrop of cinemas and dance-halls. There are more pretentious buildings too with archways and gardens; they are empty and dilapidated but not with age for carved in the stone doorways one can often read 1905 or 1908 or 1912. Those were the great days of Riga strand when wealthy merchants from Moscow and St

7

Petersburg or noblemen who did not despise Russian resorts came here with their families. Mineral springs and mud-baths were discovered and exploited; though Riga Strand was not beautiful like Finland yet it was close at hand and it was not as expensive or as exclusive as the Crimea; at least it only excluded the Jews and they were excluded as a matter of course from every chic imperial resort. There was an imperial decree forbidding them to Riga Strand.

For a decade or more all went well; new wings were constructed, new gardens laid out, fashionable specialists built up practices, more and more medicinal baths were opened – then all at once the same fate overtook the villages of Riga Strand that extinguished all the pleasure resorts of Western Europe. But the Great War, which cast only a passing blight upon the others, eclipsed for ever the brief splendours of the Latvian shore. The Baltic lands fell out of favour with the Russians, their 'barons' were suspected of intriguing with the enemy; for years it was discovered they had been employing German spies as their foresters and now from being courted they were shunned.

Then began the long campaign among the swamps and forests of Northern Europe. . . slowly the Russians fell back and their armies melted away; Bolshevik and German and White Russian swept over land and devastated it. In Riga telegraph wires were pulled down; rope had run short but there were still men to hang.

Riga Strand has emerged from the terror now and there are visitors there once more, but the clients for whom the casinos and the dance-halls and the rickety palaces of 1910 were built are gone for ever. Where now are her wealthy St Petersburg patrons, where is St Petersburg itself? Even if they wished to come, there are barbed wire entaglements six foot high, manned by armed sentries, that can only be crossed with a stack of passports. The Japanese garden with its little bridges and artificial jungles is knee-deep in groundsel and toadstools; there are trenches still and tangles of rusty barbed wire round the sulphur springs at Kemmeri, and the fashionable specialists have no prodigal Caucasian Princes to diet in their sanatoria, they have to haggle with Jewesses about mud-baths and superfluous fat. The disinherited have come into their own, the Jews have descended like locusts on Riga Strand. . . for them it has the fascination of a forbidden land. Synagogues begin to oust the gleaming onion towers and Assari, the farthest of the resorts, has almost become a Jewish village. Jewish ladies emerge with blonde curls from the hairdressers, for there are two or three 'frisetavas' in every street and Lettish gentlemen prefer blondes. But the Jews have still to mind their step, for the Letts have inherited many of the prejudices of their masters; they too fear and despise the Jews, just as they themselves were despised by the Russians.

In the afternoon the sun beats down scorchingly on Riga Strand, the pinetrees are too far away to lend their shade and even beneath them the sand is parched and burning. There are a few boatmen, a few bathers, some ladies stretched in deck chairs under the shady walls of a sanatorium, and in the long coarse grass between the pinewoods and the sand the day-trippers lie like logs. It is so quiet that one can hear a baby crying in the next village, the hoot of a steamer on the Aar, a man knocking the sand out of his shoe upon an upturned boat. It is nearly five o'clock and soon the bells begin to ring for tea in all the pensions and lodging-houses along the beach. The sanatorium bell clangs like a fire-engine, the ladies in the deckchairs clap their hands to their ears and scream at the matron, but she has been preparing the tea while they were sleeping and swings it all the harder.

After tea the beach becomes awake again, the dacha residents come out with watering-cans and make puddles in the grey powder of their flower-beds. The earth has forgotten how to drink and for a moment the water sits in a curved bubble on the surface or forms little pellets with the sand. In any case a garden in Latvia is an unnatural thing. . . the flowers in the dachas are tenants for the season like their owners. None of them looks permanent or settled; geraniums and petunias flush up a dizzy scarlet or purple for a month or two like a local inflammation, and die down the moment the owner and his watering-can have departed. The big restaurants do not even bother about bedding plants but on a gala night, the night for instance, of the firemen's ball, a cart arrives from the country piled high with branches and in half an hour the café is embedded in a luxuriant forest and flowers and shrubs have sprung up out of the dry sand. There are no gardens in the country either; sometimes someone will stick a peony or a dahlia into the grass, but if it does not look after itself, no one else will – and its life is usually a prolonged battle.

As the night falls more people stream out on to the strand,

9

for the air is cool and the sinking sun has spilt a pink light across the shore. It is the hour for the evening stroll, and from dacha and sanatorium the same familiar figures emerge. There are three robust Finnish ladies, the wives of foresters, a German financier and a Lithuanian governess. There is an Estonian gentleman who is very popular with many different ladies in turn; he has friendly charming manners and is always beautifully dressed and carries a cane. He varies the ladies not because he is fickle but because sooner or later they each of them discover that he is stupid almost to mental deficiency. There is a Swedish lady who has come over to cure her pale small son from vomiting. She has a jealous husband who condemns her yearly to dull provincial watering places and Riga, she thinks, is the dullest of them all. She has a new dress for every meal but her evening parties with kisses for forfeits are not well attended. She started to have English lessons from a British officer and amid shrieks of merry badinage learnt 'I luv you so' and 'keessmequeek' and then she got bored again. All the upper classes are bored on Riga Strand. 'Ochen skoochno!' 'Sehr langweilig!' 'I'm bored stiff!' It is only good form to be bored.

A more independent type is the Russian lady who lives with her widowed mother in a dacha up the strand. She is severe, uncompromising. Every morning she does Catherine wheels, nude, on the beach for the good of her figure and in the afternoons she mortifies herself by giving Russian lessons to French and English officers. It is a degrading occupation for an aristocrat, and she slaps down her instructions with callous, disdainful efficiency. They want to study Bolshevik idioms and the new alphabet and she has forced herself to master even that. In the back room she stows away her lonely garrulous old mother and the Lettish husband, whom she married to get out of Russia, and sometimes when she is late for a lesson, the old mother slips out and gossips with the pupils. What revelations! What merry undignified chuckles! She is delighted to have someone to talk to but suddenly she hears her terrifying daughter outside and slips back shamefacedly into her room.

There are many other Russians on Riga Strand, the remnants of the wealthy patrons of former days. All that they could save from the Revolution they have brought with them but they have no homes or estates to return to; they have to be thankful for a refuge from their own countrymen among a people they have always despised, and to get jobs in Latvia they set themselves to learning Lettish, a language they have always regarded as a servant patois. Life is very hard but they contrive often to be gay and self-confident and outrageous. They still take short cuts across flower-beds if they belong to Jews, and are condescending to Letts at tea-parties. They are ingenious at finding ways to restore their self respect.

There is also a Soviet Commissar holidaying on Riga Strand, but it is unlikely that he will join the crowd that watches the sunset in the evening. He is neither gay nor sociable. Even at meals he talks to no one but gazes intently at his plate of food, frightened to look up in case he should intercept a glance of hate. He is pale with enthusiasm or under-nourishment and he obviously enjoys the fleshpots of Riga Strand.

As the evening grows colder the strand empties, and a group of boys come out of the pinewoods where they have been collecting sticks, and build a bonfire on the shore. The rest of the sand sinks back into the night and they are islanded in the firelight. As the flames burn higher it is easier to see their keen, Jewish faces. They have not yet lost the colours of the Mediterranean, though it may be many generations since their ancestors travelled up from Palestine to the shores of the Baltic. The leaders are a woman with loose black hair and a Messianic youth of seventeen. Are they making speeches or telling stories? The eyes of twenty boys are fixed, black and burning in the firelight, on the woman as she cries passionately to them in Yiddish. Three or four boys reply to her and they sing strange, unhomely Eastern tunes. Only a few yards away are the cafés and the sanatoria but in the darkness the sand seems to stretch away interminably and the Jewish scouts seem to be the only creatures alive on the shore, a nomad tribe camping in the desert. They are of the same race, the same families perhaps, as the predatory blondes in the beach costumes, but the spirit that fills them now is alien from Riga or from Europe. Persecution has hardened them and given them strength to survive war and revolution and even to profit by them and direct them. Perhaps it is they in the end who will decide the future of Riga Strand.

At last the fire dies down, the boys make ready for sleep, and once more the small, scarcely audible sounds of the waves break upon the silence.

[1930]

11

2

IN THE ADRIATIC

I. FIUME, SUSHAK AND THE NUGENTS

Lately I have been reading Elizabeth Hickey's *Green Cockatrice* (1978) which is in part a history of the Nugents of Westmeath and in part a celebration of one of their most interesting members, William Nugent, the Gaelic poet. It reminded me that nearly thirty years ago I had visited Fiume and its neighbouring town, Sushak, where the last of the Nugents, an elderly woman well remembered in the town, had recently died.

Fiume, at the head of the Adriatic where Italy and Yugoslavia meet, takes its name from the river or 'flumen' which divides it from Sushak. This small stream was for twenty years the frontier between the Slav and Latin peoples, but now the Yugoslavs have joined the two towns with a broad flat bridge and under it the little Fiume or Rijeka as stream and town are now called, never very impressive, has become almost unnoticeable. The bridge is more like a big square than a bridge and is planted with rows of chestnut trees under which the citizens of Fiume and Sushak mingle and listen to the band. It is a symbolic bridge.

For d'Annunzio too the bridge, an earlier narrower bridge, had a symbolic significance. He had with his young Arditi seized the towns in 1919 from the Yugoslavs to whom they had been awarded by the peace treaty. The Arditi were the forerunners of the Fascists and their cry 'Eja, Eja, Alala!' with which they marched across the bridge was adopted by them. When shortly afterwards by a new treaty, Sushak, but not Fiume, was awarded once more to the Yugoslavs, the bridge was not abandoned without a struggle in which it was destroyed. It was photographed and widely advertised as the saddest of all the casualties.

When I was there the Italians and Croats had almost forgotten the hectic days of d'Annunzio, and I bought a history of his short reign for a few shillings. The first page was covered with a dedication in his own dashing handwriting to his glorious comrade-in-arms Attilio Bijio and there were fifty photographs of ecstatic triumphs and processions and conquests of Dalmatian islands – all now forgotten. Or are they entirely forgotten? I was told how a little before a foreigner missed his wife, Eva, in a crowd at Fiume railway station. He called after her shrilly 'Eva! Eva! Allo! Allo!' It was almost his last cry because he was battered by his fellow travellers with suitcases and umbrellas. They thought he had been crying 'Eja, Eja, Alala!'

A steep rocky hill rises above Sushak. On top of it are the castle, church and village of Trsat. One tower of the castle is Roman, for there where Sushak now stands was the old Roman town of Tersatica. The rest of the castle was built by the Francopans, an ancient Italian family of unknown lineage, who claimed like Dante and Thomas Aquinas to be descended from the Patrician family of Aricius, and who ruled Croatia for several generations and became more Croatian than the Croats. At the beginning of the last century it was bought by the Irish General Laval Nugent. He had left Westmeath some forty years before and taken service with the Habsburgs. When Napoleon had set up an Illyrian state in Croatia the Austrian emperor had been powerless to evict the French. So Nugent had taken the matter in hand himself. Mustering the Croats of Istria and Dalmatia he had pushed the French far back into Italy. By the Austrian emperor he was later made a count and a marshal. He restored in part the old castle, built a chapel there and below it a pleasant modern house for himself.

I found a remarkable old man living in the Nugents' house, which was badly battered by bombs. He had been a Feldwebel in the Austrian army, then he had become an Italian, now he was a Yugoslav. He had known well the last of the Nugents, an old woman who had died aged ninety in 1941, blind and alone, and he had read and knew by heart all the history of the neighbourhood. The Yugoslav government had made him a curator of the castle.

From the square Roman tower, we looked far down on the two blue harbours of Fiume and Sushak, separated only by a spit of land and the small river. Eastwards the Croatian littoral ran past the big bare islands of Krk and Cres and Dalmatia, and behind it, gauzy grey, we could see the high Velebite mountains that lie between Zagreb and the coast. On the west there was the rocky Istrian shore curving southwards at Abbazia, an elegant but now deserted resort. The old man pointed out the route by which Charlemagne's generals had met the Croats in battle and after some reverses had checked them in Istria, so that they never came into Western Europe. He sketched the campaigns of the Francopans, of Marshal Marmont and Laval Nugent. He had none but local visitors for a long time and he was pleased to talk.

The chapel that Laval Nugent built lies above the dungeon of the Francopans. It is a big classical building but it and one of the Francopan towers has been badly damaged by war and vandalism. There was a stack of planks lying beside it and the old man told me that the Yugoslav government were going to spend large sums in restoring it. 'Some young Communists in the village said it should all be thrown into the sea', he remarked, 'as a reminder of feudalism, but I told them that even the Russians respected old things. When the Finns could not pay their reparations in cash, they said, "Then pay us in antiques."'

A huge double-headed Austrian eagle in stone perched on a coat-of-arms was lying on the ground. When the Italians came first they had brought a row of lorries to take anything valuable away but the village boys had anticipated them by pulling down the eagle and hiding it in the earth. Countess Nugent liked the Italians and so they had tied her in her chair and put a handkerchief in her mouth while the digging was going on. That was during d'Annunzio's raid. In this war she had been too old to interfere and the Italians had pulled the lids off Laval Nugent's marble sarcophagus and rummaged for gold, and they had smashed holes in all the other family vaults as well. After the fall of Italy a German general arrived at Trsat. 'What barbarians the Italians are!' he had exclaimed and the Nugent bones were collected and the vaults re-sealed again. A modest vault, which the Italians had not bothered to break into, had the name JANE SHAW carved on it. 'I wonder is she a relation of Bernard Shaw?' the old man said, and he told me that some time before the war the playwright had come to Fiume in a yacht and that he had stood on the bridge at Sushak and sung a song. 'We all crowded round and laughed and were very pleased.'

He brought out a big portfolio from the house and showed me photographs of the village boys grouped round the Austrian eagle in their best clothes after they had dug it up again with ceremony. Also there was a photograph of Countess Nugent talking to him on a seat. She had a mass of white hair and a cross, distinguished face. 'She was very fond of reading Nietzsche,' said the old man, 'and knew every language but Croatian though she had lived among us for fifty years.' She always called herself an Irishwoman. Her house was perpetually full of visitors, French and German and Italian and English sailors from the ships; it was only the Croats she did not like. When she grew old, she became very dirty and suspicious and would let nobody near her. Though she was stone blind she went down every day to eat in Fiume or Abbazia and knew her way about the streets perfectly! She had not survived the war long. Her last words were 'Wo ist mein Geld?' She had been a remarkable ascendancy type and the old man had learnt much of his history from her.

When we left the castle of Trsat, the church bells were ringing. One little chapel lay just below us, but as I came towards it the bell stopped and I saw that there was no one inside; it was bare and small and cool with a delicious scent from a vase of Madonna lilies. Outside there were two men lying on the grass on their faces. I think they had been ringing the bell in this deserted chapel of the Nugents simply to reinforce the sound from the belfry in the large church in the square towards which the crowds were streaming. Trsat village still has a feudal appearance in spite of the hammer and sickle and Communist slogans stencilled on the house walls; many of the people had the look of old retainers and their cottages were lined deferentially along the road to the castle. Their gardens were full of flowers and oleanders were already blossoming in empty petrol cans on their window sills.

The church of Trsat has been for centuries the focus of pilgrimages from all over Europe, and outside the door there is a cluster of beggars and a row of booths selling candles, sacred mementoes, pictures and a small book about the Blessed Virgin of Trsat written by a former priest of the parish. The story is well known but he writes with some charm and tells many details that I have not seen elsewhere.

In 1272, as is carved on an ancient archway through which a long flight of steps descends into Sushak, the house of the Blessed Virgin at Nazareth transferred itself to Trsat; in December three years later it left again. The first to notice the strange phenomenon were some men cutting wood early one morning in March. The Adriatic below them had stormed all night but all at once it had become peaceful and still and they heard a chime of silvery bells behind them in the wood and smelt the fragrance of spring flowers. They followed the bells and came upon a small house, shaped like a tiny church, and inside it a picture of the Virgin. They went straight and told the priest, who was ill. He seemed to be expecting them for he tóld them he had that night had a vision in which the Blessed Virgin had appeared to him and told him what had occurred. She explained how after her death the Apostles had used her house as a church, and that was the reason for its tiny belfry. The priest recovered from his sickness and there was great excitement in the village. Count Francopan quickly took charge of the matter and sent down builders to make a fence to protect the house from cows and repair the damage that had been done in its voyage. Yet lest he be thought superstitious and trivially minded he sent a priest and two skilled engineers as a deputation to the Holy Land to bring back evidence. They took with them the precise measurements of the house in Trsat and when they got to Nazareth they had no difficulty in discovering the foundations of the house of the Virgin. They compared the two measurements and finding that they completely coincided, they brought back the happy news to Count Francopan. Soon afterwards some Franciscans were put in charge of the chapel.

That was the start of the great fame and huge concourses of people that came to the village every year. However, very soon in 1295 there was a sad rebuff for Trsat; one morning it was found that the Virgin's house had flown across the Adriatic to a village near Ancona. It did not stay there long but after several further flights it finally settled at Loreto, where it has remained ever since.

The great stream of pilgrims was diverted from Trsat and even the Croats travelled across the sea to Loreto. One day Pope Clement visited Loreto and saw a group of Croat peasants, wailing with tears in their eyes, 'Come back to us Holy Mother and bring your little house!' The Pope was touched and to console them he sent a famous miracle-working picture of the Virgin, painted, it is said, by St Luke himself. In a very short time this picture attracted as many pilgrims as the house itself had formerly, and Trsat recovered its celebrity and has retained it ever since.

In the early eighteenth century it was decided in Rome that the Virgin of Trsat should be crowned, and there was a three days' ceremony of incredible pomp and magnificence at which a strip of gold was fixed to the Virgin's head and the picture paraded through the streets of Sushak and Fiume. Boys dressed in white sprinkled flowers before it, trumpets blew and cymbals clashed, guns from the ships in the harbour roared salvoes and there were fireworks and torchlight processions in which all the civic dignitaries of the state played a part. Unfortunately, the cardinal who was to have performed the ceremony was detained by the plague, but there was a vast number of bishops and monks, in particular Franciscans, for it was they who had charge of the picture.

If one were to study the story of the Virgin's house and its wanderings against a background of mediaeval history, much that is perplexing would become significant. Trsat may well, through the Franciscans, have been a sort of bridgehead for the Catholic advance on the Byzantine and later the Moslem world, lying as it does on the frontier of Slav and Latin cultures. When the Franciscans of Bosnia were driven out by the Turks, many of them found refuge in the monastery at Trsat and later, when they returned to Bosnia, they still seem to have kept in touch with Trsat. The part played by Franciscans in Yugoslavia in recent years has been perplexing and anything connected with their former crusading days cannot fail to be of interest. In Western Europe the story of the Virgin's house is treated more or less allegorically. Aviators are under the special patronage of the Virgin of Trsat and Loreto. In Ireland there is a small chapel at Baldonnel Aerodrome where she is honoured.

During the war the Franciscans of Trsat supported the Ustashe, the pro-Nazi Croats, who, led by the regicide Pavelitch, crusaded to eliminate or convert to Catholicism the two and a half million Serbian Orthodox who lived in the newly created independent state of Croatia. The Serbian Orthodox claimed that it resulted in the greatest religious massacre in the history of Christendom, and the account of the discovery of 289 mass graves at the Ustashe concentration camp of Jasenovac in Croatia, published in *The Irish Times*, 1 September 1977, seemed to bear this out.

At Trsat the guardian, Father Ignacije, and three friars received minor decorations from Pavelitch 'for their long and selfless toil on behalf of the Croatian people, especially at the time of the return of Sushak to her mother, Croatia, in 1943'. I do not know whether they were punished for this, but though the church has 'Long live Tito' written in huge letters across it there was no evidence that there had been any interference with the worship there. When I got inside the priest with his gold cape held back on either side by two small acolytes was walking up the aisle swinging his thurible towards the large crowds on either side. The church is almost like a picture gallery, and I was sorry that I had not come at a time when I could look at it more carefully. In front of me was a column on which was suspended a glass case containing a big stone and a picture of a ship, the *Ban Mazuranich*. While sailing from Havana in 1897 the ship had sprung a leak which would have sunk it, had not the stone fallen into the hole and miraculously stayed there. The captain, Bertini, a native of Trsat, had given the stone and the picture as a thank offering to the Virgin. There are many other pictures of ships through the church, of Austro-Hungarian merchantmen which had been saved at the last moment from imminent destruction in places as far apart as the Bristol Channel and the China Seas. In the back of the church which I was not able to visit is the Virgin's picture and many magnificent trophies, a silver candlestick presented by a Croat warrior to the Virgin of Trsat, who had nerved his arm to cut off a Turk's head, and a curious ornament presented by the wife of a Serbian king.

In Fiume and Sushak, as in all the other towns of Yugoslavia, the walls are covered with stencilled slogans and in shop windows and in the halls of public buildings printed exhortations to brotherhood, voluntary labour and socialism are displayed, yet I did not, as in Russia during a similar revolutionary period, see any posters deriding the Church or its practices. An Italian in Fiume told me that he believed that the Communists would try, as the Fascists had done with success, to exploit the Churches in their interest. They would make no direct attack on the Christian mythology but would hope that by tact and perseverance it might be assimilated to their beliefs. He told how

Mussolini had adapted Christian phrases, practices and festivals, so that those whose Christianity was one of ritual observance found an easy passage into his fold. The Fascists had had their 'pilgrimages', their 'martyrs', their 'Hierarchs'. He told me how the King of Italy himself had gone on a pilgrimage to Mussolini's birthplace, and that there had been a Fascist festival of 'Mothers' Day' on Christmas Day, which was by slow degrees to supplant it. In the same way the Christian festival had once supplanted the birthday of the Sun, which had been celebrated by Mithraists on December the 25th.

Yugoslav Communists are often angry and insulted when accused of attacking the Church, and it is certainly possible that the more ingenious of them may be unwilling that a spiritual machinery which was of undoubted use to the Fascists and Ustashe should be sabotaged without an attempt to run it in reverse. The Communists of Yugoslavia still keep Sunday and various Saints' Days, and foster the same cult of birthplaces, processions and martyrdoms that was once fostered by Mussolini and the Francopans before them.

II. NAZOR, OROSCHATZ AND THE VON BERKS

At the beginning of a revolution artists and writers find themselves in a position of unaccustomed importance. Their support is eagerly canvassed, and it is very hard for them not to be flattered by these attentions. In Yugoslavia the writer must depend on a very small public, perhaps, owing to the differences of dialect within the country, on only a fraction of the reading public, which is not large. Even though some writers are of outstanding merit, they have very rarely been translated so that, when a writer parts with his country, he says good-bye, too, to his craft and his livelihood. Painters, sculptors and musicians are less tied by their medium, and a man like Mestrovich, with an international reputation, can choose his politics without reference to economic considerations: a writer can't.

A French writer, when asked to explain why certain artists collaborated in France, said 'Collaborate? But in politics artists are just children, you know!' It would be truer to say that artists are passionate individualists and there are certain temptations to which they succumb rather easily. They will tolerate any system which gives scope to their temperament. They are restless, discontented people in modern democracies and are unusually open-minded in regard to any change.

Pavelitch and his German patrons took very great pains to conciliate the artists and writers of Croatia; a novelist, Budak, was the first President, and a number of literary papers of excellent quality were produced. I do not think the artist was much molested at the start; for example, Krleza, the best-known Croatian dramatist, lived on peacefully through the Occupation in Zagreb, though a Communist. In the early numbers of *Spremnost* there are constant flattering articles about Mestrovich and Augustinchich, the sculptors, and Nazor the poet, and the most prominent of the Croatian painters. The articles hinted, often incorrectly, that the subject of their praise was a supporter of the government. Sometimes the artist or writer responded to this flattery with an ode or a picture; sometimes he contributed something non-committal to the papers. That was good enough. The editors felt they had netted him. They did not insist on ideological conformity, his name was what they were after, and because of that these papers of the occupation have much admirable material in them.

There was a curious technique if the writer or artist did not respond at all to their advances. He suddenly found himself whipped off to prison for no reason he could understand. . . as suddenly he would be let out; soon after some friendly, casual person would come up and say to him, 'Oh by the way, I'm getting up an exhibition (or bringing out a new number), I'd be awfully pleased, old man, if you'd let me have something.' One artist told me that he was only able to resist this technique by pretending that his mind had been unhinged by prison. Very few said flatly, 'No'. But the painters had difficulty with paint or materials or found their inspiration drying up, the producers found the plays were quite impossible to cast. The mercurial artistic temperament was freely invoked and as it was wartime, there were often plausible excuses for doing nothing. Mestrovich, after he had been in prison for some weeks, found there was only one subject to which he could do justice at the moment. He must go to the Vatican and make some busts of the mediaeval Popes. He knew Pavelitch could not refuse so praiseworthy a suggestion. On the way there he was asked to accompany the

Croatian exhibition to Venice where his sculpture was to be displayed. He did so. He then made the busts in Rome, got a visa to Switzerland through the Vatican, and never returned to Croatia.

Soon after the liberation a magazine was published in Zagreb with the intention of disconcerting the government. It published various odes and declamations, photographs, busts and pictures that had appeared under well-known names during the Occupation and in which the Ustashe and the Germans were glorified. The editor pointed out that these people were now ardent Partisans and supporters of the government. It was, I believe, the last freely critical paper published since the liberation and it was very quickly suppressed. I do not know whether the editor was making a gesture against corruption or whether he was being just malicious. What he proved, I think, was that while the power and influence of the creative mind is acknowledged, only unrepresentative governments are prepared to subsidize it. They invite the writers and artists to compensate with their enthusiasm for the frigidity of the electorate.

But it was not only creative minds that the Ustashe tried to buy, it was also cultivated and educated minds. With the collapse of several empires in 1918 a number of men, product of the wealth and leisure of this society, found themselves deprived of the climate in which their talents developed and needed to be maintained. I suppose they were considered greenhouse plants in a society which could not afford a greenhouse, but, as it turned out, their talents, which needed artifice and privilege for their development, were missed in a thousand ways in the new states. Alexander during his dictatorship made a great use of the Russian émigrés in Belgrade, and under Pavelitch in Zagreb the remnant of the Austro-Hungarian ascendancy, which was all but moribund, began to show signs of life; they were, I think, not quite so militant, embittered and combative as the Russians, their days of glory were further in the past, but they could not forget that Zagreb and Croatia had once been a great greenhouse for the forcing of their talents and that the civilization of the Croatian towns had been given an indelible stamp by the Austro-Hungarians. Probably it was the most idealistic and disinterested of them who took part in the new Croatia, the ambitious would find more scope under Hitler in Germany or Austria.

I can think of one Austro-Hungarian poet who for the first time in his life found in Pavelitch's Croatia an outlet for his remarkable gifts. As an Austrian, whose family had been connected for centuries with Croatia and Slovenia, he felt himself qualified to act as interpreter between Croat and Austrian and for three years he filled the Zagreb newspapers with remarkable poetry and prose. The new Croatia was as indulgent as it dared to the old ascendancy; its temper was romantic and pseudo-mediaeval but as all the Croatian aristocracy had disappeared or been absorbed generations earlier into the Austro-Hungarian upper classes, much compromise and connivance was essential. Poets, if they can't be anarchists, are susceptible to the romance of aristocracy, and I think it must have been this spurious pretence of aristocracy, with its bogus titles and resurrected pomps, ceremonies and traditions, that seduced for a time some of the better Croatian writers. I am told that the great poet Nazor was induced at the beginning to write praises of the new régime, but though I found many articles in the Occupation papers praising his work, I could not find anything written by him.

After a year he had had enough and in the New Year of 1943 the Partisans sent a car to Zagreb for him to fetch him 'to the woods'. He was an old man in poor health, and victory for the Partisans was still a long way out of sight, so his courage in leaving his comfortable home in Zagreb and a devoted sister in order to undertake this arduous journey across the frozen rivers and through trackless mountains of Bosnia will not be forgotten. The Partisans on their side paid a fine tribute to his fame and to poetry in undertaking the task of transporting, often by stretcher, this distinguished old gentleman with eczema and digestive troubles. He had his reward when he became the Vice-President of the Federal Republic of Croatia and was the first to address in Zagreb the liberated citizens.

If it is true that romance and poetry disappeared under the Communist government in Yugoslavia, there was an abundance of both in the Partisan warfare. There cannot be many wartime descriptions to equal Nazor's; it is not ordinary reporting. . . the enchantment of the Bosnian woods in the early morning and the hallucinations that the interlacing branches and mists weave in the mind of a sick old man recall Turgenev. The hero-worship and the comradeship of the woods was the real kind; not till it was transferred to the streets and newspapers and the election platform did the metamorphosis begin. The process is, I think, inevitable. Nazor prints in his book the poems that his comrades wrote, often about Tito; they are monotonous and uninventive as the song of the blackbird but in the woods they have their own appropriateness. Tito is their Achilles, he has the head of a young lion, says Nazor, and like the heroes of Homer he is only partly real; he becomes the symbol of what men admire in each other and everything he does and says becomes charged with significance. It is not till the symbol has to appear on the election platform that some spell is broken. 'Tito with us and we with Tito' they scribble on all the walls. But it is not the same. Some appalling catastrophe happens which should be explained not in terms of politics but of social psychology.

Nazor's diary has great documentary interest.* As an old, bourgeois poet campaigning with young revolutionaries, his elderly attempts to share their thoughts as well as their hardships are sometimes embarrassing, but the reader gets the feeling that he is trying sincerely to interpret the virtues of the old world in which he grew up in terms of the new, and that he is trying to save a good many venerable but discredited idols from the first fury of the iconoclasts.

A staff-officer, Major Moma Djurich, looked after him and saw that he had very quiet horses and refused to allow him to carry arms. In a rebellious mood Nazor wrote him a poem:

> When will you give to me, Commandant Moma,
> Rifle and horse, not a broken old screw?
> Did you forget how Nestor of Homer
> Was older than I but a warrior too?
>
> Did you forget how, when Doichen was dying,
> They strapped on his harness? Come harness me well,
> And set me on horseback! I'm weary of lying.
> I too would be after the black infidel!

One day they arrived at a castle in Bosnia where Tito had his headquarters. It had been built in 1902 with turrets and battlements by a romantic landowner, Frau Isabella von Berks. She herself was of Croatian descent but her husband's family came

* Vladimir Nazor, *Partizanska Knjiga (1943-1944)* (Zagreb 1949).

originally from England to Austria during a time of religious persecution under James I. They had been Earls of Berkshire but had been deprived of their estates, and that may have influenced her in spending her dowry on erecting this imitation Anglo-Norman castle on the banks of the stormy river Una. Inside it was furnished with four-posters and rich canopies, with carved Gothic presses and cabinets and refectory tables, no doubt in polished pitch pine. The long gloomy passages were hung with trophies of the chase, there were mirrors in heavy gilt surrounds, and ranks of ancestors in the dining-room. The library was full of ancient tomes in lofty book-cases, German and French and Italian, but there was not a single book in the Croatian or any other Slav tongue. There was literally nothing in the whole castle, said Nazor, to indicate the country in which it was built. It was as if the owner had deliberately set out to ignore the people of whose blood she was. The castle had been ransacked by all the armies which had passed through it in the last year, Italian and German and Ustashe, as well as Moslem fugitives, and insults about the von Berks family were scribbled in Italian on the walls. Now it was the temporary headquarters of Marshall Tito and Nazor describes the speed and vigour with which water and electricity and telephones were installed by the Partisans and Tito. 'May he do as well', he cried, 'when they come into possession of the derelict and plundered castle which is Croatia!' Outside there was deep snow so that the burnt and deserted villages, the unburied corpses, were hidden from view, the stumps of the plantations along the Una which the Italians had cut down no longer offended, even the rocks gleamed like silver in the sunlight. On the wireless the news came through of the victories of the Partisans in the Lika, of the Russian armies by Rostov. It was easy to believe, in this castle, that the worst was past.

In the night Nazor was restless with his illness and could not sleep, so he got up and wandered round the castle. There was no one about except the two guards on watch outside the little room where Tito was still writing up his despatches. In the dining-room the bright snow outside the window made such a lovely light in the rooms that he found his way around without lighting his torch. He was looking for a ghost, the inevitable tenant of an English castle, and what ghost was he more likely to see than Isabella von Berks? If she was ever to appear it would be now, when 'barbarians' were desecrating this creation of her romantic soul. There was no ghost, and he did not know which of the portraits was Isabella, but he persuaded himself that if he flashed his torch into their faces, one after the other, the proud owner would surely move in her frame, if only to turn her back on him. He had an obsession that one day he would meet her and know more about her; he would find her perhaps sitting at the head of the dining-table, reproachful and indignant, waiting for him. He felt that he understood her, for he too had a nostalgia for the past. He had lived for twenty years on his Dalmatian island in the shadow of a tower, and wherever he had moved to afterwards, conscious of being ridiculous, he had built himself a tower. He went back to bed disappointed but confident that all the same he would somehow get to know her.

The next day the doctor would not allow him to move and while Tito and his men were ranging the countryside, Nazor was confined to the castle watching from the large window the snow thudding and slipping down from the evergreens and tossed off irritably, like premature flowers, from the bare and spindly twigs of the lilac. There was a slight thaw. The Una was black between its snowy banks, and the devastation on either bank was revealed. Where were the woods in which the animals, whose heads hung in the dining-room, had ranged? Where was the bridge and little mill? When Isabella lived here and sat on the terrace the hills must have been clothed in greenery and filled with songbirds. (Now there is nothing but bleakness and in the distance the minarets of a mosque.) The voices of the villagers and servants must have come up to her. What a place for an old person to live and forget the past!

Every day, as they did repairs, something came to light in the castle; a muffin dish from behind the panelling, some candelabra from a hole in the wall, silver fruit dishes from the roof; but the Partisans had not time for a thorough investigation. Only Nazor had the leisure to explore, but that was not the sort of research in which he was interested. He wanted to re-create the life of Isabella.

He had luck, for Lisica, the wife of the caretaker, a sly and lazy person, still lived in the castle, and she took Nazor to see Isabella's room, and showed him an old photograph of Isabella, an unpretentious looking woman in a white blouse and Edwardian *coiffeur*. Lisica told him she was tall with blue eyes, did not talk much, and as a mistress was kind but firm.

But Isabella sent him a second messenger, a Serbian in Tito's entourage called Tsrni, who had lived in Soviet Russia and spoke and read Russian and French, a hard, dry but prompt and resourceful man. Somewhere or other he discovered the 'Stammbuch' of the von Berks, one of those monstrous, illuminated books, all gold and azure and crimson, compiled at the end of the last century to please the parvenu wives or unmarried sisters of the Austro-Hungarian nobility. He also found two packets of letters from Isabella to her son written in 1922 and 1923.

From these letters Nazor learnt that Isabella's last years had been spent in struggles and difficulties and not peacefully and romantically in the castle of Oroschatz. Her son was looking after it for her; his own house in Slavonia had been burnt by the Communists (that is what he called them but probably they were Serbian nationalists) in 1918, and she was living with a married daughter and nine grandchildren in Germany. It was the inflation time and they were in great poverty and wretchedness. But she wrote with patience and courage and an utter absence of that pride and self-dramatization which Nazor had anticipated; she seemed to have given up all her dreams about the castle, there was nothing left of all her romantic fantasies. 'She had only her Croatian mother's heart,' said Nazor, 'the cold misty romanticism of the foreigners from the North had been purged and chastened on the day of wrath, and it had given way to our Slavonic sensitiveness, warm, plebeian, creative.'

Isabella, said Nazor, was not buried here, and it was useless to look for her ghost, but if the hopes of Tito were realized and the castle was turned into a holiday home for poor children or for veterans, perhaps her kind shade would appear under the roof.

It seemed to Nazor that she had not spent her dowry in vain. 'Build!' he exclaimed, as he ended this entry in his diary. 'Build! Even though you do not know for whom or for what you are building!'

I had read all this with interest because I had stayed with Isabella's son, to whom the letters had been written, at his house in the village of Podgorac in Slavonia. I had come as a friend of his children's tutor, Christopher Cooper, whom I had met in

Zagreb. Von Berks had been murdered early after the invasion of Yugoslavia, I suppose by the same people who had burnt his house thirty years before and whom he called, with more justification than then, 'Communists'. They were probably just his neighbours and employees. He and such neighbours as he considered his equals were living precariously and resentfully on the edge of the abyss into which they were shortly to plunge. If he had been told that he would be murdered and his wife and sons have to fly, and his daughter, to whom he was devoted, only save herself by marrying a village Communist, what would he have done? I think he could have done very little, except juggle a bit more with his and his wife's investments and see that his sons got a good English education.

They all of them refused to see anything inevitable about their fate; they had a personal grievance against Destiny which had permitted them, intelligent, educated, fastidious and honourable people, to be ordered about by people of low breeding and semi-barbarous culture. Yet when I read Nazor's diary it seems to me that there is nothing inevitable about ruthlessness, that it comes from a misuse of words; that it is the business of men of education to keep words flexible and rich in significance and to keep them free of crude antitheses. Mr von Berks and most of his friends indulged freely in antitheses. There were good people and bad people, Communists and democrats, educated and uneducated, Slav and Teuton, us and them.

Mr von Berks had none of his mother's romantic nature nor was he a snob; he valued wealth and privilege for the power they conferred, not for prestige. He had been in a bank in America after the collapse of Austria-Hungary and he had a superstitious belief in science. This did not interfere with his support of the Church, which he thought exercised a stabilizing influence on those incapable of independent reflection and without scientific training. Archbishop Stepinac was an honoured guest at his table but when the parish priest came to meals this polyglot family used to joke about him in different languages and their superior education showed itself not in the power to deflect or soften the impact of cultural difference but in giving the contrast extra pungency and force, which they did with eloquence and skill. International politics entertained him, local politics hardly at all. I think that he derived his extraordinary arrogance less from his pride of birth than from scientific

27

enlightenment and American bumptiousness.

When the Mayor's daughter in Podgorac was married Mr von Berks asked me and Christopher to the interminable banquet in the village hall. He enjoyed himself on equal terms, arguing, quarrelling, drinking in the most convivial way with his red-faced sweating neighbours. He knew all their failings, just as they knew his, but there was not a trace of real comradeship in this reciprocal knowledge. He was an individualist more than a democrat. I don't think he had any confidence such as his mother had in the glamour and prestige of his ancestors. What he admired was science and power and American nationalism which he mistook for internationalism. He regarded small nations as nonsense and was humiliated by the imputation that he now belonged to one. It was degrading to have to ask permission of Belgrade to travel though the land of the former Austro-Hungarian empire, so he had provided himself with a special stamp and ink eraser so that he could organize his own passport and travel to Budapest or Vienna without ridiculous formalities.

I think his generation, Americanized and internationalized, was less easily assimilated than even his mother's. They were of more common fibre: they could capitulate or dominate but not live on equal terms, and with the disappearance of the feudal relationship with all its vague reciprocal obligations, the stark antitheses of wealth and poverty, pretension and powerlessness, became more pronounced than ever before.

The von Berks lived in an ugly mansion at the end of the main street of Podgorac. It had been rebuilt after the Yugoslav nationalists had burnt it in 1918, as splendidly as was consistent with comfort and practical good sense. The grandeur had been laid on afterwards on the side that faced the street. At the back was a straggling garden with a large rickety greenhouse which did not look as if it were much used. Paprikas and tomatoes drying on the edge had stuck to the woodwork. There were aubergines there, some like polished ebony but most had gone a dirty brown. Obviously the von Berks took no interest in their garden.

The second day I was there the Count, a local magnate, came to lunch. I had met him at the wedding banquet and had found him a very congenial person. After we had eaten we all four walked up the street together. It was October and the broad flat fields round Podgorac were full of dried stumps of maize stalks

28

with golden pumpkins crawling around them, some of them pale green, some frosted and rotten. Four Podolian oxen were dragging a one-furrow plough across one of the fields. The ploughman shouted at them as they reached the headland and they trudged round as if in a trance, dark-eyed and blue-grey. 'How beautiful,' said the Count. 'Horses would do this quicker,' said the steward, 'oxen for harrowing.'

I never learnt the Count's name or saw his house, but the fields at the eastern end of the village must have been his as he showed us his wine-cellar under a mound in the Turkish cemetery. 'I won't have much wine this year, I'm afraid, as I've had lumbago and I could not go round and see that the vines were properly sprayed.'

I think that, unlike von Berks, the Count was proud to be Yugoslav. He spoke Croatian, not German, to the steward. He had been born an Austro-Hungarian citizen but remained proud of his Croat nationality. Many such had cherished the Yugoslav ideal and, when the empire collapsed in 1918, had given their support to it. The man who had earlier pioneered the Croatian revival, Lyudevit Gai, had been half-German. It often happens like that. In an empire subject peoples are ashamed of their language till someone of the imperial blood urges them to value it. That was the story of Douglas Hyde and the Gaelic League, of Yeats and Synge and the Irish Literary Renaissance. They were all Anglo-Irishmen.

As elsewhere in the formerly Hungarian parts of Yugoslavia, each cottage had a strip of land behind it. In the Austro-Hungarian days the landlord ruled the village and had the right of life and death over the villagers and kept a certain routine going, which still partially survived. At four o'clock on summer mornings the cow-boy blew a horn under the priest's window and the cows went off to their grazing. The broad street was criss-crossed with the tracks of the cows. It is very muddy in the autumn but there is space enough for the traffic to use one half of the road till the other half has time to dry.

Podgorac on my last day seemed amazingly tranquil and beautiful. Turkeys and geese strutted down the street. There were maize cobs stuck away for the winter under the tiles. There was a short, rather noisy interruption. The fire-brigade band, having got out their uniforms and instruments for the wedding, marched up and down a couple of times extra before they put them away. The second time they collided with the cows coming back from the pastures. Each cow knew its own home and made for it, but they were wildly alarmed by the drumming and trumpeting and for a few moments man and beast were helplessly interlocked.

Before I left, the Count insisted on my visiting the village school. There were little boys with books and little girls with embroidery crouched round the central stove. They must have had an imaginative teacher. He had helped them make a map of the country round Podgorac and another map of the Dravska Banovina, the province through which their river, the Drava, flows. It was constructed out of coloured matches, powdered paint and little bits of a sponge dyed green for the trees. They were growing cherry trees from cherry stones and later were going to learn to graft them. The Count had given them a drawer full of oddities from his home and also an 'orrery' to show the movements of the planets round the sun. And there were two large coloured posters on the wall, one to illustrate the growth of a lobster, the other the formation of a molehill. The children all looked lively and interested. I complimented the Count from my heart for what he had done for the school. I thought that, as he trotted away behind his white pony, he looked pleased.

Years later, when I heard what had happened to the von Berks, I wondered how the Count had fared when the Partisans arrived in Podgorac. Is it true, as a Roman poet thought, that the good man is his own protection? 'He does not need Moorish javelins and poisoned arrows.' I doubt if that applies in the post-von Berks world, where one is judged not by one's temperament but by one's presumed politics.

III. THE RUSSIAN CONSUL

On the night journey to Split, the other berth in my compartment was taken by a solid, youngish-looking man whom the wagon-lit attendant told me *sotto-voce* was the Russian Consul at Split. After we had shown our passports to the next official, the Russian told me that he had never met an Irishman before, though he had read about our agricultural problems in Engels. He was the first Russian I had seen after three weeks in Yugoslavia, though I had been told they would be ubiquitous, so we were both of us ready to be talkative. He discovered a catch in the window-frame which released a small table and in a remarkably short time he had it covered with bottles of wine and beer and mineral-water and two tumblers.

He disposed quickly of Engels and Ireland and then he asked: 'What do they say of us in your country? Do they say we are savage illiterate mouzhiks?'

'No, not exactly that,' I lied, 'but they are convinced that you are trying to get control of Eastern Europe.'

'They're always saying that but it's not us, it's the people in these countries themselves. In the old days democrats used to look for their models to England or America or France; nowadays Communists look to us as we are the only Communist nation. Is that not natural enough? As for the propaganda, look at this country! We have only fifteen representatives here, the British have about thirty . Look at the English reading-rooms and clubs and the British Council. Do you know in Belgrade there's a French, and an American and a Czech and a Polish and two British reading-rooms, but not a single Russian one? And look at the other towns too, Zagreb, Maribor, Dubrovnik and the rest!'

I knew he was right about Belgrade and Zagreb, but I also knew that English people would say that Russian influence travels through unofficial channels and is applied through direct and sometimes violent measures. The Russians, they say, can dispense with reading-rooms. But I had only started to mention this when the Consul began about American intervention in Turkey and Greece, which I had to counter with remarks about Russian penetration in Hungary. I realized we were launched on one of those barren newspaper arguments from which there is no exit but silence and ill-temper.

'You see,' he said, 'we have never forgotten that Churchill and the Western powers intervened against us after our Revolution in 1917; we know that they'd like to do it again now. Why should we trust them?'

I was not sure how to reply to this, because I had been in Trieste and had met many Yugoslave émigrés and their British sympathisers and I had heard the cry raised a score of times:

'England and America must fight Russia now, while she is weak; in ten years' time it will be too late.'

I could only repeat to the Consul the platitude: 'Because everybody knows that the next war will be the end of civilization,' but I was not convinced myself. I had read its refutation in the eyes of the Triestan émigrés: 'We must all die soon anyway, and if civilization dies with us our personal tragedy will be, if anything, less anguishing.'

There are numbers of broken and frustrated people with no great love of life nor expectations from it, who look forward to Armageddon with an almost religious excitement. Communists, on the other hand, never developed a mystique about war as a cataclysm that purges and sanctifies and, at the worst, releases. That kind of thinking is a disease of the West. Communists only like wars which they win or profit by. It is the saving grace of materialism.

The Consul told me how much he and his family were longing to get back to Moscow. Split was nice enough – and he made a few deferential remarks about its antiquities – but it was not like home. His wife found Split women stand-offish and unfriendly. Though he had only been a year in Croatia, he spoke Croatian fluently, so similar is it to the Russian language. Yet he seemed to feel himself almost as much a foreigner in this country as I did. Croatia is honeycombed with ancient prejudices and idiosyncracies and a Soviet citizen, used to the size and shapelessness of Russia, soon loses patience. He finds himself constantly obliged to move circuitously around some venerable taboo.

The Consul's father had been an illiterate Moscow factory worker, and he spoke with immense pride of the campaign against 'analphabetism'. Soon there would be no illiterates left in the Russian army.

When I asked him about the devastated areas of the Ukraine he had the usual inhibitions. Sympathetic enquiries are always treated as attempts to spy out the nakedness of the land. He said quickly that in spite of Russia's vast sufferings she would in two years, because of her gigantic efforts, be stronger than ever before.

We spent a large part of the night talking like this, never entirely frank but always affable. The light was coming in under the blinds and the wine had been of the stimulating not the soporific kind. When I lay down in my berth, I knew I could not sleep so I tried to give some shape to the ideas left by his conversation and my experience of Russian influences in Zagreb and Belgrade.

The competition for cultural influences is one of the newest and nastiest features of international relationships and so far the Russians, preoccupied with economics, have played rather a small part in it. The Pan-Slavs were associated with reaction and the Communists have not yet abandoned their belief that genius is international. Yet there are signs in Slav countries that they might modify this creed in the interests of a reformed Panslavism. At the Zagreb fair in June, for instance, much honour was paid in the Soviet pavilion by means of busts and books, pictures and articles to the great Russian writers, even those who, like Dostoievsky, have been considered reactionaries.

Undoubtedly this Panslavism was inflamed by the German and Italian assault upon Slav culture; it might be still further stimulated by the cultural competitiveness of the Western democracies. When in the course of a friendly article in the *Manchester Guardian* on Yugoslavia Professor A. J. P. Taylor wrote quite accurately that Croatia had always had closer cultural ties with the West than with Russia, he was venomously attacked in the Moscow papers.

How can this Russian distrust be overcome? In their contacts with the West it is impossible for Russians to make those admissions of insufficiency or indebtedness which as individuals they will make so generously. I found circulating in Zagreb a well-written article on the corruption of the British press. It was only by accident that I discovered that the Russian writer had drawn most of his material without acknowledgment from a book by Wickham Stead. A comparable analysis by a Russian of the Russian papers would at present be impossible. I see only one way in which a breach might be made in the wall of Russian suspicion, and that is by demonstrating constantly that other communities can criticize themselves and flourish; also by emphasizing always the cultural inter-dependence of nations and the international character of genius. Communists in theory believe this too and opportunities for cultural collaboration in small ways might open up.

Unfortunately the Western powers in their official contacts are much more concerned with prestige than with candour or real cultural reciprocity. There is a kind of self-advertisement that many British mistake for self-criticism. 'We may be slow-witted,' say writers like Mr Arthur Bryant,'but somehow we "muddle through" in the end, thanks to our glorious. . . etc,' or again, 'Maybe we attach too little importance to book-learning, too much to what we English call character. . .' Only very ingenuous foreigners mistake this for the real thing. Handed out by the British Council in liberal doses, it acts as an emetic or perhaps I should call it a virus, because it induces something akin to rabies in the sensitive foreigner who comes into contact with it.

Leaving all the prestige-business aside, an attempt should be made to show how extensive is the literature of criticism and revolt in Western countries and how closely inter-related and what deep roots Communism has in Western thought. It could be shown that Western revolutionary theory is still developing and that Communism is only one of its offshoots. In England, for example, Wells, Shaw, Russell, the Huxleys, Orwell and Koestler are the legitimate heirs of the revolutionaries.

Yet such ideas have made little headway. They were not reflected in the collection of English books displayed by the British Council last June in Belgrade and Zagreb, nor in the small present of books given by UNO to Zagreb University. Typical of the nine or ten dozen presented, I found *The Life of Charlotte M. Yonge*, *The Later Life and Letters of Sir Henry Newbolt*, Vols II and VI of Ben Jonson's Plays and a mass of belles lettres by Alfred Austen, etc. The idea behind this choice was probably a kindly one. 'The patient is in a nervous state; give bromides!' An alternative possibility would be that there was no idea at all.

At present there is little organized resistance to Western cultural propaganda. The British reading-rooms in Yugoslavia are always crowded, the exhibitions of British books had a huge attendance and a couple of Yugoslav ministers at the opening. A large shop in Ilica now stocks a big collection of British books, and the demand is not only for bromides. A professor of Zagreb University has just translated *The Years* by Virginia Woolf: 5000 copies have been published and are likely to be sold. In the universities there are five or six times as many students of English as of the Russian language. All this does not suggest a severe censorship or a cultural subordination to Russia. Yet such a subordination is so constant a theme in American and English circles that it is impossible not to believe that it derives from pique that any other cultural influences besides their own should be admitted. The constant marching about of children with flags and songs is regarded as a direct import from the Soviets, but actually the embarrassed godfather of marching, singing, over-confident children was Baden-Powell. As for sport, English influence is still supreme with Futbalkup, Boksmech, Dirt-track, Fiskultur, Ping-Pong. Only the earnestness with which they are regarded comes from Russia, as does the enthusiasm for chess. (There are special chess-match excursion trains.)

I am sure that the strongest foreign cultural influence still comes directly or indirectly from Hollywood, and though an attempt has been made to counter it with French, Russian and home-made films, it has not been successful. A good Russian film like 'Alexander Nevski' would not even today draw as big a crowd as a million dollar American production.

Russian example is no doubt responsible for the new State bookshops in Zagreb and Belgrade. There are a great many, and in structure and display they are a vast improvement on what preceded them. The books are largely political pamphlets, but there are foreign classics as well. Dickens, of course, is the favourite English author, Upton Sinclair, Steinbeck, etc, among Americans. Of the Russians the great writers are all represented. A window in one shop was given entirely to Lermontov.

The Zagreb Theatre, which is being very lavishly subsidised, is certainly not under exclusive Communist control. While I was there *Othello*, as well as *A Midsummer Night's Dream*, was staged, a Molière, an Ostrovski and two Croatian classics. In Fiume, Shaw's *Widowers' Houses* was showing. Owing to the advent of a left-wing government, the greatest of Yugoslav dramatists, Krleza, a revolutionary, has after a generation of suppression come into his own. In three months his chief play, *The Glembays*, has been staged more frequently than in the previous two decades.

Unquestionably there will be an increase of Russian cultural influence, but it is as likely to be exercised through the Russian classics as through their Soviet successors, and in view of the affinity of language, and race it will be natural enough. Unless there is pressure from other nations it will not inevitably be chauvinistic. Yugoslavia should be regarded not as a cultural battlefield in which Russian influence must at all costs be defeated, but as a meeting ground in which propaganda might take a rest and friendly reciprocity begin.

After Ogulin the train passed through the Lika and I drew the blind up cautiously to see, if I could, that savage country of massacre and reprisal which Father Chok had described. The tiled houses were more substantial than I had remembered but they were scattered in lonely clusters around these forbidding mountains. Round each settlement were maize fields and cow byres and well-tended lettuce beds. Here and there a settlement was scorched and roofless. These were the crimes of neighbours, not of enemy bombers, and that much the more horrifying.

The blind slipped from my hand with a snap and woke the Consul. We talked again till Split, where he was met by a lively and charming family. When he said goodbye the Consul added with warmth: 'I do not see why two different systems cannot exist side by side in friendliness.' In print this reads easy and meaningless; as he said it, it carried conviction. A sociable and inquisitive people, the Russians do not enjoy the isolation into which a conflict of principle has forced them.

[1947]

3

IN RUSSIA

I. A VISIT TO YASNAYA POLYANA

Yasnaya Polyana is one of the famous homes of Europe, like Voltaire's house at Ferney, Goethe's at Weimar, Rousseau's near Chambéry, and our own Edgeworthstown. It survives by a mere chance, for it was occupied by the Nazis for forty-five days, and after their withdrawal orders came from High Command that it was to be destroyed. Some motor cyclists arrived to do the job, but time was short, and the Russians pressing on their heels. Though it was set alight in three places, only a couple of armchairs, some doors, floorboards and a bookcase were burnt before the Russian fire hoses were turned upon the house. Though about a hundred articles were looted, the loss was not a serious one, for at the time of the German invasion all the major treasures had been removed to Tomsk in Siberia, and they have now been replaced.

The house and property have had a complex history since the Revolution in 1917. The early years of the struggle for its preservation have been described with great candour and detail by Tolstoy's youngest daughter, Alexandra, who for five years dedicated herself to the task of preserving Tolstoy's home, defending his reputation, his ideals and social and educational enterprises, and securing the continued publication of his works.

Her book ends in defeat, for she gave up the Russian part of the struggle in 1922 and left for Japan and America. Yet her story is mainly concerned with personal disappointments and betrayals and day-to-day frustrations. The Tolstoy family could not today be wholly dissatisfied with the course of events. Tolstoy's position as the greatest and most widely read of Russian novelists seems to be firmly established and, though Tolstoyanism as a creed is dead in Russia, it was moribund long before the Revolution. It is impossible to believe that so great a genius as Tolstoy does not still exercise a powerful influence in unexpected ways and places.

Certainly I have never seen a national shrine preserved with greater taste and reverence than Tolstoy's two homes, his town house in Moscow and this country house near Tula, two-hundred kilometres south of Moscow. In both cases the caretakers are enthusiasts; one of them, Mr Loshchinin, has written a book about Tolstoy's early life. As far as the dead can speak through the books they read, the houses they built and furnished, the trees they planted, the places they loved, Tolstoy and his family are allowed to say their say without any tendentious interruptions.

Yasnaya Polyana is not as large or grand a country house as one might have expected. In the 1850s there was a big central block with two wings, but when Tolstoy was soldiering in the Crimea he wrote home to his brother-in-law, who was minding the estate, that he wanted funds to start a soldiers' magazine. 'Sell something, please, to raise about £5,000!' So without more ado the brother-in-law sold the central block and a neighbouring landowner carted away stones and woodwork to his estate. Tolstoy heard of this surprising decision with dismay. He had not even the soldiers' magazine to console him for the government forbade its publication. Tolstoy erected a commemorative stone on the site and planted elm trees round it. As an old man he would sometimes point out one of the upper branches to his guests: 'I was born up there in those twigs.' As his family grew up he twice enlarged one of the wings, and the house is now as it was when he died.

Apart from the final outrage, the Germans seem to have behaved with moderate propriety. The trees were not cut and an ancient elm, called the Tree of the Poor (because the peasants used to come there to tell Tolstoy of their troubles), still stands outside the front door; the old iron bell which summoned the Tolstoys to their meals is now half-embedded in its trunk. Tolstoy's grave, in a far corner of the woods, was not desecrated except insofar as the Germans buried their dead beside him. (The indignant Russians have disinterred them.)

The continuity of tradition has scarcely been interrupted. Here, for example, is the room, an old store-room with hooks for hanging hams on, which Tolstoy converted into a study where he started *War and Peace* and completed *Resurrection*. And it was in an upstairs room that he finished *War and Peace*, as always weaving into his stories many of the familiar features of his home. It was under one of the big oaks in a grove behind the house that Kitty and Levine sheltered from a thunderstorm, and the Prospekt, the avenue that runs from the village to the house, is the same Prospekt that occurs in the novel. It was the occasion of an unfortunate misunderstanding between the steward and his employer, the old prince, who shared the peculiar autocratic-democratic views of Tolstoy's grandfather, Prince Volkonsky, and indeed of Tolstoy himself. One day the prince remarked to the steward that the Prospekt had been cleared of snow. The steward, gratified that the prince had observed it, explained with modest self-satisfaction that he had cleared it because one of the Tsar's ministers was coming to dinner. 'What!' the prince had exclaimed. 'You will not clear the snow for my wife and daughters, but you will clear it for a minister? What do I care about ministers? Put the snow back again!' And the snow was put back on the Prospekt.

We were shown the hut below the orchard and the Wedge Grove (so called because paths radiate from the centre, dividing it into eight wedge-shaped segments) where the coachman lived. He had been roused up that October evening in 1910 to drive Tolstoy, accompanied by his doctor and close friend Makovitzky, to escape for ever from that aristocratic existence that had become intolerable to him. Surely it was the most ill-timed and uncomfortable act of literary escapism that has ever happened. They did not get farther than the railway station, and a couple of weeks later Tolstoy's body was brought back to Yasnaya Polyana and given, as he wished, a pauper's burial.

The second wing of the old house was used by Tolstoy and his daughter as a school, and is now a museum with many fascinating family portraits and photographs. I saw there the photographs of Tolstoy's funeral which was attended by all the peasants for miles around. All the birch trees round the grave were black with boys and men, perched in the branches to see the burial.

There is an upper room in which the old man lay ill for a long period. There is a striped armchair, and on the iron bed a gaudy bedspread embroidered by Countess Tolstoy. Above it is a photograph of Tolstoy sitting on the same bedspread, on the same bed, talking to Dr Makovitzky who is sitting in the same striped armchair. Beside it is another extant memorial of the past, a frightful leather cushion presented by the municipality of Tula and stamped with its compliments in gilt; it has survived the revolution and the Nazi occupation.

When we left Mr Loshchinin gave us each a green Antonovsky apple from the orchard but he scrupulously disclaimed for it an unblemished Tolstoyan heredity. The Antonovskies which Tolstoy had planted had died in the frost of 1948, and these were replacements. The great birch trees on the Prospekt had also died and been replaced, regrettably enough, by gloomy conifers.

I expect Mr Loshchinin's Antonovskies taste much the same as Tolstoy's, but the flavour of Tolstoyanism and the circumstances which produced it are harder to recapture. Yet, Mr Loshchinin and his colleagues (I was told that Tolstoy's last secretary still works in the museum, but he was absent when I was there) have done their best. And, if one is to believe that the past can ever be satisfactorily potted for posterity, it can seldom have been done with greater care and conscientiousness than at Yasnaya Polyana.

II. SIBERIAN JOURNEY

Though it is more accessible than it has every been, Siberia has never been so little known to us. Forty years ago it was liberally sprinkled with governesses from the West and reports came back to English rectories and Scottish manses about their remote and snow-bound lives. At the time of the Bolshevik Revolution an excitable French minister, who wanted allied intervention from Vladivostock, reported the murder of some fifty French governesses at Irkutsk, a frontier town on the edges of Mongolia. Unfortunately for his plans the governesses had not been murdered at all, and perhaps he had exaggerated their numbers also; as the French are reluctant travellers it would be sufficiently extraordinary if even ten French governesses had ever reached the pink shores of Lake Baikal. In the struggle for cultural supremacy, English, Irish, Scottish governesses pressed hard upon the French and had the Revolution not happened it is likely that English rather than French would have become the drawing-room language of the Russian upper classes. There must have been many English teachers in Siberia.

Nowadays few of us see anything of Siberia but its airports; we accomplish in a couple of days vast journeys which up till recently took several weeks, and as we grumble a good deal about sleepless nights it is wholesome to read of Anton Chekhov's journey across Siberia in 1890. We passed great cities without noticing them, while in his mind small villages were to be indelibly engraved. Here he spent the night in the ferry-man's hut waiting for the storm to abate so that he could cross the Irtish; his sodden felt boots were turning to gelatine on the stove. Here his buggy crashed into the post waggon and he was hurled onto the ground with his portmanteau on top. But there were no such landmarks for our journey. Even the airports are inextricably confused. Was it at Sverdlovsk that we ordered omelette and got fried eggs, and was Sverdlovsk the new name for Ekaterinburg where the imperial family were murdered in 1918? Yes, I think it was, and I know it was at Omsk that mud prevented us reaching the airport buildings and some peasants told us that it was the centre of vast state-owned farms as distinct from collectives. But I cannot be sure whether it was at Novosibirsk, the greatest city in Siberia, that we saw the jet plane that is to do the journey from Moscow to Peking in eight hours and the little garden of frost-bitten asters encircling a marble Lenin sitting on a marble sofa and patting paternally the marble shoulders of Stalin. In general one Brobdignagian air palace was much like the next; heavy plush curtains divided the saloons and the cavities between the Corinthian columns were draped and decorated with epic gentility. There were chrysan-themums girdled with paper lace, tubs of castor-oil plants swathed in velour – even the wooden chairs had canvas covers. There were pictures five feet by ten feet of local heroes of the Revolution, of dying horses, wild duck and melons. At Kazan one big wall had a mural of Lenin, the boy from Simbirsk, head-ing a students' rebellion at Kazan University.

I regretted that so few now try to penetrate behind these imposing façades. Life could hardly be drearier for a teacher of English in Novosibirsk than it was for these Edwardian rectory girls whom fate had stranded in some isolated manor house beside the Kama or the Ob, but we are more poor-spirited than they were. It would not be necessary to be a Communist to have such a job and one would learn something of these formidable people who present such a challenge to us and whom we fear so much.

Sometimes a traveller after poking his nose into one of these teeming cities brings back a report of dreariness, overwork, dowdiness, provincialism. But it tells us nothing because it has always been like that. Chekhov sent back just such reports, but horror was blended with love. Of Siberia he wrote:

The people here would make you shudder. They have high cheek-bones, protruding foreheads, tiny eyes, gigantic fists. They are born in the local iron foundries; it's a mechanic, not a midwife, who officiates. . . The cabs are inconceivably squalid, damp, filthy, spring-less and the horses' hooves are stuck onto their spindly front feet in an astounding way. Here, I'll draw it for you. . . And, O Lord, that sausage in Tyumen! When you stuck your teeth into it, it lets out a fearful puff, just as if you went into the stable when the coachman was unwinding his puttees. And when you began to chew it, it was like sticking your teeth into a tar-smeared dog's tail.

But another day he writes:

My God! How rich Russia is in good people! If it were not for the cold which deprives Siberia of summer, and were it not for the officials who corrupt the peasants and exiles, Siberia would be the very richest and happiest of lands.

At Irkutsk on the return journey fog delayed the plane for eight hours, and at last the opportunity arrived for pushing through the plush curtains into Siberia. We were a long way from the town and a taxi was impossibly expensive, so we considered hitch-hiking. One of us got a lift from some workmen carrying sand to a great Orthodox monastery which is now a cinema. They stood him a drink and exchanged friendly remarks in sign language. We two who remained were overtaken by an official from the airport who offered to help us with a difficult bus route to the town. It was a crowded factory workers' bus. The first frost had come and the passengers were swollen to twice their normal size with sheepskin shubas and padded jackets. At every pothole those who stood collapsed into their neighbours' laps with cheerful cries of dismay.

Irkutsk is a town of 300,000 inhabitants, and if my description is depressing I have to record that though the town and the river Angara which traverses it and the grey sky might all have been made in corrugated asbestos sheeting at the foundry, the people were human and friendly. A great deal should be forgiven to those who have to live in Irkutsk and I record as a fact, not an accusation, that all the women who have graduated (and it is not I think unconnected with a university degree) from being female bundles in gum boots, head scarves and padded bodices like life-belts, all wore vertical tam-o'-shanters with a small feather in them. You will meet this hat all the way from the Pacific to the Ural mountains and beyond.

There was a touch of the iron foundry about our airport friend Mr Kardin. He wanted to impress us with the progressiveness of Irkutsk, and those who lagged behind schedule; the ancient female bundle, for example, who was moving leaves about with a broom and did not leap out of our way nimbly enough, got a good hammering. But he indulged our less progressive tastes in a friendly way. He showed us the bronze plaque of Chekhov, bearded and pince-nezed, which still decorates the wall of the hotel he stayed in. He showed us the theatre where classical plays are acted: Lermontov, Ostrovsky and Sheridan were billed. 'Sheridan was an Irishman,' I said. 'Oh, yes we know quite a lot about Ireland in Irkutsk,' he answered. 'We do Irish history after the fifth class. We had two Irish films here lately. One was called "The Road to Freedom", the other "The School of Hatred" . I had not heard of either of them, but the first sounded as if it was about the Desmond Rising, the second – was it Russian, English, American? – was 'about an Irish boy, who was taught in an English school to hate Ireland'. These themes seemed unsuitable enough for Irkutsk but were they more so than Sheridan's eighteenth-century gallantries, than Lermontov's Byronic tragedies – than Ostrovsky, who wrote about the amours of wealthy Moscow merchants?

'We must hurry', said Mr Kardin, 'or the football match between Irkutsk and Angarsk will be over.'

On our way to the football ground we passed the bleak-looking Park of the Paris Commune, and down by the cold grey Angara we saw the baroque palace of the former governor of Irkutsk. It has a placard to commemorate a famous siege, when a group of local Bolsheviks had held it against some White generals in the first years of the Revolution. In the same street there was a row of low and charming houses made of elaborately carved wood. Mr Kardin could not share our admiration for them, and said they were shortly to be replaced by fine modern flats. But he had no prejudice against the past, and confessed that he greatly admired a gorgeous cocoa-coloured villa with turrets and gazebos – a vision from the Arabian Nights, which a timber salesman of the last century had built himself and which is now an old people's home.

The many-tiered gateway to the football ground was also vaguely Arabian and had half-hearted minarets from which the grey paint was flaking off. The short avenue that led to it was lined with framed posters praising the cult of the body and urging application to sport. One of them was a quotation from Lenin, who was not noted for athletic powers. The soccer match was already half over when we reached the playing-field, but there was only a handful of middle-aged peasants and factory workers watching the game from some wooden benches. Nobody cheered or exclaimed, and on the opposite side of the field twenty or thirty young men and women in shorts actually had their backs to what was going on. They were working their arms and legs rhythmically up and down and sideways, and were obviously addicts of some rival cult of the body.

Behind them a tall row of buildings closed in the field. Reading from left to right, Mr Kardin told us they were the morgue, the boiler house for a vast block of flats and a technological institute. Of Angarsk, from which the visiting team had come, he told us that six years ago it had been a wooded valley on either side of the Angara, but now it has a population of 120,000. Petrol is made from coal there and nearby, at Bratsk, is the largest hydro-electric factory in the world. The match went cheerlessly on and it seemed to us that the players were as bored as we were. If it was Dr Arnold of Rugby who invented compulsory games, I could not wish a better punishment for him than to be an ever-lasting spectator of the match between Irkutsk and Angarsk.

Some way off I saw the bulbous dome of a cathedral on a hill and I suggested to Mr Kardin that we should visit it. He smiled at this strange caprice but came with us willingly enough up the rough cobbled road that led to it. It was closed and empty except for the inevitable old woman with the broom who pottered about in the porch. Mr Kardin gave her a few brisk words of command

and she trotted off to look for the key. She soon came back with a group of excited women. They were touchingly pleased to show us the church and led us through chamber after chamber, gorgeous with ikons and murals and candlesticks. It was all in good order and there was a fine ikonostasis. Our admiration obviously gave pleasure and one of the younger women asked with gentle patronage: 'Haven't you any churches where you come from?' They told us that the evening service was just over and that on Sundays the large church was full.

I can well believe this because, on the way from Moscow to Yasnaya Polyana, I had stopped one Sunday morning to see the church in Lopasna, which is now called Chekhov, because Anton Chekhov lived a few miles east of it at Melihovo. The church had been so full that I could scarcely get beyond the door. There, too, the congregation was mainly of women and older men; it is hard to make deductions about the survival of Christianity in Russia because one does not know how many former parishes each church now has to serve. In Irkutsk, apart from the large church which was used as a cinema, the large monastery church which dominates the town from the crest of a hill is now used as a planetarium.

I regretted that I had not been able to visit Melihovo, because Chekhov, though he was an unorthodox Christian and called himself a 'materialist', had given to the local church a gleaming spire which could be seen for miles around. I would like to have seen it if it still survived and if reference was made to it in the Chekhov museum at Melihovo. About Christianity in Russia there is great need for an unemotional record such as Chekhov made of the convict island of Sachalin. For he not only made a census of the inhabitants but interviewed many hundreds of officials and peasants. Listening to their life-stories he had to reckon the part which fear, dishonesty, simplicity and ambition had played in what they told him. No one had believed that the Tsar's government would permit such a survey to be made by a humanist of unorthodox views. But the unbelievable happened; he had been allowed.

On our way back to the bus Mr Kardin lingered with pride through the main square of Irkutsk, which is like an iron-founder's dream of a university campus. A huge square of scraggy grass is surrounded by vast academies and institutes of scientific research. They wear on their pediments, carved in stone, abrupt, congested titles, such as Vostsibugol, which is short for the Eastern Siberian Coal Research Institute. Among them is a colossal library, a museum, students' hostels. They are vast factories of learning, where moujiks are smelted and hammered into scientists. As on an endless conveyor belt a stream of geologists, mineralogists and plant-physicists passes through these buildings and falls, in a thin spray of professors and engineers, over backward and thinly populated regions of Russia.

The province of Irkutsk is one of the great centres of industrial development in Russia and perhaps in Europe. Every conceivable mineral lies beneath its soil and only the men and machines for mining it and converting it to some higher purpose are absent. More and more of the experts are now bred locally, but the working-class populations to fill the great new cities are drafted in from all the regions of Russia.

Sir Eric Ashby, Vice-Chancellor of Queen's University, Belfast, once gave formidable statistics about this great drive for scientific education in Russia. From a population which was 75 per cent illiterate in 1918, so many science teachers and experts are now being trained that they not only satisfy Russia's present needs but can be lent to the backward countries of Asia. In 1954 250,000 science teachers were working in Russia as against 20,000 in Britain.

Walking with Mr Kardin through Irkutsk, one could easily persuade oneself that all this was very regrettable and alarming. Vostsibugol soars above the decaying villas and ugly tenement houses like some sinister intellectual forcing-house from the Brave New World of 1984, that vision of the future with which two disillusioned Etonians have clouded our judgments. But had one seen Irkutsk as Chekhov saw it in 1890, surely one would judge it less harshly? To the grandson of the ferryman who sheltered the writer on the banks of the Irtish, Vostsibugol must seem the gateway into a world of unimagined opportunity; it must offer to his young heart the same glamorous illusions of emancipation that Christchurch or King's holds out to the middle-class youth of England.

Perhaps if one were to spend several months in Irkutsk one might be able to make some sense of this extraordinary jumble of colossal enterprises and mean economies, of generous ambitions and spiritual poverty, of desperate ignorance and brilliant speculation. On the credit side, one would have to note the complete absence of one kind of vulgarity, advertisement-hoardings, beauty queens, comics and film stars, and to analyze the new negative vulgarities which are replacing the old.

Without sharing the lives of these people, one could make no guess where they are going. Is all this vast activity merely a stage on the way to war and universal annihilation or is it a short step towards that world which the heroes of Chekhov so often predicted, when, after two hundred or three hundred years of weary intellectual and spiritual struggle, life will at last be 'unspeakably, amazingly lovely'?

[1956, 1957]

4

IN CHINA

I. SMALL FEET AND BIG NOSES

In the old days a visit to China was a relatively simple affair and you were not expected, after a month's sojourn, to have formed any private opinions. Uncle Fred was in the Shanghai Police; Cousin Harold was in a bank in Canton and Aunt Alice was in Fukien province teaching in a mission school. They were all strongly opinionated people and would have been very snubbing to any relative who started, after a few casual meetings with Chinese, to have independent views. The idea of a cultural delegation to China would have seemed to them preposterous.

They are all gone now and an easy, if at times unreliable, channel of communication is blocked for ever. We have to form our own opinions without any friends, relations, compatriots to help us, and we are definitely expected to express them. I took with me the *Marlborough Chinese Word Book* (1914) in the hope that it would at least help me to break a small hole in the language barrier. But a glance at it showed that even that was written for Uncle Fred, Cousin Harold and Aunt Alice, and by no means for us. There are no fewer than eighteen pages for Uncle Fred: Charge! Eyes-Right! Defaulters' Drill! Reveillé, Rations, Right Wheel! There are twelve pages for Cousin Harold: Affidavit, Arrears, Assets, Demurrage, Dividend, Double Entry. There are seven pages for Aunt Alice: Offertory-Box, Parable, Sunday School, Temperance, Temptation, Wickedness. But I looked in vain for a single page to help a cultural delegation. Pictures, Plays, Pagodas, Poetry, Publishers – such things can never have been a topic of Anglo-Chinese conversation.

For an analogous reason, the editor is hopelessly misleading about the five tones of the Chinese language. He says that if you get the idiom right you need not bother about the tones: the chances are you'll be understood. But in fact the tones are as impenetrable a barrier to mutual understanding as the character-writing, and only one or two of our delegation tried to leap it. In the early hours before breakfast you could hear them going through their scales with a teacher: 'Má, Má, Má, MA,' their voices rising and falling; for only one of these Ma's means 'Mother'. The others mean 'hemp', 'horse', 'curse', or an exclamation of surprise; and a single fault will fuse a whole sentence.

There is very little English of any kind, or indeed of any other European language, spoken in China today. It has become once more a land of mystery, as in the days of Marco Polo. But there is a difference. Everyone is friendly and interested, and we were treated as equals and brothers. Only a few generations ago the Emperor of China had written to George III forbidding all social intercourse. He realized, he said, that later on a visit to the Celestial Empire might possibly be of moral value to the Western barbarians, but he did not think that they had as yet reached a cultural level to profit by it. The average educated Chinaman disliked the Big-Noses, thinking they smelt unpleasantly and finding something sinister in their round eyes, irregular pigmentation and hairy cheeks; and, of course, they were keenly and justifiably frightened of the Pink Peril. Till Sir Henry Pottinger brought his warships up the Yangtse in 1842 there was very little intercourse and no diplomatic relations between China and the West.

The intimacy, started in such an unpropitious way, was never cordial. At the time of the Boxer Rebellion the last Empress ordered a massacre of all the Europeans; and there was continuous constraint and suspicion. No doubt today, too, a spark would set the old passions flaming, but we certainly were only aware of friendliness and courtesy. It was not the old ceremonial courtesy of the imperial China of the London music halls ('My humble doorstep is not worthy that your honourable shadow should fall on it') but an imaginative and unobtrusive sympathy and solicitude. This was not laid on for our benefit, for we met it also as we wandered on our own round the streets shopping or sightseeing.

Once or twice we were mistaken for Russians; but it was not because of Stalin's big nose and Marx's beard which decorated

so many club-rooms and lecture halls that our Western idiosyn-
crasies were smiled upon. Such few Russians as we saw were
as little acclimatized as ourselves. They held together, sightseeing in depressed bus-loads and poking mournfully with their
chopsticks at Chinese delicacies. 'When you get to Canton,' one
of them said to me, sadistically and quite incorrectly, 'you'll have
to eat cat-and-snake pie.'

How much of the fascination that we found in Peking was a
relic of the imperial or bourgeois past which will disappear in a
few years? Much of it, I suppose. Peking is a city of trees and
gardens, because the Emperor liked an uninterrupted view from
the imperial palace and two-storeyed houses were forbidden.
The middle and upper classes expanded sideways, so that their
homes usually consisted of a group of low buildings of brick
and glass and latticework, set lightly like summer-houses round
quadrangles filled in September with Michaelmas daisies and
tubs of lotus. The father and mother lived in one of them, the
grandmother, perhaps, in another, a married son in another.
There might be seven or eight separate establishments, and one
could picture them living a willow-pattern existence, walking
across rustic bridges to take tea with each other and composing
ironical couplets in the shade of a magnolia tree.

These houses took up an immense amount of space and pre-
supposed a life of leisure which is not now possible. Yet an
elderly clergyman with whom I took tea contemplated with
equanimity the ultimate disappearance of his home. He was not
being hustled, he said, change was inevitable; he had left one
of the summer-houses to the Church. Nor was he frightened of
the materialism of the age. A materialist philosophy had prevailed in the Sung dynasty, yet the arts had flourished. The
Chinese peasant was not a primitive person. And if he was
emancipated, he too would display creative talents. Each
dynasty had ended like this in social revolution.

Listening to him, one could believe that the Chinese were the
most rational and practically minded people in the world. If they
occasionally ate cat-and-snake pie, it was because they had been
experimenting with the material world for three thousand years
and had shed all vulgar prejudices. For example, he said,
modern medical science in China is now justifying and exploit-
ing the empirical observations of the Chinese herbalists.

I could take most of this. The Chinese can make something

exquisite and refined out of the most unappetizing spiritual and material ingredients. But, of course, every now and then something happened to shake this belief in Chinese common sense. Occasionally one heard behind one a small patter of two feet and a stick, and an elderly lady with her hair screwed back in a serious sensible bun hobbled past on small doll's feet fitted into triangular pockets of leather. Instantly all that I had read of bound feet and infanticide came back to me; perhaps it was true, as a sailor had told me twenty years ago, that he had seen the weirs in the Yangtse choked with the bodies of unwanted female infants. We saw women as young as thirty with bound feet. Plainly, long after the practice had been officially forbidden, upper-class parents must have crippled their children deliberately so as to give them an aristocratic helplessness.

To the passing stranger Chinese children are certainly enchanting. If you get up early in the morning you may see them rolling by in their school pedicabs, glass boxes like greenhouses on wheels drawn by a bicyclist in a coolie hat. Behind the panes seven or eight tiny scholars are fidgeting and chattering like sparrows. We never heard a child cry, except one who was seen having a surgical operation in a barber's shop, and they seem without shyness. Once at a créche we were mobbed by thirty or forty infants. They left their play-pens and their educational toys and swarmed round us thrusting their arms stiffly into the air, pleading for picky-backs.

But once up in the air they focussed all their attention on the mysterious un-Chinese growths of hair on our faces, exploring them with speculative fingers. One of us who was hairier than the others had babies hanging all over him in clusters, like leeches, insatiably curious.

How can one reconcile these happy children with the cruel traditions of their ancestors? It is not sufficient to say that those customs have been abolished. How could they have survived so long in a highly civilized people? That is one of those questions which we had to leave unsolved.

II. TEMPLES AND CHURCHES

One of us developed the dubious theory that the Chinese language is descriptive, not informative, and that place-names are not meant to locate but to explain. Certainly if you asked the name of a hill or a lake, there was always the greatest difficulty. One day we stood with a Chinaman on a sacred island, looking at the marble slab on which its name was written in flowing characters. 'You want its name?' he answered doubtfully. 'Well, it's rather hard to translate. There was a king, you see, and he saw the shadow of the moon falling between two Tangs.'

'What is a Tang?'

'Those are Tangs, those stone things sticking out of the lake. When it has a stone cap on it, it's a tomb, otherwise it's just a monument. They were made in the Tang dynasty.'

'Is that why they are called Tangs?'

'Oh, no, that's quite different. I said Tang, not Tang! Ho, ho, ho! Ha, ha, ha!' (A lot could be written about Chinese laughter. It comes from lower down the throat than ours and is an immensely warm and sociable noise. It is seldom derisive, but often used to cover up the traces of someone else's embarrassing stupidity.)

'Yes, but what is the *name* of the island?'

'Please, I am telling you now. Ho, ho! You see, this king had a dream. . .'

Another temple's name was a very long story about a tiger, another was concerned with some blue clouds. Large crowds reached it by bus, so plainly the Chinese have some device for telescoping these anecdotes for the purpose of a bus ticket, but they had difficulty in sharing it with us.

The Chinese are expert acrobats and jugglers, and I think they can keep as many contradictory ideas dancing about in their mind as they can plates, parasols, eggs and coconuts. Otherwise the government's curious attitude to these temples and the Buddhism to which they are dedicated is hard to explain. Buddhism, at least in its material manifestations, is in violent conflict not only with Marxism but with all the ideals of the West. Yet our path crossed several times that of a world Buddhist organization which was touring China. Draped in robes of orange, lemon and saffron, bald-headed, spectacled, they were to be seen trooping in and out of taxis, hotel lifts, museums, in Hangchow, Peking, Shanghai. They were always delighted. 'The government is doing wonders for Buddhism and spending large sums on its temples.'

We saw evidence of this ourselves. The repair of a Buddhist temple is not a matter of an odd coat of paint. Scores of dragons, lotus buds, whales, phoenixes, camels, souls in agony, six-headed cows, as well as Buddha in several manifestations with his many attendants, have all to be carefully redecorated. Swallows' nests have to be taken from the intricate woodwork under the eaves and the protective wire-netting carefully reinstated. Real hair whiskers have to be replaced on gilded demons and acres of porcelain-tiling, camphor-wood columns and carved stone pillars have to be renovated.

There are many possible explanations for this energy, some of them credible, some not. Cynics say that the government is still wooing the Tibetans, the most religious people in the world (a third of their male population are monks), who are still imperfectly assimilated to China. But Buddhist temples are usually charmingly situated, surrounded by groves and streams and carefully tended gardens. Fat carp, orange and dun-coloured, swim about in sacred tanks, and from the tops of the temples you look down on doves nesting in lime trees. Or perhaps a very small bird is perching in an ornamental cherry tree, and a holiday-maker is stalkng it with an air-gun. These places will always have a secular appeal, and that is maybe why a secular government can afford to spend so much money on them.

Many of the large Buddhist temples north of Peking are in excellent repair, but we visited one near Hangchow which was being rebuilt from the beginning. (Its collapse was attributed to Chiang Kai-shek, but I expect that time and disbelief were the real offenders.) While still some way off we could hear the whirr of saws and the hammer of mallets, and inside the temple we found scores of craftsmen chiselling dragons round stone pedestals, shaping wooden columns or painting arabesques upon altars. The back of the temple was completed and, passing a score or more of half-finished gods and goddesses three times life-size, we came to a screen sixty feet high of painted wood and plaster.

I do not know whether it was an apocalyptic vision of Heaven or Hell, but it left us speechless. We had never in our lives seen such a profusion of intricate and horrific detail. Let me describe one corner where there is a sort of vertical cavalcade. Surrounded by jelly-fish and snakes, a naked man is riding a sea monster, which is vomiting on to an umbrella, which is carried by a demon, who is riding a griffin, which is swallowing. . . but no description can do justice to these strange works of art, and nobody could tell us what they meant. 'Who is that man roaring and stamping his feet?'

'He is a god.'

'But why is he beating the naked woman with his guitar, and why has he two eyes in the soles of his feet?'

'Because he is an angry god.'

Nobody could be blamed for not knowing, for only a specialist could unravel these complex mysteries. But it was very puzzling to witness the elaborate reconstruction of a symbolism in which, it would appear, very few now believe.

Possibly the Communists argue that popular Buddhism is innocuous and politically moribund. In the old days the landlords used to have an annual feast in the temple of the City God, and he may have seemed to some 'a symbol of feudalism'; but these feasts have long been discontinued and the City God is worshipped for himself alone. The God of Shanghai and his temple have been for a long time completely swallowed up in the market. To buy cabbages or peanuts you must go through the innermost sanctuary and pass his four gigantic guardian gods; in front of the City God himself is a bowl in which some joss sticks are smouldering, a box of matches, a dish-cloth and a copy of the *Shanghai Daily News*. There is no evidence of disrespect, but none of awe either, and for the simple surely awe is an essential part of Buddhism.

But perhaps I have no right to argue infidelity from absence of fervour. The Chinese have always been a sceptical people – 'Worship the gods', said Confucius, 'as if they existed' – and it is possible that their Communism will be as individual as their religious beliefs, and as liable to be submerged in ornamental accretions.

We visited also a Taoist temple. Taoism used to be a deeply spiritual faith but, like the others, it has through the centuries become encrusted with a gorgeous and fantastic mythology. In the central shrine we found the usual pop-eyed divinities with bared teeth and furious tomato faces, but in the rear was a very benign god, Tao's father, the creator of the world. He had a black wedge-shaped hat upon a knob of hair. Some attempt has evidently been made to modernize his worship, for he is said to have appeared in the sky over Peking one day in June 1927, and just below him there is a framed and enlarged photograph of his apparition. The clouds have parted over the tops of trees and roofs of houses to reveal him. There is his wedge-shaped hat right enough, and the very same benign smile.

There were still five priests in the temple, gentle creatures, one of them quite young, busying themselves laying out on plates in front of the gods little pyramids of buns and apples. But they have had to let a part of the monastic premises to some workers' families and ten or a dozen small children gazed at us from behind the latticed windows.

Confucianism is perhaps at present more discouraged than the other ancient religions, because Chiang Kai-shek, who was in fact a Methodist, tried to base a new social order on its revival. It is an ethic rather than a faith, but it has shaped Chinese life for so many generations that it is unlikely that its influence will ever disappear.

What has happened, and what will happen, to the Christian Churches in China? This is a vastly important question for us; to the Chinese it does not appear so, since only an infinitesimal percentage of the population has ever been Christian. Two or three of us heard much about the Churches and saw many clergy, but what we heard and what we conjectured were sometimes in conflict.

Everybody knows how hard it has been for the Christian Churches in China to dissociate themselves from the political and commercial aspirations of the Western powers, and how often they have failed. Toleration of missionary effort was grudgingly granted after humiliating defeat in the Opium War, and, now that the concessions then extorted have been withdrawn, it would be very strange if the old suspicions did not revive, taking their colour from Marxism rather than from the moribund creeds of imperial China.

Must it be a case of war to the death? I can only quote a distinguished Chinese Christian scholar of Peking. He told me that the government is not hostile to Christianity, but it is challenging, and that the future of the Churches in China depends on the Christian answer to that challenge.

III. THE BRIDGE OF FU KO CHOW

When you are a guest in a foreign country and like it very much, a wholesome corrective to any excessive infatuation is to visit some European embassy. You will usually find there some very knowing, disapproving person who will puncture your naive enthusiasms and explain how far you have been led up the garden path. He will sometimes hint that your judgment has been warped by caviare and civic receptions. To those of us who loathe caviare, these insinuations can be irritating; but I am glad that some of us took the the risk of visiting two foreign embassies in Peking, that of a large democracy and that of a small one.

We had been told things that we found it very hard to believe; a resident who was also an outsider might be able to help us. Was there some catch in the tremendous slum-clearances we had seen in Shanghai? Was it true that the war on dirt and disease had improved the general health? And if it had, were they as little worried about over-population as they claimed to be? Then we had just seen the Peking gaol. Was it really true that 1800 prisoners went to bed every night in unlocked cells, that the warders were unarmed (or rather that there were no warders, but only teachers, cooks, experts in the manufacture of socks and textiles, etc.), and that the only guard was a military one outside the walls? Had we been shown special cells suitable for visiting delegations, or were they all as airy and clean, with gay wall decoration and Chinese lanterns in the corridor? Had they all cotton counterpanes, printed with tractors in a ring of rosebuds? What about brainwashing and mob-trials?

We got the expected douche of cold water from the great democracy, but administered with intelligence and charity. From the small one we got a less guarded approval of the social achievements of the Chinese government. We had not been deceived on these points. The cells were not locked, but the prison we saw, where two-thirds of the prisoners were political, was not the only one in Peking. There was another one where 're-education' often took the form of interminable cross-examination. But there was nothing secret about this prison or its methods; it had been frequently visited by foreign correspondents, we could have seen it had we asked.

And indeed, to a large extent we made our own programme, visiting whom we chose; and had we, as a cultural delegation, refused to see any 'non-cultural' spectacles, our wishes would, I think, have been indulged, if not approved. But naturally we were interested in the future of China as well as its past. For the middle-aged and set in their ways, the future certainly did not look rosy. Or rather, among the rosebuds there was always a tractor. The willow-pattern world of leisure and cultivated conversation had gone for ever. One of us visited a banker friend who had remained behind in Shanghai to 'wind up' as best as he could the last tangled shreds of his Shanghai bank. He was thirsting to be gone. Every day's delay was torture. 'It's all right for the Chinese. What they have done to clean up Shanghai is beyond belief. They have checked corruption and disease, but they have made life intolerable for Europeans.'

That was more or less what we had heard, too, in the embassies. For generations the Chinaman had been considered a backward, ridiculous fellow, who for his own good must be forced into the main streams of Western progress. The Chinese put up a feeble, but persistent resistance to Westernization. They clung to their old traditions, building tombs for their ancestors and solving all social, moral and political questions by reference to the teaching of Confucius. Western pressure became stronger and stronger, and by the end of the last century it seemed almost certain that China would be carved up, like Africa, among the European powers. Only their mutual jealousy prevented this from happening. The Chinese had watched Japan becoming in a few generations a great power, able to challenge successfully the Russian Empire. She had done this by adopting Western civilization. It was plain that for China, too, Beelzebub had to be thrown out by Beelzebub.

The Europeans were so securely planted in China that it was more or less inevitable that the Chinese should choose the most explosive of Western philosophies to dislodge them. Long before Mao Tse-tung, Chiang Kai-shek had applied to Moscow for assistance in the shaping of the Kuomintang, and Borodin had been sent as an adviser for a few years. But the opposition leaders considered that a bigger charge of Marxist dynamite was needed. In 1949 there was a gigantic explosion; not only were the Westerners thrown out, but the old China was blown sky high.

In so tremendous a cataclysm it is difficult to count the casualties or to estimate how soon, if ever, the new energy which has been released can repair the damage which has been done. Whole classes have disappeared – landlords, bankers, scholars, civil servants, priests; and such things do not happen without appalling wastage and suffering. Obviously there must have been peaceful ways in which the same force could have been generated; but who was likely to find them? Certainly not the Europeans, to whose interests it had been that China should remain weak and divided.

All that is clear is that the energy *has* been generated. For good or evil, China has become a force to be reckoned with; she is more united than she has been for a century. And even the most unsympathetic visitor could not fail to be aware that the air was charged with excitement and enthusiasm. Dreams were not, as in other countries, divorced from reality, but were being realized daily. What right had a Westerner to complain that they were mainly Western dreams, and were being fulfilled in ferro-concrete and not in jade and camphor-wood and marble? A vast bridge, one of the greatest in the world, was being built across the Yangtse, and every province had its own schemes for factories, power-stations, irrigation projects.

But, of course, we did complain. The old China was being swept away, and the energy for these achievements was being diverted from those pursuits which we had come out to observe. Probably as much manpower, skill and enthusiasm had been applied to the Ru Ko Chow bridge near Peking as has gone to spanning the Yangste, but it will never be applied in that way again. The balustrades are sustained on either side by a hundred stone lions and supported at either end by stone elephants. Each lion is slightly different; they seem to have their hearts (or are they heart-shaped lockets?) round their necks, and their cubs are chewing them. Nobody, of course, could tell us why.

There are thousands of such monuments all over China, most of them betraying high craftsmanship. There is a replica of Ru Ko Chow bridge in the grounds of the Summer Palace built thirty or forty years ago, but already it bears traces of the Age of Progress and the detail is slipshod and inferior. The Summer Palace itself was burnt by the English in 1860. A cultural defeat can often be as serious as a military one. Those who rebuilt it, decorated it and furnished it had obviously caught the contagion of the Great Exhibition and of Balmoral Castle, and the portrait of the Empress Dowager in the vestibule bears a striking likeness to Queen Victoria.

It was plain that the museums were admirably kept, the temples and palaces were being restored; there were galleries and cultural institutes where none had been before. But all that was a matter of maintenance and organization, not of creation. It is probable that the creative impulse has shifted away from the arts. The best painter, Chi Bai She, is well over ninety, and did not seem to have any obvious successors. He spent his life not in movements and revolutions, but watching the shape and colour of a jackdaw's tail-feathers, the tendrils of the vine, the veins in a maple leaf. And that is the tradition of old China, an intense concentration on small things. A Chinese took as much pain in writing his name as in painting a flower, and his signature is an integral part of the picture. Can this delicacy of perception be carried over into a hydro-electric proletarian civilization? It is not, of course, a Chinese problem only but our artists and sculptors did not appear to get much encouragement for its solution from China. Looking at exhibitions of contemporary art, they found abundance of skill, unsurpassed mastery of technique, but something, perhaps the proud independence of the artist, was missing. Where Chinese art became the accomplice of contemporary politics, appalling outrages were often committed.

On a lower plane, the Chinese decorative sense seemed infallible. At the mid-September Moon Festival in Canton, every lantern was a triumph of inventiveness. They were shaped like dragons, griffins, camels, elephants. It was easy to fall into the old trap and to mistake the unknown for the magnificent. The Canton moon, the guest of the evening, seemed far larger and brighter than ours, and if we could have seen the gay and ubiquitous Chinese script as words and not as pictures, possibly we should have been disillusioned. Someone asked the meaning of a gay arabesque that ran round the brim of a coolie hat. It meant: 'We must hit the bullseye on the target of productivity.'

IV. THE BIRD CHING-WEI

'The bird Ching-wei carried small twigs
In her unshakeable determination
to fill up the Eastern Sea.'

I am not certain whether the poet was here making fun of Ching-wei, but in her patience, optimism and industry Ching-wei was a very Chinese bird. In Russia one hears only of Five-Year Plans, but in China Hundred-Year Plans are discussed. Time is of no importance.

If the Chinese had wished to dazzle us with the speed of their accomplishments rather than to exhibit the problems to which a solution had to be found, they would not have taken us to that collective farm near Peking. It was a very large one, containing 2443 families, 94 more or less absorbed and assimilated ex-landowners, 560 pigs, 494 mules and donkeys, nine schools, two lorries, 33,000 library books. They grew wheat and cotton and maize and millet, peanuts, kaoling and sweet potatoes.

I would consider that I had made a mistake about those two lorries if I had not seen some collectivized peasants engaged in old-style farming on their own private allotment., An old donkey with some blue cotton pants over his eyes was walking round a mill-stone, pulling a roller which was crushing some maize. As the maize scattered outwards to the edge of the stone a little girl pressed it back under the roller with her fingers. From time to time the little girl gave some handfuls of crushed grain to her mother, who sat on the ground beside her and sieved it in a bowl through a coarse-meshed sieve. When she had filled a bowl, she went across to a kitchen colander and resieved it all into a cardboard box. There were some pans of wheat and millet waiting to be done in this way, too.

The collective threshing of the soya bean was scarcely more up-to-date. The dry haulms were stacked on some square yards of trampled mud and lashed about with forks. Then they were tossed to one side and the grain was swept up with brooms. Twenty of the thinnest pigs I have ever seen looked on from their sties at this process; to reach them we had to paddle across a small channel of disinfectant.

I dare say that, apart from the little stream of disinfectant, in itself a cultural revolution, things were much the same in the days of the 94 landowners. The old donkey looked as if he and his ancestors had been walking round the mill stone for thousands of years, and as if his children – but, I think, not his grandchildren – would follow in his footsteps. Behind one of the barns a vast stone tombstone lay on its side and beside it the stone tortoise, the symbol of longevity or enduring memory, on which it had been reared. No doubt the Chinese characters recorded the rank and virtues of a former landlord, but no one could tell us much. 'It's just a tombstone.'

'What are you going to do with it?'

'Nothing. It's no use.'

Apart from the splendid tombstone, there was no trace of former parks and gardens and architectural splendours. Aristocratic families were large, and the properties divided or shared among innumerable descendants; so it is likely that the 94 landlords were quite simple people, extravagant only in their devotion to their ancestors. It was against the ancestors as much as against the landlords that the revolution was directed, and there had been friction for some generations between them and the agricultural experts. All the way from Peking to Canton the fields had been dotted with grave-mounds like large ant-heaps; sometimes a marrow or a pumpkin had been planted on top of them, but usually they were bleak islands in a sea of rice or soya bean. In the spring the descendants used to come out and, laying an embroidered cloth on the grave and seating themselves on crimson satin cushions, used to have a commemorative picnic.

Only occasionally did one notice a concentration of these graves, where they clustered round a triumphal arch or two stone columns with stone clouds, the symbol of eternity, projecting from the summit. In the office of the collective farm there was a poster of some fresh-faced, productivity-increasing pioneers tackling some tombstones with spades and pick-axes. It was inscribed: 'The dead must not stand in the way of the living.' But after seven years of Communisim the paddy-fields are still speckled with millions of graves. The bird Ching-wei is in no hurry. It has not occurred to her to use a bulldozer.

Yet the mechanical revolution is on its way. When it comes, it will surely transform society as much as it transforms the countryside. Can it fail to bring with it the usual problems of over-population and unemployment? The contrast with the empty plains of Siberia, where there often seemed to be as many tractors as men, was startling. Looking out of the railway carriage windows, we seemed to see every few yards a Chinaman in a large hat hoeing or transplanting rice seedlings, steering a tub across a pond to collect water chestnuts, stripping the foliage of hemp or soaking the long hemp skeins in tanks, working a long-armed wooden pump to irrigate the rice fields. Only the ox and the buffalo and the mule were there to lighten their labours. There were not many horses, but sometimes we saw one drawing a wagon with basket sides like an old-fashioned governess cart, loaded with sacks of lime or piles of bamboo. A donkey, as often as not, trots beside the horse; he does not seem to be pulling very hard, but he is said to have a pacifying and encouraging effect on his big brother. Some wear eye-shields, but others have been blinded by the dust and lime.

What will be the ultimate effect of mechanization on unemployment? In so vast and enigmatic a land as China perhaps one man's guess is as good as another's. In one of the great courtyards of the Forbidden City a long blue-tide of crouching Chinese was creeping slowly across the cobble stones. They were rooting out weeds from the crevices with knives and putting them in tins.

'You could do the whole thing with a couple of gallons of weedkiller,' I said to Mr Pu, but he replied: 'We want to save our foreign credit for really vital imports.'

'Surely', I said, 'the real reason is that you would not know what to do with all these people if you used weed-killer?' But Mr Pu would not agree that there is or ever could be an unemployment problem. 'And why not a garden-hose for all those flower beds and lotus tubs, instead of those old men dropping roped buckets into the lily-pond?' Same answer.

The Nazi solution for unemployment was intensive militarization but I think only fear for its frontiers could shake China out of the old Confucian prejudice that the soldier ranked lowest in the order of society. It was because of that prejudice that Messrs Jardine and Mathieson were able to build and defend with force their commercial empire in China.

Though frequently exploited, I don't think the prejudice is extinct. Yet one would hesitate now to presume on it. On October 1st, the National Day, we stood for five hours at the

Gateway of Heavenly Peace watching many thousands of soldiers and sailors march past in the pouring rain. Their legs moved like pistons, their white gloves like bobbins in a weaving machine. There was not a solitary mistake or misadventure to relieve the awful tedium, but every hour or so there was a frivolous interlude, a procession of dragons or a van load of cardboard vegetable marrows, each the size of a horse, or all at once the sky was full of multicoloured balloons.

The evening ended auspiciously in superb fireworks, and we recalled the old tradition that gunpowder had been known in China centuries before it reached Europe, but that this sensible people had used it only for social and religious purposes, pyrotechnics at parties, ceremonial salvoes and squibs to scare away demons. It will be of painful interest to us to discover how much of this common-sense has survived Confucianism.

V. JOURNEY TO SHANGHAI

Chinese railway journeys are usually immensely long and begin with ceremony. As the doors slam, the railway porters stand to attention and the vendors of roast chicken and water chestnut fall in beside them in a wobbly, courteous line.

The engine gets up speed and the music starts, an exceedingly squeaky and alien sound with a gay refrain that jingles round and round with the wheels. After a time it breaks off, and a female voice, squeaky like the music, pronounces: 'Comrades! This train is yours. Keep it clean. Put your cigarette stubs in the ashtray. Leave the toilet as you would wish to find it. Make sure you have your tickets. Dinner is served at seven.'

Then the music starts again, sad, nostalgic, gay, round and round, like the nursery musical-box. Surely we are not just a delegation going to see the slums of Shanghai, but Gullivers off to visit some socialized Land of Prester John where golden apples are graded for export and red lacquer dragons give a record yield of brimstone.

Every twenty minutes a smiling Lilliputian comes in with a large watering-can of boiling water with which he fills and refills our tea mugs. As the last flush of colour fades from the tea we speculate whether by jamming the lid on tight we can keep it warm till we are ready to shave, for in this beardless land shaving is attended with difficulties.

Once or twice a day an attendant, with a cotton pad over mouth and nose, grins us out into the corridor, souses our compartment with disinfectant and brushes out the floor. This is a part of the great and successful crusade which is purging China of flies, mice, sparrows, germs. The waiters in the dining-car also wear pads, but my waiter has not quite caught the spirit of the crusade, for he has his thumb in the fruit salad, just as he might at home in Ireland.

At the opposite table two students are spitting their chicken bones on to the tablecloth. This is quite normal good manners, though, for a Chinese chicken is sliced up whole into small pieces that can be handled by chopsticks, and the bones, which are thought to give an indispensable flavour, are not extracted. The disintegrated chicken sits on a single plate between the two students, who demolish it with chopsticks from opposite sides. The tablecloth, which always returns freshly laundered, is meant to be spat on.

At Shanghai we decided that in all that really matters the Chinese must be among the cleanest people on earth. In the slum district of Drug Lane there are 18,000 inhabitants; the streets are cobbled and so narrow and crowded wth wash-tubs, primus stoves (they cook out of doors), vegetable stalls and babies, that only a man-drawn pedicab could pass down it, and pedicabs are now disappearing as 'degrading to human dignity'.

Imagine the symphony of smells that would arise from such a street on a hot day in Naples! There were no smells at all in Drug Lane, except such as are appropriate to a summer afternoon. Many of ther residents had made their own houses out of bamboo, wood and bricks, thatched them and whitewashed them. They are small and crumbling, and till not long ago all their water had to come from the canal; the Kuomintang gave them twelve taps and now they have thirty-two.

One of the cottages has been made an office, and there the Secretary holds meetings of the six Welfare Committees of the neighbourhood. The only one of them that seemed convincingly Chinese was the Reconciliation Committee. Looking at the passers-by in the street, we could see that the Committee would have to reconcile not only squabbling neighbours but whole epochs of civilization. Two small boys passed by with cotton pads over their noses; they grabbed them off and grinned at us in case we should think they had some terrible disease.

Behind them came an elderly sage in a black skull-cap, a wisp of white hair projecting from his chin; he wore a lilac dressing-gown and a scarlet umbrella slung across his shoulder in a case. After him came a little girl swinging in her hand a willow-twig to which two large grasshoppers were tethered. Her skull was shaven bald except for three pig-tails, plaited tightly with red ribbon. We were told she was probably a dearly loved only child and that she had pigtails so that her parents could hold on to her.

A great deal of Chinese superstition is an elaborate kind of ancient fun like this. In Peking the old streets sometimes had a sharp bend, so that if you were chased by a demon you could dodge him by an abrupt swerve.

I do not know if there is any place for this ancient fun in the new suburb into which 6370 families from Drug Lane have been transferred. It has broad roads and Savings Banks, fifteen buses in a row, hot and cold communal taps, television aerials and a tall painted tower to carry slogans about cleanliness, flies, productivity, Formosa. Apart from the tower and the hot-water taps, it is indistinguishable from a million workers' suburbs in Western Europe.

It is too easy for the travellers to repine for pigtails and pedicabs and to say that good plumbing and well-built roads do not lead to contentment. But what Western government has discovered a better route?

The 'cleaning-up' of Shanghai is one of the most remarkable achievements of the Communist régime. The Chinese, when they decide on a moral objective, are frighteningly whole-hearted, Lowes Dickinson, who travelled in China after Sun Yat Sen's revolution, relates how in the campaign against opium, smokers were flogged and beheaded, and in Hunan seventy farmers who resisted the destruction of their poppy-crops were shut up in a temple and burnt alive.

I do not know the method by which vice was suppressed in Shanghai, but few can dispute its success. We visited one of the famous haunts of sin in the city, formerly called the Great World, and found it transformed into a Peoples' Recreation Palace. It contained fourteen theatres as well as club-rooms for table-tennis and chess and many other blameless games and hobbies.

You can see acrobats and opera, puppet shows, tragedies,

comedies, ballet. It is a gay but noisy place, for the Chinese like to beat gongs behind the scenes to emphasize the emotional crises on the stage; these make a furious barking sound, as though one of those enraged bronze animals that decorate the terraces of the imperial palaces were suddenly to find a tongue. It is the most characteristic of all the many Chinese noises.

On my way out I passed through a reading-room where a number of elderly people were sitting round a pile of small fat books three inches square. These books are the Chinese equivalent of comics, but better than ours. I looked over the shoulders of a serious spectacled man expecting to see that his comic would be about stakhanovites or spacemen, but judging from illustrations it was about a wicked magician who had swallowed his own evil potion by mistake. His nose had grown ten feet long and was coiling round his ankles.

Perhaps the Chinese endure their revolutions so calmly, because, despite their four thousand years of civilization, they have retained the lively imaginations of childhood. No catastrophe, either natural or supernatural, can really surprise them.

[1956]

5

A VISIT TO ONEIDA

I was in luck. It was Thanksgiving Day in upstate New York and, though this meant that the factory was closed and the official guide was away and the stall of Oneida silverware from which tourists were expected to select souvenirs was closed, some of the leaders of the community were taking the day off in the Mansion House and could show me round. Many of their names were familiar, that of Mr Inslee, for example, who took charge of me, for I had read of their fathers and grandfathers in Pierrepoint Noyes' books. In an age of conformity, the Mansion House has kept its continuity with the America of revolution and experiment surprisingly well, better perhaps than more distinguished shrines like Mount Vernon or Monticello, or Brigham Young's house at Salt Lake City. I suppose this is because it was never just the family home of a revolutionary. It was itself built as the workshop in which a revolution was planned and carried out. Then it became a besieged fortress, which surrendered more or less, but was never quite abandoned or assimilated to ordinariness. It still has an air of not impolite disengagement. The big trees and the lawns which the community laid out still make a small but perceptible psychological barrier against the encroachments of its post-revolutionary prosperity, the factory workers' ranch-type and colonial villas and the social annexes to the factory. There is a charming library where the books on the shelves and periodicals that lie on the table are serious, adventurous, unprejudiced. There is a big saloon at the back where some of the staff from the silver factory were playing cards, talking or reading and I recognized over the big fire-place a portrait of Pierrepoint Noyes. While I was looking at it, his son, a director of the firm and Dr Noyes' grandson detached himself from his card game and, learning that I was Irish, told me that the Oneida firm was about to start a branch in Belfast. I followed Mr Inslee to the music room with its big gallery and to the council room where the community had its meetings to discuss the future and to listen to addresses from the founder. On the staircase there are framed daguerrotypes of the community, sitting or standing in rows like rather relaxed college groups. The men all have beards or side burns and the women have rather odd but reasonably feminine garments of a Victorian cut. Walking on beyond them I saw through a big window a magnolia tree shedding its petals onto a demure well-kept courtyard. Some decades ago H. G. Wells visited Oneida and was struck by the contrast between these prim photographs in their quietly prosperous setting and the wildly adventurous social experiment which had drawn them together and resulted in the Mansion House. And indeed I do not know of any Utopia which dissolved into such elegant and agreeable ruins, for, of course, from the standpoint of Utopia, the large efficient factory and its branches spreading as far as Belfast, and the village that has grown up around the Mansion House and Mr Inslee and Mr Noyes and their pleasant and contented-looking companions, are all of them ruinous symbols of defeat, pitiful distortions of the intentions of their progenitors. For the silverware factory is run on what are roughly speaking ordinary commercial lines, though in a very enlightened way, and the group that lives in the Mansion House is married or celibate according to the normal pattern. Yet there has been no express repudiation or recantation. In the library I felt an air of patient expectation as though the final report on the great adventure had not yet been published, and as though somewhere there was a great chest of psychological exhibits still to be ticketed and displayed and nuggets of social experience which had, if anything, appreciated in value as the years passed by.

I think that the caretakers of all this still thought of their grandparents as famous explorers. That is how they appeared to Pierrepoint Noyes, one of the planned children of the second generation round whom the experimental society in which he had been born and reared had crumbled. He was deeply proud of his origins: 'We had made a raid into an unknown country, charted it and returned without the loss of man, woman or child.'

While I was still in the library waiting till my bus back to

Albany was due, I heard a group walking towards me down the passage very ponderously and slowly. The door opened and a very old man – he must have been ninety – came into the room led by a young girl. 'This is Mr Leonard,' Mr Inslee who accompanied them explained to me, 'the last surviving planned baby.' Mr Leonard was too old to make any articulate comment, but, as the conversation moved round him, he contributed some proud and smiling acknowledgments. Then after a few minutes he was led away again by the girl. His name, like most of the other names I had heard in the saloon, was familiar to me, since a century before it had been borne by one of the pioneers. But only when I got back to New York was I able to collate what I had heard and seen in the Mansion House with what I had read.

How had it happened that Noyes, despite his failure, had at least left behind some proud memories and a flourishing business community, while Joyce and Lawrence and their numerous imitators had achieved so little? Lawrence had aimed at being a sexual reformer in a bigger way and Joyce, engaged on his cold, private conjuring trick, had tried to see how many obscene words he could balance chastely on his towering literary integrity. What had been the result? They had liberated a few condemned words, but the ideas and images which they released loiter uselessly in the mind like an audience reluctant to believe that the show to which they have been summoned has been postponed. And ideas that loiter, disengaged from reality however fine in intention, are specially corruptible. Despite all the serious criticism, the Ph.D. theses and the championship of the high-minded, they have as paperbacks found appalling companions on the bus-terminal book stall.

As a pioneer Noyes had two obvious advantages over Lawrence. Firstly he was a God-believer in a God-believing society, and like other religious leaders could call on divine authority to strengthen his own convictions and to bind his followers to him. Secondly he lived before buses and telegrams could publicize or vulgarize an adventure whose development depended on patience and privacy.

Pioneers who find causes by examining their hearts inevitably assume that what they find there comes from some source that transcends reason. And in Noyes' day the common name for such a source was 'God'. And religion was a bridge between the consciousness of divine purpose and the obligation to assist others to understand and acquiesce. That is to say one might at any moment become the authorized interpreter of God's will to others. New England had for half a century produced a succession of leaders to whom some truth had been revealed. Ever since the Puritan revolt against popes and bishops and the whole hierarchy of interpreters of God's will, it had been easier for an unofficial mediator between God and Man to sway the minds of men who had thrown off ecclesiastical tyranny yet retained the habit of obedience. Then too there was still the Bible, a great bran-pie of intoxicating poetry, of stern exhortations and luminous phrases, on which a man could draw to explain and justify and enforce the revelation which he had received.

Can one assess the value of one man's revelation of the divine as against another's? Not easily. One man with a command of words may describe some not very startling spiritual adventure so luminously that we follow him. Another man, who is ignorant and reared in platitudes, may be able to express only in nonsense words and a discredited mythology some great spiritual disentanglement from our worldly prejudices and preoccupations. Perhaps indeed Joseph Smith of the Mormons did have some dazzling revelation of the divine such as was never vouched to more sober prophets like John Wesley. Truth against which the study and the drawing-room windows are barred is obliged to force its way through the basement.

Noyes could never have embarked on his revolutionary programme or acquired any converts if he had not felt the hand of God guiding him and been able to justify his revolutionary ethic from the scriptures. I do not think he indulged in any more self-deception than is natural to the human condition. One of his biographers called him 'a divine madman' and we shall have been fair to him if we add to this that like so many of America's great spiritual prophets, Brigham Young and the leaders of the Mennonites and Moravians, he was extremely practical and domesticated, an expert at turning lathes and water-pumps and pig-mash, with informed views about pedagogy and medicine. Giving to God the credit for all his ideas, he was able to propagate them more vigorously than if he claimed them as his own. And in his immense unconcern for public opinion there was indeed some of that superhuman detachment to which our ancestors gave the name 'divine'. By degrees the elaborate pattern of Oneida evolved. Little groups of explorers in the domain

of love, human and divine, approaching each other, were sometimes attracted, sometimes repelled. Public pressure moved the
gathering communities from one New England village to
another. They converged with the slow uncertainty of a swarm
of bees that scatters and swirls and first appears to coagulate on
one twig and then on another. Finally, around the caprice or
the instinct of a single bee, the firm decision of the multitude
takes shape. They settle in a large symmetrical bag and a new
stage of consolidation and differentiation begins. At first the
scandalized neighbours observed only a random patchwork of
adulteries, but as the families gathered and merged, it was seen
that on chaos and confusion a master hand was imposing an
orderly design. On territory which the Oneida Indians, recently
moved to Wisconsin, had evacuated, the Mansion House was
rising by degrees, the religious basis of the community had been
secured and Noyes established as their God-given leader.

Noyes preached that monogamic marriage was founded on
selfishness but that unselfishness is the fundamental principle
of the heavenly state. All sins come from selfishness, and true
love alone excludes it. In the New Testament there is a problem
which we must resolve for ourselves. When the Jews asked
Jesus, 'If a man marries seven times, whose husband shall he
be at the resurrection?', and when Jesus replied 'In the resurrection they neither marry nor are given in marriage but are as the
angels', what did this mean? Noyes maintained that the angels
were not celibate but that in some etherialized form, far above
the crude possessive monopolies of this world, 'sex intercourse
did take place in Heaven'.

This was the gospel which was preached and elaborated in
the meeting hall at Oneida and published in *The Oneida Circular*.
Writing about the community in 1900 Allan Eastlake has
described it as 'the most extraordinary and the most valuable
enterprise which has ever been undertaken since the foundation
of Christianity, one which hints at the direction in which the
world at large should gradually move'.

This was not how it appeared to the Methodist Meeting which
gathered to consider it at Perryville in 1873. They named it 'the
hideous thing that hides itself away from the light of day and
revels in debauchery and shame, corrupting the very fountains
of social and domestic virtue'.

The best account of Oneida comes from Pierrepoint Noyes'

books. He was one of the nine children whom Noyes fathered from different mothers when he was in his sixties. Some years after the community had dissolved under the threat of a legal prosecution, Pierrepoint had reassembled as many as he could of the fifty-eight 'planned babies', his cousins and kinsmen, who had been born in the Mansion House, and together they revived the lapsing industries of the community and forged a new solidarity, strictly in accord with the laws and the proprieties, on the foundation of the scandalous one which had collapsed. Pierrepoint had even before his birth been carefully planned to fit into an imaginary society different in every detail from that in which he was to prosper as an adult; everything had been done to make him 'maladjusted' and yet he felt immediately at ease in the great world into which he was so suddenly plunged. He had his first glimpse of it on a visit to Niagara Falls; it was already organized for the American tourist and coming from the complex society of Oneida it struck him as amazingly simple. He was filled with 'confidence of his ability to compete in such a world of sham and futility'. He had no grievance then or later against his father or his upbringing. He had not disliked the communism in which he had been reared and he claimed, from his own experience, that 'the desire for exclusive ownership of things is not a primal human instinct'. He had not, for instance, resented the communal best suit which he and other boys of his age would take out in turn when they paid visits away from the community. Looking back on the Oneida discipline with its odd blend of rigours and laxities, he recalled with contentment 'the pleasant aroma of spirituality so humanized as to be inoffensive to a boy'.

For the first twenty years of the Oneida community only two babies had been born every year because a form of contraception was in use, the result of long and careful training. It depended on the indefinite postponement of the orgasm, a difficult feat in which the young men trained themselves through intercourse with elder women beyond the age of child-bearing. Noyes believed that 'the normal man loved the normal woman and only exclusiveness is abnormal', and he added, surprisingly, that exclusiveness was 'fatal to the highest type of romantic love'. This last seems contrary to the usual opinion. Desmond MacCarthy, for instance, once wrote that if men ever lived and loved as Lawrence had preached, two things would disappear from the earth, the smoking-room story and the love-lyric. There were certainly no smoking-room stories in the Mansion House, but were there love-lyrics? Noyes seems to have firmly blocked all the normal channels of romance and to have scrutinized carefully the sources of pleasure. The community was not in the habit of expressing affection openly. Like the Chinese, they did not kiss much – nor did they shake hands. Noyes distinguished the Oneida system sharply from Free Love which was only for 'irresponsible pleasure-seekers'. Men were not entitled to pleasures 'beyond the freedoms licensed by their degree of perfection'. What did Noyes mean by perfection? Just as the Mormons considered themselves saints redeemed from sin, the Oneida community did in fact believe that in some respects the Kingdom of Heaven had arrived and that their love affairs were as innocent as those of the angels. They did not claim 'perfection in externals', but they claimed to have attained 'purity of heart' and 'salvation from sin'. Perhaps this meant that if all those sins which derive from encroachment upon the conjugal rights of others (and that means perhaps the majority of the traditional sins of sex) had been abolished and women were freed from the obligation to respond to demands which they did not desire, sin could only survive where love was tainted with the old egoisms. It survived where men introduced sexual thoughts disharmoniously or soiled the expression of love by the furtiveness or the calculations of the everyday world. As one advanced towards perfect understanding, the temptations to such sins became fewer and a more exquisite, because a more refined, pleasure came within reach. Was that what Noyes meant? Was that where the love-lyrics began? One might get contradictory replies from the community; they were explorers in an unknown land and it might not be easy to harmonize completely the reports, the explanations, of the different travellers.

Noyes believed that righteousness would ultimately triumph and that glimpses of the predestined paradise appear to us from time to time to strengthen our courage and illuminate our path. I cannot quite reconcile this with his statement that on 1 June 1846 the Kingdom of Heaven had actually come. This perhaps is one of those inner circle observations which an outsider finds it hard to interpret, especially as at this time he was deeply engaged in launching his small industries and had started to play golf.

Noyes believed that the pioneers must prove themselves more conservative than the clergy, that is to say that they must strictly observe the rules which they had made for themselves by breaking through the apathy and laziness on which conventional morality depends. The rule against exclusiveness in love was rigorously applied and after a time the community adapted itself to it and ceased to consider it onerous. Pierrepoint Noyes relates how one day his mother was playing with him very affectionately, when his father came in. 'Harriet!' he said firmly, 'this is idolatry!', and took the little boy away. Pierrepoint says that he thinks his mother grieved at this restriction on their intimacy (they were only allowed to meet at fixed intervals every week), but he himself did not, though he was a devoted son who looked after his mother when the community dissolved. He was happy in the shared affection of forty or fifty kind and varied aunts and uncles. For the young adults often there were very hard decisions to be made. For instance Charles C. became attached to Miss B. with a love that transgressed the law against exclusiveness. But he overcame it. One day he found another member of the community making love to Miss B. while his baby lay in a cradle beside them, making some demand. He walked gently into the room and removed the baby which was disturbing them to comfort it himself.

In March 1843 the community numbered twenty-eight adults and nine children; they had originally developed out of small converging groups but once established, they attracted miscellaneous outsiders. Mr Herrick came, a New York episcopal clergyman, and Mr E. Hamilton, an architect. The cook at Oneida had been a lawyer and other professional men took up work with them such as stokers, lamp-cleaners, farm-hands, proof-readers, laundrymen. They had a severe critic in one of the governors of the New York YMCA, a man who had brought life into that institution and been active in the Ragged Schools. He was converted to Oneida and taken on a five years' probation, which was described in this way: 'He was stood on his head and allowed to drain till all self-righteousness had dripped away.'

Another converted enemy was E. P. Freeman, a journalist, who attacked Oneida fiercely in *The Schenectady News*. His son joined Oneida and the journalist in his old age was supported by the community. And of course many distressed people joined. Though they were careful in their acceptance of new recruits, they laid themselves open inevitably to the exploitation of charlatans.

In its early days the community had sold vegetables and fruit and other country produce and then had branched out into a factory for animal traps and another one for tea-spoons. In the evenings the women made artificial flowers out of shells, fish scales and silver thread, as well as other ornaments and toys. They had no regular meals except breakfast; for the rest of the day they helped themselves off shelves in the pantry.

Later on the community was helped by the fact that its land adjoined the newly built Midland Railway and by degrees they got the reputation of having the best farm and grazing land in the state. They won prizes at the Lennox Fair and farther afield for their thoroughbred Ayrshires, their Aylesbury ducks and Leghorn poultry. Though they had suffered bitter reverses and were often near starvation, they made progress. Between 1860 and 1869 they earned 200,000 dollars profit. In the year 1880 they bred the third-finest Holstein in the state. They started canning on a vast commercial scale, paying to those outside the community 25,000 dollars in salaries. They co-operated with Wrigley's Chewing Gum and popularized their spoons by giving away a spoon with each 5 cent cake of soap. According to Pierrepoint Noyes, who was the most objective of chroniclers, these spoons had the reputation of being the worst silverware in the country. From their animal-trap factory they supplied four southern states with twenty-foot tie-out chains.

At last after twenty years a great decision was made. It was decided that to secure the continuity of the community and in the interests of science and religion, children must be born to Oneida. This was the beginning of Oneida's great experiment of Stirpiculture. It was the practical fulfilment, Noyes believed, of Galton's theories of heredity. 'The law of God', he wrote, 'urges us on; the law of society holds us back. When Galton comes to the point where it is necessary to look beyond his theory to the duties it suggests, he subsides into the meekest conservatism.' The community considered, rather like the eighteenth-century aristocracy, that the business of love was too serious to be left in the hands of the young people themselves with their immature and unreasoning passions. They believed that one day when communal life prevailed the regulations which they proposed would be universally adopted: 'Through propagation by wise selection, higher spiritual traits would be transmitted.' For unlike the aristocrats they were not concerned to preserve property and power by their organized alliances, but to maintain and increase virtue, wisdom, strength and unselfishness. In just such a way nature and providence were wont to offer compensation for the blunders of man. 'Who can say how much the present race of men in Connecticut owes to the numberless adulteries and fornications of Pierrepoint Edwards. Corrupt as he was, he must have distributed a good deal of the good blood of his noble father, Jonathan Edwards.' Maybe even from the wicked practice of *Jus primae noctis* the human breed had been improved, but we must not leave such arrangement to chance and to ignorant and violent men. We must intervene ourselves. The community appointed a stirpicultural committee on which there were two graduates of Yale Medical School. Fifty-three young women signed a declaration: 'We do not belong to ourselves in any respect but first to God and secondly to Mr Noyes, as God's true representative. . . We offer ourselves as living sacrifices to God and to true communism.' The committee claimed that there was no diminution of liberty, even though some were excluded from parenthood. 'It was the free choice of those who love science well enough to make themselves eunuchs for the Kingdom of Heaven.'

Fifty-eight children were born of this experiment and the results must be considered to have been satisfactory. They seem on the whole to have grown up remarkably intelligent and able people. They were healthy as well. In fifty years according to the law of averages forty-five of the fifty-eight would have died, but in fact within that time only five had died. Noyes himself had sired nine of them though in his sixties, and, as I have said, one of these, Pierrepoint, was the leader of the reconstituted family group whose business enterprise still flourishes.

The community developed many practices which have been adopted by later religious or secular fraternities. For example, there was public confession as in Soviet collectives or among the Buchmanites. The competitive spirit seemed the greatest threat to the community and it was in that sphere that tension was greatest. The Oneida orchestra gave difficulties. As it got more skilled the claims of art began to conflict with the claims of perfect brotherhood. Its performances were no longer family occasions, the expression in terms of music of their fraternal solidarity. They became famous and attracted audiences and discriminating critics from far afield. The seniors feared that it was ending in 'professional sterility' because it had never been communized properly. The juniors suspected them of Philistinism. Carry had been asked to play the accompaniments only because Edith was ill, but what was to be done when Edith recovered and it appeared that Carry played better? Clearly in art as in stirpiculture the inferior had to make way for his betters, but how hard it was to do this without injuring the harmony of the group. The community tried to solve this by their criticism committees and their practice of utter openness, and candour among themselves. Lily, for example, admitted to the community that she hated Marion because Marion sang better. Marion had to decide for herself whether the applause of the outer world mattered more to her than the unity of the little inner world to which she had devoted herself. It was by meeting and overcoming or perhaps simply evading such crises that the community developed.

It appeared to the community that illness as well as jealousy could be alleviated by criticism. Did they think that illness was 'error' as the Christian Scientists think, or 'sin' as the inhabitants of Erewhon thought it. When one of the community fell ill a group of his colleagues would gather round and discuss his moral failings and, like the faith healers of all creeds, they had startling triumphs to record. A pedestrian explanation of some of these cures was given by one of the members. He said that the patient was often so appalled by the earnest, perspicacious and unanswerable criticisms of the friends gathered round his bedside that he broke into a sweat as though he had swallowed half a dozen aspirins and the fever left him. And the healthy too were criticized on regular occasions, and sometimes criticism took a highly original form. John Skinner, for example, was told he was too fond of his food to be sufficiently amative.

The community had become famous for its agricultural and industrial successes, its musical festivals and its craftsmanship. It had excellent relations with its employees and customers, with the townspeople and local newspapers. Somehow or other the neighbourhood ignored or forgave the unusual tenets and practices which bound the members together. They secured for their sexual innovations a tolerance which the Mormons only won after a slow and bloody retreat westwards as the armed forces of propriety caused them to abandon one stronghold after another.

On one occasion they were visited by a deputation of the New England Shakers. This was an extraordinary event. For the Shakers also had an overruling preoccupation with sex and religion but it had led them in a precisely contrary direction to that followed at Oneida. They lived male and female together dedicated to absolute chastity. Presumably, though they reacted so differently from the ways of the world, they felt drawn to Oneida because they too repudiated the world utterly and were driven to similar devices to make their isolation bearable.

The community had never concealed its beliefs and its sex problems were openly discussed under the heading 'The Open Secret' in *The Oneida Circular*, which was edited by Pierrepoint Noyes' mother, Harriet. Perhaps in those days of spawning sects men had a more open and experimental approach to the mysteries of God and Man, perhaps too they were less frightened of press publicity. Otherwise it is hard to understand how respectable people could have organized family picnic parties to the Mansion House grounds and should have been shown over its gardens and workshops by the members, and how even Sunday School excursions should have been organized to this pleasant and hospitable abode of sin. Even the travel agencies started tours.

It was, I think, the Sunday School excursions that finally brought into action the Methodists of Perryville and the Reverend Thatcher of the Congregational Church of Hawley, Massachusetts, and the famous Anthony Comstock of the New York Society for the Suppression of Vice, and above all Professor Mears, the Presbyterian Head of Hamilton College, and Bishop Huntington. The time was propitious for the organization of moral indignation and the crusading against vice. In 1873 Congress had enacted a Federal Obscenity Bill. Contraceptive information had been declared lewd, lascivious and obscene. Its mailing was forbidden and a mood of stern censoriousness spread through the countryside. Professor Mears summoned many committee meetings at which 'the organized fanaticism and lust' of the Oneida community was strongly denounced. Was it tolerable that this system of corrupting concubinage should 'luxuriate at ease in the heart of New York State'?

In fact it was strange that this reaction had not come much earlier and that when it did come Noyes should have received as much public support as he did.

If the local papers reflected popular opinion, as they are supposed to do, his neighbours were on his side. The *Fulton Times* praised the community, saying that 'a foul and corrupt fountain cannot send forth a stream so clean, thrifty, respectable and peaceful'. The *Utica Herald* was not prepared to go so far as this but maintained that while one might disapprove of Noyes' theories, one could not disapprove of Noyes himself for it was to him and not to 'the open secret' that the fine qualities and attainments of the community were due. 'You may call it fortune, luck or providence. I call it religion, duty and the help of God.'

The heads of all the sound business houses between Utica and Syracuse, which had dealt with the community, supported them and treated Professor Mears' crusade with icy disapproval. District Attorney Barnett of Oneida County said, 'It is easy enough to reason out that their social habits are wrong, because they don't conform with ours – that is with what we *say* ours are – but if indictments could be procured on the ground of general immorality, who would not be liable?'

My impression is that till sin is formulated and denounced by some prominent and influential person, the average person makes his moral judgments in particular and not in general terms. For as long as it was possible, Professor Mears was ignored.

The community was all the same alarmed at the publicity and it was decreed that 'the open secret' should no longer be discussed in *The Oneida Circular*. It might have weathered the attack from outside if there had not been undermining forces at work within. They had some time before admitted and tried to assimilate a Free-Love community from Cleveland, Ohio, headed by a man called Towner. There had been divergences of ethic and policy and Towner had built up an anti-Noyes faction within the community and tried to usurp his authority. In addition, a real scallywag had been indiscreetly accepted and had had to be violently expelled through a window, and he was threatening prosecution. And finally there were whispers, perhaps fomented by Towner, against Noyes himself. What had he done or allowed to be done? About this the evidence is not clear and his son, so candid about most things, is rather evasive.

Certainly some of the women were complaining that they were being treated like white mice and perhaps there had been some aggression by an older man, which, despite all the promises of obedience which had been signed, was punishable by law and there was a danger that the law might be invoked. One day in 1876 Noyes went hurriedly away and the community was left leaderless. At this time, when Noyes was in hiding and disgrace, his first cousin Rutherford Hayes moved into the White House as one of America's least distinguished presidents, and the contrast of their destinies became a theme for romantic journalism.

There was another disadvantage. Father Noyes' God was a Bible God and was going out of date. His son and successor, Theodore Noyes, an able physician, was a Darwinian. He did not believe in the angels, so could not maintain as did his father that in their sexual habits they behaved like the Oneida community. And though he accepted 'the open secret' and the community rules, there was a problem about authority. Noyes had acted as Jehovah's Vice-Regent and had been obeyed but Theodore, trying to translate the idea of leadership into modern terms, became a priggish disciplinarian, ruling through reasonable arguments rather than through divine ordinances. And, though he was a kind intelligent man, his orders were resented. The woman with whom he lived as the angels live was a schoolmistressy person and, with her as his helpmeet, his shyness and uncertainty began to look like aloofness. This was greatly disliked and the deep rifts began to widen.

Rapidly the community dissolved after this. Like the Mormons they abandoned their practices but not their principles. The ethic of Oneida was, like Brigham Young's polygamy, postponed for some distant day when mankind had more of the wisdom and the innocence of the angels. Marriage was once more to be permitted but the counsel was given that for those who had once had this brief glimpse of paradise, celibacy was to be preferred. There were weeks of difficult and tragic manoeuvering as the community paired itself off into would-be respectable married couples. Their common property had also to be equitably apportioned and it was discovered that while collectively they had been rich and secure, as solitary couples they would be miserably poor and helpless. Also they would exchange the conviction and confidence of superior righteousness for tarnished reputations and social ostracism. A handful stayed on in the all-but-deserted Mansion House; others struggled with the shattered industries.

This should normally have been the end of a chapter, the unmasking of illusions, the dissolution of yet another of America's numerous Utopias. And yet it was not; for the Mansion House is still there and so are the descendants of its founders, and the wheels of its factories are turning more vigorously than before. How can one explain this except by saying that human cohesion on an organized and personal level has a value quite apart from the principles which bring diverse men and women together. Even when the principles are rejected the memory of the cohesion remains and acts as an inspiration to the survivors.

And the cohesion of the Oneida community had been much closer than that of other Utopias, Robert Owen's for example, for not only in religious metaphor but also in fact the younger generations were brothers and sisters or at least kinsmen by birth. The tie of blood was there to strengthen the weakening bonds of fellowship. Also, genetically at least, the experiment had succeeded. These young people were vigorous, openminded and intelligent.

And so it happened that the sons and grandsons of the founder came together again and built up an economic kingdom on the foundations of the ruined spiritual one. They make cheap cutlery in greater abundance than ever before. They are not at all embarrassed by their unorthodox past but it is not relevant at present. I visited an Irish branch of the Oneida factory in Belfast and saw men and women tending small machines like church harmoniums and regulating cathodes and anodes in a tank in which sometimes a bowl is being shaped or else an ornamental curlicue is being stamped on a handle. The directors have international problems; once, for instance, the Japanese flooded the market with cheaper spoons stamped with identical curlicues. In regard to love their views are now normal and they make a 'Marriage Gift' set of cutlery. On the lid of its box there is a picture of a bridal pair leaving the church door in wedding clothes. Several of the present Noyes generation, outstanding business men, have sat on Coal Board Commissions and represented America abroad. One or two have written novels. By easy stages they have become like everybody else, only perhaps a little more talented.

Bernard Shaw thought of Noyes as a great pioneer, 'one of those chance attempts at a Superman, which occur from time to time in spite of man's blundering institutions'. There is, of course, today more unregulated sex than Noyes would have approved. Many would agree with him that 'sexual intercourse is an honoured method of innocent and useful communion', but most of those who experiment are attached in one way or another to 'blundering institutions'. The idea of collective experiment has seldom been so successfully fulfilled. It survived the collapse of its principles and retained a measure of its former social cohesion.

Not often expressed, there is still a feeling that sexual power is something like the power of wealth or intellect, which must be exercised with charity. Like money and brains it is not exactly private property. The rich ought to give to the poor. But not only are there no supermen in control but we are all centripetally organized towards some distant focus of authority and small breakaway communities are more shortlived than ever before.

[1962]

PART TWO
WRITERS AND WRITING

6

MARIA EDGEWORTH

There are some Irish writers who are so precariously balanced between England and Ireland that an Irishman often has to do a bit of special pleading in order to claim them for Ireland at all. If I had felt that Maria Edgeworth was one of these borderline cases, I might have been tempted to concentrate on her Irish stories, *Castle Rackrent*, and *The Absentee* and *Ormond*, and to treat her other work, her educational tales and English novels, as in some way secondary. But in fact from the time she was fifteen and returned to Edgeworthstown with her father, Ireland became her home and Irish life her major preoccupation. Yet though she lived in Ireland, she was far less provincial than many of her great English contemporaries; she was accepted on the continent as a European in a way that Jane Austen, a much greater novelist, never was. The Edgeworth Way of Life, expounded by her father and herself, had found them disciples far and wide. Friends in Paris once urged them to set up a salon there in rivalry to Mme de Staël, for it was thought that the Edgeworths and their philosophy of rational conduct would be a wholesome antidote to the brilliant romanticism of the de Staël circle.

All this led Maria to speak condescendingly of Jane Austen, who had found all the material for her art ready to hand in a Hampshire village, and whose novels never touched on the social problems which agitated the Edgeworths. 'One gets tired', said Maria of Jane, 'of milk and water, even when the milk is of the sweetest and the water the purest.'

One cannot wholly blame Maria for this undervaluation or for the havoc the once-fashionable Edgeworth notions made of her own talents as a novelist. Ireland in those days offered a chal-lenge to the heart as well as to the head, and in warm-hearted intelligent people like Maria and her father it was bound to stimulate ideas of justice and reform. The Edgeworths found arrogance on one side and poverty and ignorance beyond belief upon the other, and a deep social fissure which it seemed to them only education and mutual trust could bridge. They had a passion for social justice and they could not be content to be chroniclers of country manners like Jane or like Maria herself in *Castle Rackrent*.

In her old age Maria recognized clearly what had happened. She admitted that her best-conceived characters were those, like Sir Condy of *Castle Rackrent* and Thady Quirk, which she had created with a minimum of what she called 'philosophical construction'. 'Where I least aimed at drawing character,' she wrote, 'I succeeded best.' She would like to have gone on writing about Ireland but she said that passions were too high and there was no place for a writer who wished to hold the mirror up to nature. The people would smash the mirror and that would be the end.

If she was often very didactic it was because she was an invincible optimist, believing that there was no evil to which experience and self-knowledge could not discover a cure. In this she was no mere echo of her father, dominating character as he was. R. L. Edgeworth was certainly dynamic. He invented springs for carriages, 'Macadamized' roads and early types of bicycles and telegraphs. He was an enthusiast for education and domesticity, which his twenty-two children and five wives did not succeed in quenching. As a young man he had been a disciple of Rousseau and for a time had brought up his eldest son as a child of nature. But the more he saw of the miseries of Ireland the less respect he had for primitive simplicity and for Rousseau, who had sung its praises. When the Edgeworth philosophy took its final form, I think it could be summarized in three words: 'Learn by experience', or perhaps 'Think for yourself'. That was the refrain that recurred through scores of Edgeworth novels and tales.

Perhaps it is easier for us than it was for our parents to understand how such a chilly platitude could become a slogan in a crusade. For if there is any truth in the theory that history repeats itself in cycles, have we not come round again to the problems of the Edgeworths and their friends? Then, just as now, civilization had rocked and men were slowly recovering from the intoxication of tremendous dreams. The magic of the dreams had faded but they had not relaxed their hold upon the mind. Men of opposing factions were mobilized to think in blocks and there was a stigma of treachery attached to those who chose to be independent. Edgeworth was one of those whose pride it was to think for himself into whatever eccentricities this might lead him, and Maria had inherited some of her father's uncompromisingly experimental spirit. The Edgeworths and their circle despised nothing so much as intellectual timidity. If you had a belief you must also have the courage to practise it. Maria's brother-in-law, Dr Beddoes, for example, a well-known physician, used to terrorize the landladies of Bristol by driving cows upstairs to his patients' bedrooms. Why? Simply because the doctor was convinced that in pulmonary complaints nothing was so wholesome for an invalid as a cow breathing on him. And is not health more important than stair-carpets?

Her father was more cautiously experimental than this and the success of his methods was to be read in his well-run estate, his contented tenantry and his happy children. The large plain house in the Irish midlands became famous in Europe and a focus of pilgrimage almost like Mme de Staël's house at Coppet or Tolstoy's at Yasnaya Polyana.

If you think I exaggerate, look up the Edgeworthstown chapter in Mr and Mrs Hall's famous *Travels in Ireland* and you will find those two quite hard-boiled pilgrims almost inarticulate with emotion. They seem to be on tip-toe from the moment they enter County Longford, fearful to violate this sanctuary of family happiness but at the same time anxious to draw from their visit and share with the world all the enlightenment they could.

For from this mansion [they wrote] has issued so much practical good to Ireland and not alone to Ireland but to the whole civilized world. It has been for long the residence of high intellect, well directed genius, industry and virtue. It is a place that perhaps possesses larger moral interest than any other in the kingdom.

Mr and Mrs Hall, like so many others, saw Maria working at her stories in the general living-room, children in and out the whole time, for in addition to some dozen brothers and sisters there were nephews and nieces, but her mind was so attuned to domesticity that they did not disturb her. Indeed in one of her letters she writes that she was taking her writing desk into her sister Lucy's room for Lucy, while in bed, liked to hear the sound of Maria's pencil. In most modern writers distraction like that would be almost unintelligible but with Maria it was no affectation. Affection for her family and friends was the fuel which kept her mind in motion.

Maria and her father, much more than Rousseau or Montessori or any one else, were the progenitors of the progressive school with its educational toys and uninhibited ethic. And it was as an educational reformer that Maria first acquired a European reputation. I wonder if it is her fault or ours that no modern child has an appetite for the sort of story she wrote. This may be an accident of fashion, for though to us her stories seem steeped in the most austere morality, the Victorians did not find them moral enough. Or rather they complained that the Edgeworths used all the wrong arguments for inculcating virtue, basing it on neighbourliness and reason and common sense rather than the Ten Commandments. They did not, like Charlotte M. Yonge, the Victorian favourite, link virtue to the eternal verities. Indeed *The Quarterly Review* printed what her friend, Dumont, called 'an infamous and calumnious attack' on Maria. The writer complained of 'the deplorable omission of expressions of devoutness, which from its persistence it is impossible to believe to be accidental'. Elsewhere the Rev. R. Hall wrote:

Her books are the most irreligious I have ever read. She does not attack religion but makes it appear unnecessary by exhibiting perfect virtue without it. No works ever produced so bad an effect on my mind as hers.

But what our children miss is fantasy. The Edgeworths had no use for it. Maria's stories about little Rosamond are crisp and logical, like a proposition in Euclid. There are no fairies, pirates or bunny rabbits' tea parties. Particularly about rabbits was Rosamond very rational. She discussed with her mama the idea that it was wrong to kill and eat rabbits, but rejected it as unreasonable. And when a rabbit nibbled a shrub that her mother had given her, her brother made her a humane and ingenious rabbit trap. I haven't a doubt that if Rosamond's mother lived today she would blame myxomatosis on Peter Rabbit. She would argue like this: 'If you grant to animals false feelings that they have not, you will finally forget the true feelings which they have.'

How can one explain the immense appeal that these uncompromising stories had for the children of 150 years ago? Maria tried to give a plain unadorned view of society and its obligations, scaling it down to a child's vision. She never bluffed or condescended. Children felt they were being initiated into the secrets of the grown-up world, its tabus and dangers, and perhaps this was as thrilling to them as mystery and adventure are to children today.

'Rosamond and the Purple Jar' is the best known of these stories. It exemplifies so well the remorseless but benevolent Edgeworth logic that I'll relate the plot.

Rosamond, going out shopping with her mama and a servant to carry the parcels, inevitably wanted to buy almost everything she saw in the fascinating shops, but her mama countered all her excited suggestions with cool prim logic.

'Nay, Rosamond, I have a pair of buckles, I do not want any more,' or 'Yes, Rosamond, the jewels are pretty but what use are pretty baubles to me? . . . You say I would discover a use, but I would rather find out the use before buying.'

And then they come to a chemist's shop and Rosamond can scarcely be drawn away from the delirious contemplation of a purple jar in the window.

'Oh, mama, but it would be useful. We could put flowers in it.'

'You have a flower-pot, Rosamond, and that is not a flower-pot.'

'But I could use it as a flower-pot, mama.'

'Perhaps, if you were to examine it closer, Rosamond, you would be disappointed.'

'No, indeed, mama, I am sure I shouldn't.'

A little later Rosamond starts to limp on the pavement. 'Oh, mama, there is a great hole in my shoe and a stone is got in. My shoes are quite worn out. I wish you would be so very good as to buy me another pair.'

'Nay, Rosamond, I have money but not enough to buy shoes, buckles, pretty baubles and purple jars.'

But the limp becomes worse, really cruel, and they have to go into a shoe shop, dark and smelling horribly of new leather, but they find a pair of shoes that exactly fits. And Rosamond is given her choice. She may have the shoes or she may have the purple jar and wait till the end of the month for the shoes.

After reflection she decides, 'Oh, mama, I *think* I can wear the bad shoes till the end of the month. I would *prefer* the flower-pot if you will not think me very silly.'

'Why, I cannot promise not to think you silly, Rosamond. But when you have to judge for yourself, you should choose what will make you happy and then it will not signify who thinks you silly.'

'Then mama, I am sure the flower-pot will make me happy.'

You will remember or can guess the rest. When the servant arrived with the purple jar, Rosamond finds to her dismay that it is just a plain glass jar full of nasty purple liquid. And every day her shoes get worse and worse so that she can't jump or dance or run. She offered to exchange the jar with her mother for a pair of shoes, but the calm logical answer came back, 'Nay, Rosamond, you must abide by your choice.'

Rosamond's mama would be attacked from a dozen different angles today. A woman, we'd say, who could afford a servant to carry her parcels, should be ashamed to let her child hobble round in broken-down shoes and there would be medical talk about permanent injury to the instep and so on. But the key to the Edgeworth doctrine surely lies in the mother's remark. 'What does it signify who thinks you silly, if you choose what will make you happy?' The Edgeworthian parents never, like the Victorian paterfamilias, put themselves on pedestals. They seldom preached and never punished. But nor did they hasten headlong, as we should do, to protect their children from the educative consequences of an unwise choice.

The stories themselves don't sufficiently explain the little world of mutual solicitude and patience, which Maria assumed as a necessary background to these chastening adventures. Mr Edgeworth's letters and, much more so, Maria's, make things clearer. For instance there is his letter to Maria about little Fanny who had asked him what a section was when he was busy. He tells Maria to buy a lemon for her and get a small cylinder of wood turned. Then Maria is to demonstrate with a knife what a transverse section is and then what a longitudinal section is. The Edgeworth educational system demanded a warm and constant intimacy between elders and children. Boarding schools were regarded as an easy, inadequate way out. It was only because Mr Edgeworth was dead and Maria old that the youngest of the brood was sent to Charterhouse.

Many little sisters – there were ten of them – went to the

making of Rosamond. And that rather abstract little girl becomes more intelligible if we set the reality beside the fiction. It is a little daunting to read of Maria's young sister Harriet coming in before breakfast at eight a.m. every morning to read her Mme de Sévigné, but turn a page or two and you will find Maria taking Harriet and Fanny to visit Sir Walter Scott at Abbotsford or to Mme de Genlis, Lord Edward's mother-in-law, decaying in a Parisian garret. Or dressing them up for a dance at Almacks. And then coming home again and helping Maria make a gutter in the main street at Edgeworthstown, her own idea, her own plans and 'twenty men', Maria claims proudly, 'employed for three weeks'. Those returns to Edgeworthstown were always happy. 'We look to our dear home for permanent happiness,' wrote Maria. 'We return without a regret for anything we have left behind except our friends.'

A few days pass and we read of Harriet again. She is taking the part of a fire-eater in a charade and devouring lighted spills; 'she only burnt her lips a little'. Or listen how the children organized a *fête champêtre* at Edgeworthstown in 1805 to celebrate old Mr Edgeworth's birthday. First of all they contrived to get their elders and the babies out of the way for the afternoon.

I had little Lucy in my arms [wrote Maria] and, after the chaise, on horseback came rosy Charlotte all smiles, and Henry with eyes brilliant with pleasure. We came home with no suspicion of what was prepared, when our ears were suddenly struck with the sound of music and as if by enchantment a fairy festival appeared upon the green. An amphitheatre of verdant festoons suspended from white staffs with scarlet streamers. Youths and maidens in white, their heads adorned with flowers, were dancing while their mothers and little children were seated on benches round the amphitheatre. William danced a reel with Harriet and baby Sophie, and Kitty served cakes and syllabubs and then William at present in the height of his electrical enthusiasm proposed to the dancers a few electrical sparks to complete the joys of the day. Everybody flocked after him to the study and shrieks of surprise and terror mixed with the laughter. And when we came out the grassplat was lit up by boys waving flambeaux, illuminating the beauty of green boughs and flowers.

You see it was part of the theory that when Rosamond had learnt to reason for herself and had discovered that purple jars might not be purple, she should use her intelligence and daring to its utmost limits. Not only could she play with fire, she could swallow it if she chose. So you can understand Maria's indignation when Mme de Staël gibed at the 'triste utilité' of the Edgeworth educational system. There was no evidence that it produced either prigs or pedants.

Their educational schemes had of course their setbacks. Maria's brother, Lovell, put into practice an old dream of his father's, and with the support of the Catholic priest and the Protestant rector of Edgeworthstown started an inter-denominational school there. This experiment, a unique one in those days, went well for ten years. But Lovell's business capacity was not equal to his educational zeal. He bankrupted the estate and Maria had to take it over and run it herself from her literary earnings.

It would be hard certainly to claim that even in her novels Maria was not excessively didactic. The book of hers which I prefer, *The Absentee*, is more propagandist even than *Uncle Tom's Cabin*. It is like the most entertaining sermon that was ever written. All the characters are tilted slightly from the plane of reality towards the central argument of the book: 'An Irish landlord must live among the people from whom he draws his subsistence.' Because they neglect this principle, Lady Clonbrony lives beyond her income, trying to buy her way into fashionable London society, while fashionable London merely laughs at her provinciality and vulgar Irishisms. For the same reason Lord Clonbrony is *désoeuvré* and feebly resentful. He exaggerates his Irishness from defiance. Meanwhile in Ireland, unknown to the absentee landlord, the bad agent of the Clonbrony property prospers, the good agent is squeezed out by intrigue. And among the humble tenants, we see virtue discouraged and vice triumphant all because of the canker of absenteeism.

But fortunately the young lord shares many of Mr Edgeworth's views about estate management. He travels to the family estates incognito. There is a superb account of social life in Dublin and the provinces in the years after the Union. The young lord reveals himself and establishes the rule of reason and order. And the earl and countess drive home to Clonbrony Castle to the cheers of their tenantry.

Maria's plots are complicated and ingenious as is fitting in an inventor's daughter. Sometimes one seems to hear the pulleys creak and the ropes strain as virtue is hoisted on to her pedestal. One recalls Mr Edgeworth raising by a new device his patent metal spire on Edgeworthstown church and how a bugle blew when the hoisting started and when at last the golden weather cock settled into position, a flag flew and the congregation cheered. And how that did not prevent a murmuring among the devout: 'Yes but is Mr Edgeworth really orthodox?' Maria's enthusiasm and ingenuity are no answer either to a parallel question: 'Is Miss Edgeworth really a novelist?' Compared to Jane Austen, I don't think she is, but she was a writer of great and significant books, and her integrity if not her art should secure her a place among the immortals.

Her last book *Helen* caused her much misgiving. It was rewritten several times and is as far removed as possible from the spontaneous ease of *Castle Rackrent*. Her father had been dead seventeen years, during which she had written little, and those who blame him for turning her from an artist into a moralist have to explain why the book which she wrote without any encouragement from him should blaze with such moral fervour. Maria had a horror of half-lies, of innuendo and evasion, and the plot of *Helen* hinges on a very charming lady's inability to make an awkward admission. Little lies breed big lies and at last the truth can only be vindicated by a lady as downright and disagreeable as Rosamond's mama. This lady hears the whole slanderous story from her dentist, as she sits in the dental chair. Such is her indignation that she bites his finger, and, with her toothache still raging, sets off to expose the falsehood.

These last novels seem today very archaic in construction but I think they have the same importance as some of Mr Edgeworth's mechanical contrivances, those dim foreshadowings of the bicycle and the telephone whose debris were found not long ago in an out-house at Edgeworthstown. They were experiments which, had he not been so preoccupied with moral problems and perhaps with Ireland, he might have brought to perfection. I don't mean by this that either he or his daughter failed in what they attempted, but that their proudest achievements must be looked for in their lives rather than in their art.

Maria Edgeworth was a brilliant and sociable personality who gave only half her genius to her art. As with her father, her ambition was as much to change society as to observe it. And though she left little imprint upon public life, who can set a limit in space or time to the influence of a happy and dynamic personality? Scott and Turgenev recorded their debt in print, for they said that it was *Castle Rackrent* that first inspired them to write as they did about Scotland and about Russia. But how many others had no opportunity of acknowledging what they owed to Maria! One debt to her, as a writer of children's stories, was paid in a way that delighted her. When the great famine was at its height and Maria, an old woman of eighty, was launching appeals on behalf of the stricken people of Edgeworthstown, a present arrived for Miss Edgeworth to distribute, 150 barrels of wheat and rice from the children of Boston, who had loved the stories of Rosamond and Harry and Frank.

Maria was a great family woman, so I can't do better than finish with a family tribute. In the home circle one is most likely to get impartiality from one's in-laws, and Richard Butler, the Dean of Clonmacnois, a scholar and antiquarian, was married to Maria's sister Harriet. Here is what he wrote to a friend after Maria, in the last years of her life, had paid them her annual visit.

We have just had Maria Edgeworth with us, as cheerful and as fresh as ever. Having her is like having the sunshine always about you and I think she is more in her element and puts out all herself more in strictly domestic life than any other. Her constant flow of gaiety is one of the most surprising things in nature. Neither sadness nor malice nor anything very bad can stand long in her presence.

[1954]

BOUCHER DE PERTHES:
THE FATHER OF PREHISTORY

Some years ago I was looking at the earliest records of the old
Kilkenny Archaeological Society which I had recently revived in
our neighbourhood. It had been started in 1848 by our rector,
Mr Graves, with the help of some doctors, newspapermen and
country gentlemen. Though it was later to attract the antiquaries
of Dublin and finally to be absorbed by them and moved to the
capital as The Royal Society of Antiquaries of Ireland, these first
journals belonged to its obscure and rustic infancy. I was sur-
pised therefore to find that two years after its foundation the
Society had already captured the interest of a Frenchman. He
was given the title of Honorary Foreign Corresponding Member
and his name was M. Jacques Boucher de Crèvecoeur de
Perthes, President of the Société d'Emulation at Abbeville (near
the coast some 135 kilometres north of Paris).

Boucher de Perthes (1788-1868) was the son of aristocratic
parents from Abbeville. His father, liberal enough to keep his
post as a Director of Customs throughout the Revolution, was
an enthusiastic botanist and the founder of the scientific society
of which his son was to be president; his mother's family claimed
descent from that of Joan of Arc. Boucher de Perthes adopted
his father's profession and was made Director of Customs at
Abbeville in 1825. Becoming interested in the geological strata
of a local gravel-pit, he gradually collected a large number of
hand-axes and other flint tools, undoubtedly man-made, of the
kind known later as Abbevillois. These artefacts were present,
with the bones of extinct animals, in strata described by the
geologists as Antediluvian (before the Flood). From 1838
onwards he sought to convince the scientific world that man

had existed thousands of years earlier than anyone had supposed: he had in fact discovered the Old Stone Age. He was met with the same total indifference as was later to be the lot of Mendel when he approached the leading specialists of his generation. He did receive some encouragement from the great Danish archaeologist Worsae, and eventually one of his leading detractors, Rigollet of Amiens, excavated the gravel-pits of St Acheul in order to refute him but discovered the tools now called Acheulian, and in 1854 published findings in agreement with Boucher's. However, it was not until 1859, more than twenty years after he began to publicize his discovery, that the antiquity of man and the work of Boucher de Perthes himself finally received the stamp of official scientific approval.

In France he is honoured today as 'the Father of Prehistory', but in 1850, though he had already published the volume of *Antiquités Celtiques et Antediluviennes* (1847) in which his great discovery was announced, almost no one had read it. He was still regarded by the pundits of London and Paris as a ridiculous old provincial bore. For many years he had been pestering them to visit Abbeville and sending them parcels of flint implements and bones and books. Some of the implements seemed fakes and the accompanying diagrams were very unprofessional. How could anyone believe this tedious person when he said he had discovered the implements beside the bones of extinct animals during the digging of a canal near Abbeville?

And how had it come about that our obscure Society had been the first of all the learned bodies in the British Isles to honour M. de Perthes? Were there perhaps, I speculated, champions of Antediluvian Man in Kilkenny? I looked up the *Journal* of 1859 for evidence of their triumph, for in the spring of that year Sir John Evans and Dr Prestwich had at last visited Abbeville and a month later communicated to the Royal Society their official recognition of Antediluvian Man. The old gentleman, after years of arduous campaigning, had been gloriously vindicated.

I found nothing of all this in the *Journal* for 1859. When after his victory the Honorary Foreign Corresponding Member visited Ireland, he did not come to Kilkenny. So I concluded that it was as the president of an exemplary regional society and not as the Father of Prehistory that he had been co-opted. His father had founded the Société d'Emulation in the Revolutionary year VI (1795) and he himself had revived it, when it was almost moribund, in 1825. To the Kilkenny Archaeological Society it must have appeared as a model, for both groups gloried in being provincial and were proud to have created in two intellectually decaying corners of Europe two lively, critical and fearlessly speculative associations.

It may have been Boucher who took the initiative. I found in the appendix of an early *Journal* a list of donations which included one of Boucher's famous parcels. It must have caused some surprise in the Irish Society but it was characteristic of Boucher and throws light upon the birth of a science. It contained, besides the momentous work on Antediluvian Man, samples of Boucher's philosophy, poetry and folklore, and even a satirical comedy called *La Marquise de Montalle*. The Kilkenny Society was by no means as austere as it later became and must still have been conscious of its own origins in local sentiment and belles-lettres. Evidently they did not laugh at M. de Perthes (but nor, I suspect, did they read him). Without comment, they co-opted him.

It is curious that even today the Father of Prehistory continues to irritate his spiritual children. It seems to them intolerable that fate should have selected this discursive old dilettante, who grew prize pears, wrote poems and plays, organized a swimming bath and, though a customs official, advocated Free Trade, to carry through a major revolution in geology and anthropology. Had they not dedicated their entire lives to these pursuits? And since collective jealousy is more potent than the individual kind, being laced with professional *ésprit de corps*, some have almost managed to delude themselves that Boucher de Perthes never existed. When I looked him up in my *Chambers Encyclopaedia* (1935) I found that everything was forgotten about him except the jaw-bone of Moulin Quignon, which he found in 1863 and which is now regarded as a trick played on him by his workmen. For many scholars the science of prehistory did not open till 1859, when tardily and condescendingly Prestwich and Sir John Evans accepted the invitation of Boucher to Abbeville. For those who might consider this English chronology as odd as that of the Old Testament, which the prehistorians overthrew, Miss Joan Evans, daughter of Sir John, explained in a long article on Boucher de Perthes (*Antiquity*, 1949): 'Belief indeed became possible when it was an experienced geologist, and not Boucher de Perthes, who presented the case.' In other words, truth has no status till it is endorsed by an 'expert'.

Miss Evans' article is the most agile exhibition of professional solidarity and filial piety I have ever seen,. She deplores Boucher's 'horrid little outline plates' with which he tried to convince the sceptics, and, following the Parisian critic Aufrère, she says that Boucher in his autobiography re-wrote his own early correspondence so as to ante-date by some decades his theory of prehistory. On a lower plane, she says that when he offered his collection of antique Picardy furniture to the museum at Cluny, 'it was to secure for himself more consideration in the city', and to get an excise post in Paris, a marble plaque and a gallery bearing his name. When he suggested that a local painter should paint a picture of all the celebrities of Abbeville, 'he doubtless expected to find himself in the front row'. When he claimed to have visited practically every excavation near Abbeville in the past ten years, 'the claim may be well-founded for he was an idle man and a good walker'.

Some of this is partly true, yet all is wholly false. Certainly Boucher's discursiveness could be irritating, but only in our dullest moments do we pursue knowledge for its own sake. 'Science', he wrote, 'helps us to prove but prevents us understanding.' In the Age of Science many scholars wear their learning as a well-trained carriage horse wears his blinkers. As an archaeologist Boucher was remarkably modest and open-minded. It seemed to him that it was just because he had a rather vagrant mind that he hit upon the truth, which seldom frequents the highways. 'I know about as much science as a donkey does of music,' he wrote. That meant that he had fewer misconceptions to eradicate. 'Ignorance', he wrote, 'is a field in which the nettle and the thistle never took root, so they do not have to be grubbed up.'

Boucher fully grasped that the knowledge to which he aspired could not be deep if it was to be wide. 'My science', he wrote, 'is only foresight', a form of intuition based on wide-ranging reflection and experiment in a dozen arts and sciences, and his triumph was perhaps the last and the greatest of the old polymathic humanism. He took it very lightly indeed: 'This victory proves that often it is good to be obstinate and that conviction, united to perseverance, can take the place of knowledge.'

Boucher gloried in being an autodidact, an attitude that sometimes reduced his critics to helpless exasperation. Aufrère comments on the scientific innocence of Boucher's five-volume *De La Création*, but he does not quote this extraordinary passage from the introduction.

Perhaps what I am writing is a repetition of what has already been said, for I am completely ignorant of all that has been published on the matter. No scholar has talked to me about it and I have not read the relevant books.

Boucher claimed later that in these volumes he anticipated the discovery of Antediluvian Man, but Aufrère cannot trace him there. In fact the concept of Antediluvian Man was not the child of geology but was hatched in a densely woven cocoon of miscellaneous speculation. In the same way the idea of evolution is thrown off casually in a footnote to Vol II, p. 362, of *Antiquités*, where, two years before the publication of *The Origin of Species*, Boucher suggests that as the sea retreated, marine animals may have modified their shape by jumping with their flippers. But, as a humanist, Boucher was more concerned with the implications of his theories than with the theories themselves. He sometimes called himself a Pythagorean, for he believed that the power of God is manifest in every living thing, moulding transitory forms and then discarding them: 'The creative power is great, for it is that of God himself.' This consciousness of divinity is present in every being, so that there can be no such thing as an atheist. The word is meaningless.

As for *De La Création*, Boucher said that only ten people besides himself ever finished reading it and that he never gave it to his friends so that the obligation of reading it should not weigh upon their minds. Yet Aufrère says that Victor Hugo and Lamennais had drawn inspiration from it without acknowledgment, and that it had delighted the followers of the socialist writer Fourier.

Though she gives it an individual twist, Miss Evans gets most of her disparaging comments on Boucher from Aufrère, who is in his own right an interesting character. Obliged to work for some years in Boucher's museum at Abbeville, and impatient with the traditional idolatries of the little town, he scrutinized all the drawers and cabinets in which the old bachelor had stored the débris of eighty years. In the end the Father of Prehistory came to fascinate him more than prehistory itself. He read all his novels, plays, philosophy, folklore and travel. He compared the rough drafts of letters with their published variants. He collated the labels on the exhibits with the records of their discovery. He proved (and no one can now disagree, because everything was destroyed in the bombardment of May 1940) that Boucher, in the cause of prehistory, cheated quite a bit. 'In order to get the truth accepted, he was often less than truthful himself.'

At the bottom of a drawer M. Aufrère found, ticketed as carefully as a mammoth's bones, a tooth and a chestnut curl. The curl was in a metal frame, embossed with the arms of the de Perthes and the de Crèvecoeurs, and was inscribed, 'hair of M. de Boucher de Perthes, April 1853'. Beside it was a tooth in a little box labelled, 'last molar extracted from upper jaw by the dentist, M. Catel, March 2, 1855'. Combining this with the evidence of the novels, Aufrère deduced a strong vein of narcissism or at least a preoccupation with self, which was hardly normal. He found too that Boucher's early novels were inspired by a love affair, real or fanciful, with Napoleon's sister, Princess Pauline Borghese, and he has commemorated this in the reconstructed museum at Abbeville. In the middle of a case full of Boucher's antediluvian artefacts, Aufrère has set a plaster model of the Princess's hand. This is meant, I suppose, to symbolize the intimate association of science and sentiment in Boucher's lifework. I value it more as evidence that Aufrère too was, like Boucher, an ingrained original and hence capable of appreciating the unique blend of obstinacy, clowning and ecstatic vision, in which the science of prehistory was born. Aufrère does justice to Boucher, the prophet-scientist, when he writes:

Making a discovery is not just making a lucky find, it is being susceptible to the spendour of an idea. That was what he was, for his thought is rich in resonances. It was through ruminating and writing on the history of man, his arts and sciences, that Boucher had pushed back the frontiers of human history.

But does Aufrère make sufficient allowances for the pathological quirks which may be induced in us by decades of unmerited neglect? Also something more than ordinary vanity is needed to make a man keep and label a decayed molar. What was it? If we knew, we might come to understand better the long solitary life from which prehistory was born and Boucher's

Pythagorean belief that the body was the transient lodging of the eternal spirit, which moulded it and would discard it. For his beliefs and his discoveries and the shape of his life were not dictated by his birth and circumstances. He was sociable, rich and vigorous. He had been handsome. He longed to marry, to see his plays staged, to live in Paris. But some irresistible introversion rooted him to Abbeville and to womb-like speculations, which he could share with few.

And is not the learned resistance to prehistory also very interesting psychologically? A congress of scientists had been held at Laon, only a couple of hours by train east of Abbeville. Boucher had as usual bombarded them with parcels and invitations to his gravel-pits. They had discussed Antediluvian Man and rejected him, without inspecting the gravel-pits, reading Boucher's books or visiting his collections.

I am far from considering myself a savant [he wrote] or even a very clever man, but I am not blind. What seems to me ten times worse than criticism is this obstinate refusal to look at the facts and to say 'It's impossible!' without going to see for themselves.

But many times he wrote about it more passionately and surely justifiably: 'Hate and persecution at least offer you a chance. . . but indifference is a wall between you and the light, it burns you alive. I'd sooner an enemy who flung Truth back into her well and crashed the bucket down on her head.'

The English geologists, Falconer, Prestwich, Evans and many others, who came to Abbeville after 1850 to pay their respects to Antediluvian Man and to the Father of Prehistory, were all of them pleasant, well-educated men, as their long letters to Boucher which have survived the bombardments testify. Yet they would all have agreed that, when you have a revelation of the truth and wish busy experts to accept it, you must draft your propositions in a brief business-like way. Prestwich, announcing Boucher's discovery to the Royal Society, explained his failure to convince them earlier 'as politely as he could'. This phrase is Miss Evans', but none of them would have thought it inappropriate. The contrast of their busy lives and Boucher's leisured dilettantism is one on which Miss Evans loved to dwell. When Falconer at last accepted Boucher's invitation to Abbeville, he was a day later than he said; the house was all shut up and Boucher himself was sitting in his carriage ready to drive away to the country. Instantly the Father of Prehistory leapt out, cancelled his visit to the country, had his house opened up again and laid himself out to make a convert of Falconer. He succeeded; and a few weeks later Prestwich and Evans, urged on by Falconer, were at Abbeville too. Boucher was at their hotel soon after seven a.m., and when they returned, converted, from the gravel-pits, he gave them what Miss Evans calls 'a sumptuous fork lunch'. This sounds excessive, almost vulgar. In contrast Prestwich, displaying Boucher's implements and expounding Boucher's discovery to a distinguished gathering in London eight days later, 'entertained them with his legendary sherry'. For busy men this was just right.

Hugh Falconer in a letter to Prestwich strikes the precise note of amused condescension with which the learned world allowed itself to be convinced by a donkey!

I have a charming letter from M. Boucher de Perthes, full of gratitude to *perfide Albion* for helping him to assured immortality and giving him a lift, when his countrymen of the Institute left him in the gutter. He radiates a benignant smile from his lofty pinnacle on you and me – surprised that the treacherous Leopard should have behaved so well.

Yet it was just the fantastic element in Boucher's character, which, allied to his practical earnestness, made him assert the impossible and maintain it doggedly against the experts. Falconer, Evans and Prestwich could have spent a lifetime classifying their tertiary pebbles and sipping their legendary sherry, but they could never have taken that great leap into the inconceivable that the customs officer of Abbeville accomplished with bravado and relish. If they had been capable of such a leap they would have taken it years before, for they had all the evidence beside them. In 1797 John Frere had reported the same combination of artefacts and antediluvian bones in Suffolk, and a dozen other such discoveries had in the intervening years been recorded. The geologists were responsible, gregarious people; industrialists consulted them about seams and measures. Probably they instinctively shied away from that solitude in which subversive discoveries are made. And deep in their subconscious there may have been some apprehension of the explosions that could be triggered off by Antediluvian Man. First there was the War with Moses, as Boucher called it, and round the corner they might have caught a glimpse of Evolution and

'Godless' materialism, and the sinister pseudoscience of Social 'Darwinism'. These premonitions cannot have been clearly defined, but they may have clouded that zone of sensibility that Boucher was trying to inflame, and decided them against opening the door to Antediluvian Man. Boucher himself was not at all frightened by him; there had long been a comfortable place prepared for him in his many-chambered humanist philosophy.

One could find dozens of passages in which Boucher tried to placate the professional scientists; but his main offence was that he had been right, so the more he abased himself and called himself a donkey, the worse it became. If it proved that a scientific revolution could be introduced by a donkey, all the academies in Europe would totter.

Undoubtedly many of Aufrère's semi-genial assaults on Boucher's integrity are unfair. He complains that Boucher tendentiously 'edited' the correspondence from which, as an old man, he composed his eight-volume autobiography. But, in fact, he explained in his preface that he had rewritten from memory such letters as he had not copied or could not recover. The bulk of the letters are as they were written, and give a charming picture of the life of a scholarly eccentric in a provincial town. They are fertile in imagination and invention and French scholars still glean ideas from them. Lately, for example, M. Roger Agache used a long and detailed letter from Boucher, written 150 years ago, to illustrate a thesis about the 'crop marks' visible from the air in northern France (*Revue Archaeologique de-l'Est*, 42, 1962).

Miss Evans insists that the man who really introduced prehistory was not Boucher but his dead friend, Dr Picard. 'He wore Picard's mantle', she writes, 'with such dramatic effect that he soon forgot it had not always been his own.'

Yet all the evidence for this comes from Boucher himself via Aufrère and I do not believe that Miss Evans could have distilled so much poison from Aufrère's book if that distinguished work had been wholly sweet-tempered. Are there perhaps traces in it of the old jealousy between the paid scholar, who lacks freedom, and the independent one, who lacks status? Certainly Boucher's great friend and disciple Dr Picard had taken the first steps towards the discovery of prehistory, but it is from Boucher himself, who gave Picard every encouragement till his early death in 1841, that we draw most of our information about the young doctor. It was Boucher's Society which printed his theories and gave him a forum for discussing them. In the first draft of his *Antiquités*, composed in 1844, Boucher had written a page attributing everything to Picard, of whom he claimed to be no more than an inadequate interpreter. 'He was starting his career when I was ending mine.' Why did he later leave out all but a sentence of this touching tribute? He was getting on for seventy. Recognition seemed far away and maybe he felt that by his obstinacy he had earned the greater part of such applause as his book might gain. In fact it gained none. Less than a hundred copies were sold of the book which ushered in the new science of prehistory. The booksellers begged him to take back their stock. He sighed not only for his masterpiece but also for the fine quality paper which had had to go to 'the writers' cemetery, the butter-merchant'.

Moreover in the third volume of *Antiquités* he gave ample justice to all those who had preceded Picard and himself, John Frere of Hoxney, Father McEnery, Schmerling and many others. 'I abase myself before labours like these. All that I can say for myself is that I have been the most obstinate.'

Miss Evans asserts that after his victory Boucher was 'more anxious for his own reputation than for the scientific implications of his discoveries'. Yet if you read the letters he wrote in the triumphant year of 1859, you will see how little his reputation was bothering him. When in 1908 the Abbevillois erected a statue to him, they inscribed on the base PALAIONTOLOGUE ET PHILANTHROPE, but in 1859 the Philanthrope was in the ascendant. There are long, painstaking letters about the cure for drunkenness, the rescue of horses from burning stables, and the agricultural use of a freshwater mussel which he had discovered in the Somme.

Boucher was a great giver of prizes and medals. He offered awards for exemplary working women in a dozen towns in Picardy, dispensing in this way during his lifetime 100,000 francs, and bequeathing after his death a further 150,000 francs. It would have been strange if he had not accepted medals and prizes himself, but he took this casually enough. He once wrote: 'They wanted to make me a municipal councillor. . . and even a deputy, but I was like that old soldier, who was taken prisoner by the Turks. He said: 'They offered me all the offices, Bey, Pasha, Vizier, . . . even Eunuch, but I refused them all.'

In 1860 Boucher set off for the British Isles. He describes his visit in one of his travel books, which cover all of Europe and some of Africa. He writes as unaffectedly as he must have conversed. For an old gentleman who had recently extended human history by many millennia, he was on this journey remarkably unassuming; he expected and received no acclamation whatever.

When he reached London his distinguished friends were as kind to him as if he had been their old uncle just up from the country. Prestwich asked him to supper to meet his sister and Falconer gave him lunch at the Colonial Club and took him to the Zoo. At the Athenaeum, to which he had sent one of his parcels, he met 'M. Th. Huxlevy' (he seldom got any English name right) and was given a month's membership. Most of the time he wandered round by himself, as he had done in Kiev and Belgrade and Algiers. He visited 'Kesington', 'Pale Male' and 'Hyde Parck'. He changed his linen twice a day because of the dirt and, watching rain from a hotel window, he composed one of his sad rhymes about London cut-throats and pickpockets (he had seen one of their victims running and shrieking 'Policy! Policy!'), and a young prostitute, who was killed by a resurrectionist. His happiest day was when he went to 'Escher' for a memorial service to Louis Philippe, who had always been kind to him (the Comte de Paris had accepted Antediluvian Man). The train at Esher was two hours late; he had left his overcoat on the wrong platform and, in retrieving it, was nearly run over by the train. Aufrère says of him that he was 'a man of great gaiety, with no luck!' Boucher describes these episodes with so much humour, zest and philosophical comment that the loneliness in which prehistory was conceived can only be guessed at.

Miss Evans cannot bear to agree with Aufrère that Boucher wrote extremely well and that it was often his fearless championship of liberal causes that prevented his plays, which were usually satirical, from being performed. She dismisses them with scorn and in his other writings she grudgingly allows him 'facility' and 'a capacity for eloquence, not uncommon in men brought up on the windy rhetoric of the revolution'. Yet Aufrère says of his plays: 'They had verve and observation and had a happy turn of phrase. And if he had not been dogged by ill-luck, he would have made his mark as a playwright.' And he relates how the greatest of French comedians, Potier, was an ardent champion of Boucher's plays against the censor.

In fact in an easy unpretentious way Boucher was an admirable writer fully deserving Aufrère's many comments on his excellent French and the graceful purity of his style. The problems to which he addressed himself sometimes no longer puzzle us, but his books are not all period pieces. In 1961 his *Petit Glossaire*, a satirical attack on the French administration was republished in paperback 126 years after its original appearance. A delightful anthology could still be made from his autobiographical volumes and his travel books.

Archaeology in 1850 was still considered to be a bridge between humanism and the physical sciences. Boucher planted prehistory at the humanist end of this bridge and defended it against all aggressors. The bridge has long ago been blown up and prehistory has been built into the fortress of science. It flourishes there but disturbing things have happened which would not, perhaps, have occurred in the old days of provincial humanism.

Boucher had greatness because he was a crusader for the unity of knowledge in an age when its fragmentation was already far advanced. His appears to be a lost cause but it is one that will always have adherents. Fighting his own battles, he was fighting for others too, the individualists, the provincial, the scholar who refuses to specialize. As that ill-organized community cannot now even recognize its own champions, it is good that in Abbeville at least the Father of Prehistory is still greatly honoured.

[1987]

8

ERNEST RENAN:
THE STATUE AND THE CALVARY

Very few people are interested in Renan now. Perhaps his brand
of scepticism, which was eager and voluble, is out of date. In
the West, religious disbelief is so widespread that it seldom has
to be defiant or even articulate. You do not have to repudiate
ideas to which you are indifferent. Only in the remote or very
conservative parts of Europe, where the old orthodoxies survive
unchallenged, can you startle people by disbelieving. But in
most other places, particularly in England, religious controversy
is tame and gentlemanly.

Renan was born in Brittany and came back there in his old
age. Spiritually he never left it. He could never dissociate himself
from the simple, unquestioning faith which he had challenged.
That challenge had been the Open Sesame to a magic world,
where truth, complex and progressively revealed, was adored
with all the devotion that the Bretons gave to myth and pious
legend. Renan was almost fanatical in his pursuit of the truth.
He asked that *dilexi veritatem* (I loved the truth) be written on
his tombstone. Truth, as he saw it, was friendly, not hostile, to
the imagination; it was only ruthless to those fabrications which
had grown inflexible with age and were cramping to the intelligence and the will. He saw danger and cruelty in them.

I think that Renan differed from other great sceptics like Voltaire and Lucretius by his sensitive, unscornful handling of the
ideas which he had rejected. He was neither a revolutionary nor
a self-sufficient scholar. He was a Celt whose emotions were
swayed by memories and personal loyalties. He loved the
Church to which he owed the learning and the dialectical skill
which he later turned against it. His childhood and the child-

hood of his race and all the villages and institutions of his native Brittany had developed under its care. He was bound with a cord which was precious to him; its knots and tangles had to be untied and not cut.

Renan believed that the faith of his childhood must be transcended, not simply by-passed. But the leaders of his Church preferred that their faith should be ignored rather than tampered with; they dreaded heresy more than infidelity. And that, I think, explains the fury and the fervent love which the memory of Renan can still rouse in his native Brittany, and the indifference with which he is regarded in the wider world where there are no strong tensions because there is no strong faith.

His clear and careful prose is today found sentimental and unctuous. The devout find him insidious, the sceptics find him insinuating. They do not understand what Renan was trying to do. He believed that Christianity is a still living faith, but, if it is to survive, a delicate and skilful operation must be performed on it. Renan had once operated on his own soul, amputating many passionately held convictions. After the torment of his young manhood he had reached happiness, unclouded by doubt or regret, a measured confidence in the powers of the human mind that was proof against disillusionment and catastrophe. He believed that Christianity could survive the loss of all its supernatural accretions.

I think it was partly because of this confidence that he decided to live among the Bretons, to match their fervour with his own and prove to himself that he had not broken with his past but fulfilled it. That is why, as an old man, a scholar of international repute, he chose to settle on the Breton coast, near Tréguier, where he was born and studied for the priesthood. And though Renan died nearly a century ago, he is still loved and hated there. He is a figure of controversy and a dynamic force. When, as happens every now and then, there is a celebration in his honour, it is hard to tell whether it is a challenge to the living or an act of homage to the dead.

Tréguier is a small sleepy town, but it was one of the great early Christian centres of Brittany. It was founded by the legendary half-Druidic St Tudwal, who in Saxon times led a group of refugees out of Wales. The celebrated St Yves was born there some seven centuries later. And all around there are innumerable Breton saints of marked individuality and doubtful orthodoxy. Renan himself belonged to the family of one of the most eccentric of them, St Ronan or Renan. Renan, despite his assault on the supernatural, had a tenderness for these cantankerous Breton saints whose cult had been for centuries the focus of local pieties. What he feared was not the credulity of the simple in which so often true history is enshrined, but its manipulation in the interests of orthodoxy and uniformity. When he was visited by Rhys, the great Welsh archaeologist, he sadly told him how the old statue of St Budoc had been defaced and the curate had collected a subscription of 40 francs to replace it with a Virgin of Lourdes, *ce triste miracle moderne*, to the dismay of the pious, conservative villagers. In many ways Renan, the revolutionary thinker, had a greater love for tradition than the ecclesiastics themselves.

While denying the divinity of Christ, Renan believed in the Christian traditions of brotherhood, selflessness and conscience. He believed that the Reformation of the sixteenth century had once safeguarded these by eliminating much that was idolatrous and heathen. Yet he thought that a yet greater reformation was needed which would embrace the whole of Christianity. 'The spirit of reformation', he declared, 'is being rapidly overtaken by rationalism, which knows nothing and which will destroy all that which awaits reformation before it has been reformed.' 'The reformers', he added, 'could only save Christianity by attaining to absolute rationalism themselves and joining hands with all the emancipated spirits, who will accept the Sermon on the Mount as the code of conduct.'

You can imagine what consternation these opinions caused in the Church. Long after Renan's death the battle was still being fought. And in Tréguier itself the clash of wills is immortalized in stone. Outside the church door in the centre of the square Renan's statue was erected in 1903 in the presence of Anatole France and many other leading intellectuals of France. It was a challenge which could not be ignored. A group of country people had agreed to come in and stop the unveiling, but they were prevented by a tremendous downpour of rain. A few years later, in protest against the statue, a great monument was erected called the 'expiatory Calvary'. It stands at the base of the Rue Ernest Renan, within a stone's throw of the house where Renan was born and his mother kept a small grocer's shop. Below it is inscribed: *Vere hic homo filius Dei est* (Truly this man is the son of God). In front of it, with other saints, the stone figures of St Tudwal and St Yves stand on guard. Renan's house had been a museum for a long time and some years ago it was reorganized. There was a ceremonial opening with M. Herriot from Paris, the Mayor, a naval band and a banquet for seven hundred guests. Belief and disbelief in the supernatural are in France still real issues, dividing men's minds. Evasiveness and compromise are not honoured. If this is responsible for bitterness and deep social fissures, it is also surely the source of France's cultural and intellectual pre-eminence.

Through long experience the antagonists have learnt to make graceful contact across the abyss. They can be courteous even when intransigent. I am thinking in particular of the letter Renan wrote on his first return to Tréguier, asking to be allowed to visit his old seminary and his teachers, whose favourite pupil he had once been. It is a masterpiece of delicacy and tact. But in the Principal's reply, a refusal, there is sweetness, too, as well as firmness. Perhaps the worst quarrels occur on the fringes of conviction. Renan and his teachers were not so much hostile to each other as completely unintelligible.

Renan was, of course, attacked as well as defended in an uncivilized way. He had indiscreet champions. But I think his bitterest enemies were those who never came within range of his happy, serious, friendly personality. Renan made himself loved by his Breton neighbours. He was a good man and a good Christian; on that point, their intuition was sound. But beyond the friendly circle there was no understanding or sympathy with his work. It needs generosity as well as genius to cut across the current of your age. Renan advanced fiercely unpopular opinions and yet remained smiling and unperturbed, though he was regarded by many as Anti-Christ and the Incarnation of Evil. I only know of one occasion when Renan lost his temper. He was asked to use his influence on behalf of the son of some Breton cousins of his. He paid a visit but learnt afterwards that the armchair on which he had sat had been sprinkled carefully with holy water by the boy's mother. She sent him, however, a present of some oysters. Renan had the oysters very conspicuously thrown on the manure heap.

Renan, old as he was and declining in health, by his mere physical presence in that remote corner of Brittany gave courage and confidence to many, and in particular to that small band of

Breton scholars and poets who had urged him to come home to live. He had loved Brittany and the Celtic peoples and in spite of his unpopular theology there were many there to welcome him. He was the greatest Breton of his age. A heretic? Yes, but hadn't there been plenty of Breton heretics before him? Pelagius, perhaps, and Abelard and Lammenais certainly. The faith of the Bretons, he declared, had always been detached from books and forms, orthodoxy had been imposed through French bishops and concordats made with the French. For centuries there had been no Breton-speaking bishop. The Reformation had once taken a firm hold on the Bretons and it was only an accident of politics that they had not, like their kinsmen in Wales, remained under its sway.

Renan was looking in Brittany for some affinity of spirit that did not rest on scholarship, and, if one is to judge by the small public demonstrations that were made in his honour, I think he must have found it. Once when he was so crippled that he could not walk, he was entertained on the Island of Brehat; as usual on these occasions in France, there was a canon and a mayor and a naval band, a fleet of little painted boats and a banquet and lots of little girls dressed in white with bunches of flowers. When their boat reached the shore he found that a victoria, the first carriage ever seen on the island, had been ferried across the night before to receive him. With the simplicity of genius Renan spoke to the gathering of his father, the sailor, of his neighbours and friends of his childhood. Renan would like to have felt as at home in Brittany as in the Collége de France. He believed in the natural pieties of home and fatherland. 'The memory of our native land is for each of us', he said, 'a part of our morality.' He believed in the power of natural goodness, which can in time replace that precarious goodness, as he would have considered it, which requires the support of a supernatural system. Was he anti-clerical? It is not so simple as that. 'Father-land', he said, 'and family are the two great natural forms of human association. Both are essential, but they cannot suffice of themselves. Side by side with them must be maintained an institution in which the soul can be nurtured and receive conso-lation and counsel, in which charity may be organized and spiritual masters and directors found.'

Though Renan was isolated and frustrated, yet he had confi-dence. He thought that one day he would be justified. Though

Christianity appeared inseparable from forms and ceremonies, from established hierarchies and supernatural beliefs, these things belong to the childhood of reason, while we are accustoming ourselves to the naked truth. One day we shall dispense with them. What did he mean though, by the 'institution for nurturing the soul', or 'the spiritual directors and masters'? In what respect would these differ from the Church and its ministers? It is a point that Renan has not made clear. I think he would say that certain men have a clearer vision than others of the truth and can walk undazzled in the light of it. They are the true spiritual directors, whose task it would be to nurture the soul. But the Church will have none of them. They are feared and hated. It is even asserted that the Christian virtues themselves would collapse if the supernatural origin of the Church was repudiated. Renan denied this.

In fact Renan's enemies gave constant proof of the precariousness of this supernaturally fortified goodness. When his body was laid to rest in the Pantheon, and later, when his statue was erected at Tréguier, a flood of malice poured from the press. I can think of one book, similar to many, whose author dwelt with satisfaction on the last painful months of Renan's illness. 'It was proof', he said, 'that God had deserted him, as he deserted Voltaire and Arius the Heresiarch who died of a haemorrhage in a privy at the moment of his triumph, an answer to the prayers of the pious bishop Alexander. 'The apostate', says the writer, 'was hustled away to die in the grim fortress of the Collége de France, so that he might be out of reach of the pious Bretons, whose faith he had assailed and whose conviction it was that he had been devoured by lice.' And he perfects the parallel with Arius; 'The apostate', he says, 'was a humiliating spectacle in an old coat like a soutane and a sort of ecclesiastical hat tottering in the garden, coughing, spitting, puffing, groaning, trembling, crying like a soul in pain. Two valets followed him bearing a commode shaped like an armchair.'

So the statue of Renan at Tréguier was, in a sense, expiatory like the Calvary. In the words of the French Minister at the unveiling: it was to 'repair the unjust ostracism to which the apostle of toleration had so long been submitted on the soil of his native Brittany'. The Mayor of Tréguier declared in 1903, 'This statue proclaims in the face of the whole world that our old province has not been absolutely abandoned to fanaticism.

To attack this statue will be to attack the glory of France and to do a deep injury to the dignity of human thought.'

But the statue has never been attacked. It is as safe as the Calvary in this civilized little town. The citizens are deeply divided in their loyalties, but they can cherish their differences with dignity. Renan, according to one of his biographers, will never attract followers. To have disciples is the destiny of those who 'croient lourdement', like Paul and Luther and Wesley. All the same I think that the picture of Renan, the smiling sceptic, aloof, ineffectual, impregnable, has been overdrawn. Renan the fearless enquirer, the fighter for the truth, has been under-estimated. He followed the truth without misgiving as to where it would lead him. He saw that what he had written would bring release to some, but pain and bewilderment to others. Would the ill-disposed profit by what he, in good faith, had said? He did not ask.

Renan's faith in human destiny was a very individual, almost aristocratic one. It was proof against the disillusionment that may overtake all our democratic enthusiasm. 'Idealists like us', he said, 'must approach these fires with precaution. The chances are that we'll lose our head or our wings in them!' And he remarked on that strange magnetism which plays between the opposite poles of religious and socialistic orthodoxy. 'How often', he said, 'it happens that when a man abandons the Church, he will search for the lost absolute, the lost comfort of believing friends and colleagues, in a fanatical political faith!' And the converse happens too.

Is there something rather smug about Renan's practical sobriety? Sometimes admittedly there is. I think it was not always wisdom so much as a certain physical timidity that pre-vented him from dissipating his energies in unprofitable idealism, but, whatever the reason, the clarity of his vision was seldom dimmed by passion or prejudice. He believed that truth must be pursued without any reservation. He thought that man, through advancing knowledge, would acquire the power to extricate himself from the difficulties in which his too great con-fidence might plunge him. In one of his last writings he foretold how Caliban would turn Prospero out of his kingdom, and wis-dom and goodness would have to be cherished in exile and in secret. But he thought that it would be better to endure Caliban for a space than to have Prospero restored by the forces of clerical reaction. 'Far from being a Renaissance,' he said, 'that would be in our circumstances annihilation. Let us keep Caliban.' These lines were quoted by Anatole France at the unveiling of the statue. I am sorry that he did not quote further, for Renan believed that Ariel, the spirit of religion, would survive all these vicissitudes and adapt himself to changed circumstances.

In fact Renan was convinced that Christ's teaching had a validity that needed no supernatural sanction. He thought it was only obscured by arguments based on historical facts that would always be disputed. You might entice millions into conformity by an elaborate system of beliefs and duties and catechismal phrases, but you would alienate thereby the handful of Christians who loved the truth unreservedly and were ardent and expert in the pursuit of it. Time would prove that they and no others were the best advocates of Christian love and charity.

It is nearly ninety years now since the statue was put up but I discovered in the fifties that the Breton scholar who had first appealed for its erection was still alive and still capable of inspiring and infuriating his countrymen. He was the founder of one of the leading Breton nationalist associations and, though old and half blind, was unjustly sentenced to a short imprisonment for his political opinions.

What would Renan have thought of Breton separatism? I think, like Matthew Arnold, another philo-Celt, he would have regretted that it was the lowest gifts of the Celtic peoples and not the highest, for which the modern world could find a use. Political revolt would have seemed to him merely the physical symptoms of a spiritual disequilibrium. There was no place today in the world for those excellences which the Celt had once contributed to European civilization, their gifts of imagination and of poetry, their defiance of the orthodox in thought and feeling. It would be natural that the Celts should wish to rebel against a civilization which claimed to be able to dispense with these qualities. I think here too Renan would have proved a prophet of reconciliation. For he himself had found no conflict between his love of France and his loyalty to his native land.

[1950, 1988]

9

I . . . I SUPPOSE SO:
MARIA CROSS RECONSIDERED

Much of *Maria Cross*, Mr Donat O'Donnell's important study of some modern Catholic writers, was first published in *The Bell*. His analysis is subtle and stimulating, and he avoids dogmatism without blurring the outline of his arguments with too many qualifications.

Broadly, he is enquiring whether there is a particular climate of thought and feeling in which art flourishes that is specifically Catholic, and to what extent these eight diverse writers are the product of such a climate. Much in them that appears 'Catholic' in its origins he traces to other sources. For example, one cannot study Mr Waugh, 'the embattled Jacobite', without reference to his adolescent romanticism and adult snobbery; M. Mauriac's curious obsession with 'Property' and the 'Home' also has its roots in the emotional conflicts of childhood. Mr Greene's 'Pity' is shown to be a clever piece of joinery from the literary work-shop, and, less convincingly, Mr O'Faolain's strong loyalties are said to be diluted with nostalgia for ancient politics.

Then there are Bloy and Bernanos, Péguy and Claudel. Most people would be content to lead Bloy to the psychoanalyst's waiting-room and leave him there, but Mr O'Donnell, more patient, manages to distil some vapour of Christianity from his misery and megalomania. He is judicious about Péguy and Claudel. He sees that their poetry, in its intimate relation to their faith, has a strange 'uterine' preoccupation. But, while he will accept a Freudian diagnosis, he rejects the anti-poetic, anti-religious inferences that a materialist philosopher – he produces

* Donat O'Donnell, *Maria Cross* (London 1953).

an archetypal one called Dr Joystone – would draw from it. He finds in Bernanos an un-Christian 'hatred of reason' shared in a lesser degree by Mauriac, Péguy, Greene and Waugh, but traces this terrible disease to our impoverished environment, in which the imagination and the heart are starved. But he shows that Bernanos' integrity has not been impaired by its ravages.

Later, Mr O'Donnell tries to see whether these writers have been led towards Fascism by their feeling of exile from the modern world. He take their cases separately, and few will dispute his conclusions.

In a final summary, Mr O'Donnell, if I do not mistake him, discovers that the most valid link between these Catholic writers is the sense of communion which ascends from parochial loyalties to the conception of the community of all mankind. And he concludes by saying that even those who do not share their beliefs are susceptible to 'this intuitive harmony of mystery and suffering, the reverberation, even at the oblique touch of a finger nail, of the great Catholic bell'.

Mr O'Donnell is here addressing a 'mixed' audience, and will not be suprised at the angry scraping back of a chair and a rasping voice saying: 'You mean the ROMAN Catholic bell, Mr O'Donnell?' This crude person has just been reading on page 257 that modern Protestantism is 'dead from the waist down', and he is threatening to bring out his drum in order to drown that 'reverberation'. Alas, I can't dissociate myself from his vulgar interruption, because he and I also have our communion and are linked together by many common thoughts and feelings and five centuries of history. To pacify him, I have promised that half-way through this essay I'll consider some 'non-Roman-Catholic' writers. I haven't warned him that he'll dislike my opinions as much as Mr O'Donnell's.

But to return to *Maria Cross* – for the majority of these writers the consolations of religion seem to be balanced against an almost bottomless despair. Mr Greene pours his cockroaches and dead pie-dogs, his loveless lechery and betrayed innocence, into the scale of material pessimism in order that the scale of divine grace may mount and mount. Mauriac and Bernanos add their pimps and blackmailers, Bloy his 'torrent of scatology', Waugh his Mayfair cannibals and Californian corpse beauticians. It seems as if a touch of natural happiness would upset the precarious equilibrium.

Obviously if there is Christianity here, it is of a very specialized kind, not immediately recognizable to us all. Mr O'Donnell's task of stripping away what is adventitious in order to rescue what is unmistakably and imperishably Christian is therefore of great value and importance.

Mr O'Donnell rightly treats *The Heart of the Matter* as the most revealing of Greene's novels, 'telling more about the people of our time than many more honest books', and his long analysis of it is as fascinating as it is ingenious. By the seduction of his craftsmanship Greene can draw the most Protestant of us into his curious twilight world in which the policeman and the priest cast such gigantic shadows. Though we feel the unreality of this world he deftly forestalls our protests by putting them into the mouth of his more foolish characters. 'To me it's all hooey!' says Helen Rolt when she hears of Scobie the policeman's moral dilemma. She is a nice but very silly woman, and we are flattered by the suggestion that we are different.

Scobie's problem is that his wife suspects him correctly of adultery, but, in order to make sure, she urges him to go to confession. To obtain absolution he will have to give up Helen, so that if it is withheld, his wife will know the worst. Having to choose between discovery and renunciation, Scobie lies to his confessor and commits suicide. His dilemma, if it is really insoluble, seems to me to expose a small flaw in the machinery of the confessional. Its secrets can sometimes be deduced by a simple process of reasoning. It can be used for the purpose of detection.

It is, of course, the flaw in Scobie and his world, rather than the flaw in the machinery of confession, which Greene here explores. He approaches it very tenderly and, in Mr O'Donnell's eyes, with incomplete candour. Scobie, it would seem, despite six or seven grave offences ranging from connivance at smuggling (inspired by charity) to the false confession and the suicide, has earned divine forgiveness, because in each case he acted from pity, which in an imperfect world is the nearest we can reach to the Love of God.

Mr O'Donnell's analysis of Greene's 'Pity' is a very distinguished piece of research. Scobie, at each stage of his moral decline, finds his heart touched by the suffering that befalls the innocent, the childlike, the simple. His derelictions of duty – first to man, then to God – are all attempts to alleviate this undeserved misery. But, under Mr O'Donnell's microscope, Scobie's pity is seen to have ragged edges from which less respectable emotions have been torn. For example, was it just pity, as the author seems to imply, that motivated Scobie's adultery with Helen? The web of circumstances which Greene has woven round his hero could not, I think, have strangled a more candid, less inhibited, man. The Lilliputians would never have tied up Gulliver with their tiny threads if he had not been dozing. To that extent Scobie and his fate, despite the narrator's skill, lack the universality of great art.

I am puzzled by Mr O'Donnell's essay on Sean O'Faolain. He considers that O'Faolain has smothered some of his talent under a blanket of nostalgia for rebel Ireland, as it was known to him as a child through the Parnellite talk of his elders, and as a young man through his own experiences in the twenties. Mr O'Donnell reproves him for his obsession with an out-of-date and parochial conflict, and contrasts him with Mauriac, whose tenacious love of his native place was never complicated by political partisanship. The land serves only as a carefully delineated background for 'human action which has the universality of sin'. But surely Mr O'Faolain's work captures the imagination just because it is three dimensional. We are creatures of time as well as space, and the Parnell struggle seems to summarize our past as well as to shape our future. It marked us permanently like an unhappy and quarrelsome adolescence. It could not be ignored any more than George Eliot in her provincial studies could ignore the social and moral commotion that attended the passage of the Reform Bill.

Of the two writers, French and Irish, Mauriac has undoubtedly the more repressed and repressive genius. Mr O'Faolain's creative powers blow like a fresh and salty wind through the forgotten, stupefying villages of the south-west. He is the least excluding of these writers. Perhaps it is because his Catholicism is native to him and he has sympathy for those who were born and bred to different loyalties. In his lovely story 'The Broken World' the old priest-narrator is looking for 'an image of life that would fire and fuse us all', and in many other stories, too, his love of his native land seems a liberating and enlarging passion, and not a restricting one, as Mr O'Donnell considers it to be. A Christian community is not warmed, like a Rotary Club, by the number and importance of its foreign affiliations. The neighbours whom we are enjoined to love are those nearest to us.

But, no doubt, I have misunderstood Mr O'Donnell's use of the word 'universal'. To the outsider 'universal sin' is an almost unassimilable notion. It stands on guard over many of the novels under consideration, but I am sure that to most of their non-Catholic readers it means no more than the stuffed policeman at the entrance to an exhibition. He gives a momentary thrill, and then they pass on, giggling, to the waxwork horrors within. They, too, recognize wrong-doing, but use a different idiom.

It is strange to find that five out of eight of these celebrated writers are converts, and a sixth, Mauriac, though always a Catholic, changed into top-gear in the middle of his creative period. The transition was so abrupt and rasping that Mr O'Donnell is surely right in calling it a conversion. He does not discuss the special 'convert-psychology', but it is important to the Protestants and other children of the Reformation from whose ranks some of these writers seceded. These converts have made a breach with the past. There has been tension and sadness, and they have had to meet accusations of apostasy. The peace of mind which they at last attain is often like the peace of a deserted battle-field. It is strewn with the corpses of massacred ideals and traditions which still show faint signs of life. For example, the dying wriggles of the Protestant respect for private judgment are surely the clue to some of the inconsistencies which Mr O'Donnell observes in *The Heart of the Matter*. If Protestantism was really 'dead from the waist down', its renunciation would be a more cheerful, less murderous affair.

But, in fact, the Churches have always been writing these acid obituary notices for each other. Here is one from a Victorian religious novel, which I have just been reading: 'The hold of Catholicism and its analogues on the guiding forces of Christendom is irretrievably broken,' said Friedland, 'and yet the needs of the soul remain the same.'

I am quoting from *Helbeck of Bannisdale*, a successor of *Robert Elsmere*, a once-famous book which in the late 1880s disturbed the complacency of the conventional much as *Brideshead Revisited* and *The Heart of the Matter* have done today. These books by Mrs Humphry Ward arose out of two crises of faith – two storms which landed their victims, a father and his daughter, on opposite shores. The tense atmosphere of emotional upheaval which hangs over them recalls closely the convert literature of today. If there is such a thing as a liberal Protestant novel, they are landmarks in its development. They are full of excitement and repudiation and moral certainty. They offered a prescription for the needs of the soul which thousands of readers found satisfying. I don't think anyone has a right to say that Protestantism is dead till he has proved that these prescriptions are no longer valid or devotedly followed, and are not a legitimate amendment of the ferociously intolerant Protestant dogmatism of the past.

Nowadays, as it was a century ago, the most notable conversions are to Catholicism, but in the intervening generations the children of the Tractarians grew up, and here and there faith snapped like an elastic that has been drawn too tight. Thomas Arnold, the brother of Matthew and the father of Mary Ward, was one of Newman's disciples and, on conversion, he threw up his job and dedicated himself to his faith. There was little therefore that Mary Ward did not know about the psychology of conversion by the time she had deserted to the liberal Protestantism of her Uncle Matthew.

So, let us consider Bannisdale. It is, like Brideshead, a crumbling home of the ancient Catholic aristocracy. It is dissolving under the hammer-blows of a world which Mrs Ward, in her Victorian innocence, believed to be catastrophically 'modern'. Alternate waves of sin and contrition have thinned out the woods and swept the historic furniture to the auction rooms. The Helbecks had in their time been splendidly, dynastically, bad like the Marchmains, but now the pendulum has swung to repentance, and the last of the historic pictures, a Romney, is being sold to pay for a Catholic orphanage.

It would be fascinating to compare Mrs Ward's heroine, Laura the Liberal, with Mr Greene's hero, Scobie the Catholic. Both of them are spiritual exiles in an alien milieu, both hopelessly entangled in an affair of the heart. They shuffle helplessly towards a self-inflicted death by roads that seem often to converge. They follow their two different prescriptions for the needs of the soul, believing that compromise is death. The novel, which has, I guess, about the same lease of immortality as many of those considered by Mr O'Donnell, is old-fashioned in style but not in subject; it illustrates and confutes that strange Catholic delusion that Liberal Protestantism is dead, because in many educated people there is little emphasis on dogma. The climax approaches when the heroine's step-mother, a lapsed free-thinker, is dying and a relic of St John of the Cross is brought to her bedside.

'Wasn't it kind of the dear nuns?' asked Augustina, fervently.

'I. . . I suppose so,' said Laura, in a low, embarrassed voice.

'I. . . I suppose so' is a stammering and fragmentary confession of faith, to be compared to Scobie's aposiopetic 'Dear God, I love. . . ' It brings tears of grief to the eyes of the dying step-mother, convulses Laura's lover, Helbeck, with stern anger, and fills her own heart with anguish. It leads her by a chain of complications, which are melodramatic and contrived, but not more so than what we find with Greene and Waugh, to the brink of 'the Otter Cliff'. Below it next day Helbeck finds her, 'her bright hair tangled among the drift of branch and leaf brought down by the storm'.

Rewrite all this in the idiom of our day, putting in cockroaches and dead pie-dogs where necessary, and recalling how much more realistically Waugh or Greene would describe a corpse in a creek (Scobie's wife, under a mosquito net, appeared to him like a joint under a meat cover), and here, too, will you not find unreserved loyalty to a living faith which is not dimly conceived?

It may be said that 'I. . . I suppose so!' is the last faint echo of the apocalyptic bellowings of Luther and John Knox, and that no Jenny Geddes will ever again fling her stool at the preacher and scream, 'Out, thou false thief! Dost thou say Mass at my lug?' But Laura is as resolute as Jenny. There is no cause for alarm if Protestantism appears to be coming out of its protective shell of dogma like a too trustful snail, for its apparent defence-lessness is the measure of its assurance. Nothing has happened to discredit the Liberal Protestantism of the Arnolds. For example, free what follows from its Victorian idiom – Friedland again speaking:

Behind the Church, as she moves through history, the modern sees the rising of something more majestic still, the free human spirit in its contact with the infinite sources of things! The Jerusalem, which is the mother of us all. . . But she is not only a material and generative power: she is chastisement and convulsion. . . There is a great elaboration of conscience. . . and an almost intoxicating sense of freedom.

There is nothing wrong with that except that we are now more conscious of the chastisement and the convulsions than of the intoxicating freedom. Is it, maybe, rather academic and chilly? There is fervour there – the fervour that is associated with religious upheaval – but is there natural warmth, love? I think the Arnold-Huxley clan were as deficient in warmth as most of the writers studied by Mr O'Donnell, but they tried to fill the gap with integrity.

Liberal Protestantism is perhaps waiting for some new spokesman to fuse the new knowledge with the old charity, or will we have to wait till the children of today's converts grow up before the fusion is effected in the heat of spiritual crisis? I hope not, for love seems to be linked as insecurely to religious fervour as to intellectual brilliance. There is in these six converts a lack of natural warmth so startling as in itself to explain the need for a theological heating apparatus. There is certainly an 'elaboration of conscience', immense subtlety of perception and detailed self-scrutiny, but the natural juices which convert sensibility into charity cannot, it appears, in these writers function unaided. Their books, as the most casual glance will show, are lumpy with angry prejudices. If you think it naively blasphemous of me to link such a disposition with their ardent pleas for the love of God, read George Eliot on the celebrated Protestant divine, Dr Cumming:

It is in vain for Dr Cumming to say that we are to love man for God's sake. . . the love of man for God's sake (Dr Cumming's God) involves, as his writings abundantly show, a strong principle of hatred. . . According to him, a man is not to be just from a feeling of justice; he is not to help his fellow-man out of good will to his fellow-men. . . All these natural muscles and fibres must be torn away and replaced by a patent steel spring – anxiety for the 'glory of God'.

George Eliot's religion was as unorthodox as her personal relationships, but there is no evidence that her divergences made her insensible to beauty or mystery or human suffering. She had no difficulty in reconciling reason and charity. These convert novelists, in contrast, appear to have projected their own spiritual turmoil onto the human scene. The shadow which darkens it is theirs. For have people altered very much in the intervening generations? Have they really started to function either according to the principles of Dr Joystone or by an artificial steel spring? Or is it possible that the sad company of Bannisdale and Brideshead would find their troubles understood in *Middlemarch*, and could be judged adequately by its author's assured, but liberal, standards?

[1953]

122

10

A REPLY TO SILENCE

In Ireland there has been for many generations a truce between Protestant and Catholic. The missionary activities of Swaddlers and Bible classes all but ceased a century ago and the last Protestant miracle by which a Popish boy had his eyes opened to the Protestant faith happened a generation earlier. The truce had been faithfully observed by both sides. The huge Protestant emigration is due to political not religious friction and the conversions to Rome, now more frequent than those in an inverse direction, are not (if we overlook the consequences of the *Ne Temere* decree) due to clerical interference. The principal influence that is likely to affect us comes from overseas. A militantly anti-Catholic novel like *Westward Ho!*, or an anti-Catholic film, is today unheard of, but Catholic books and films directed at the heretic as well as the faithful are frequent and often good. We, the children of the Reformation, from over-confidence or apathy, do not retaliate. Though we still exert an influence on the press of Ireland we do not often use it. However, our silence might so easily and dangerously be thought to convey acquiescence that now and again it should be broken. We are members of a great European community that took its rise at the Reformation. We are not the dwindling rearguard of English misgovernment.

Thomas Merton's *Elected Silence* has the praise of Evelyn Waugh and Graham Greene on the cover. It has had huge sales in the USA and now enjoys wide publicity in England and Ireland. Waugh believes that the book is the symptom of a great monastic revival in the USA. 'There is an ascetic tradition deep in the American heart, which has sometimes taken odd and unlovable forms. Here in the historic Rules of the Church lies its proper fulfilment. As in the Dark Ages the cloister offers the sanest and most civilized way of life.'

Merton, an American of Protestant extraction, had a restless youth and an unsatisfied temperament; at last he found peace in a Trappist monastery. His story is presented by himself and his publishers as a parable for us all; his problems are our problems, his tragedy the world's tragedy; in his conversion he has found a way out that is the Way-Out for all mankind. In fact this is not a book but a battleship; we cannot ignore its threat, for the captain came from our ranks and deserted us with scorn. He makes no secret that he is after our blood.

Some will say that we are taking too seriously this earnest, striving, imperfectly educated young man. But give his story a different but equally possible climax and indulgence will vanish. Suppose he had found the deep peace his troubled heart craved in the Communist Party (he had once looked for it there), should we not be alarmed to find his book a best-seller? Kindly feelings for the poor young man and his sorrows would be swept away in a panic that other sick souls might retreat as he did into this fortified refuge from the chaos of the world. Pity would dry up in our hearts.

Though the children of the Reformation are today a motley herd with little solidarity among them, this book by Thomas Merton may reawaken in us some long-buried awareness of common ideals. Fundamentally we believe that freedom and truth and happiness and the light of reason are not hallucinations of the worldly and foolish; they really exist and after infinite strivings may be reached. We do not believe with Merton and with Waugh that the world has to be repudiated or that its ambitions and pleasures may only be indulged under clerical supervision.

The book must have merit of some kind, though it is not that of distinguished prose, because the character of this emotional young man and his companions emerges vividly enough. The stupendous falsity of the book lies not in the narration of facts but in their interpretation. Merton's method of reasoning is so debased that the prodigious sales of this book must mean that over vast stretches of the English-speaking world the power of logical thought is dying out. How did this happen? Bertrand Russell had diagnosed a specifically American disease. 'From the highest flights of philosophy to the silliest movie the distinctive feature of American thought and feeling is the determination to have done with the notion of fact. Truth is a mistaken concept. Dewey the leading philosopher of America replaces truth by 'warranted assertability'. For the asssertability of *Elected Silence* there is a five-fold warrant from five ecclesiastics behind its title-page, but its truth requires closer investigation.

Thomas Merton was born in the heart of a strange world where for a living you had constantly to assert things which you did not believe. His grandfather was a pioneer in publicity for the movies, and Merton himself, from choice, not necessity, took advertising jobs. Once he had to demonstrate for the manu-facturers of paper cups how you get trench-mouth through drinking from glasses; another time, after his religious quest had started, he was for a few days 'barker' for the *Streets of Paris* at the World's Fair at Chicago. I do not know what a 'barker' is but we are encouraged to suspect the worst.

Merton relates all this and much more to show how in a world of sin he was a sinner only to be redeemed by renunciation. But the careful reader will come to the conclusion that he was a good and serious person but very silly. It is his intellect and not his morals that life has corrupted most dangerously. For example Original Sin might seduce us all into being furtive patrons of the *Streets of Paris* but most would be restrained by intellectual fastidiousness from acting as showman for it. His own incapacity to distinguish degrees of sin and folly seems complete. No doubt he would profit by some severe and simple code of ethics. Yet, I think from vanity, he tries to present his problem in a universal light. He is like the fox without a tail who wanted all foxes to be tailless.

And what in fact were his sins? I would make a guess that he contented himself with being the 'barker' for a great many delights he never tasted. He is never precise. He talks of the 'iron tyranny of moral corruption that held my whole nature in fetters', and again, 'My soul was simply dead. It was a spiritual vacuum . . . it was rotten with the corruption of my sins.'

I think the physio-chemical laws of self-hatred have yet to be discovered. Men cannot project so much loathing inwards with-out a counter-balancing thrust outwards or they would disinte-grate. In the case of Merton this outward blast is like the 'kick' of a mule or of a black-plumed undertaker's horse. He hates the world as much as himself. This is how he refers to his old uni-versity: 'I swept into the dark sinister atmosphere of

Cambridge . . . a cloudy, semi-liquid medium in whose dregs I was ultimately destined to settle.' Even an Oxford man would regard this as an overstatement, and this is how he tells us that he was reading Dante while training for the Clare College fourth boat! 'And now in the Christian Lent, which I was observing without merit and without reason, for the sake of a sport I had grown to detest, we were climbing from circle to circle of Purgatory.' Later on a visit to an uncle in Ealing, he found he 'had fallen through the surface of the old England into the Hell, the vacuum and the horror which London was nursing in her avaricious heart'.

It would, of course, be crude and callous to dismiss in a breezy way these torments of adolescence and young manhood. They can be unbearably real and acute, yet the perception of the misery, futility and coldheartedness of men has no more direct connection with religious orthodoxy than with the Clare College fourth boat. That is why it is offensive to see it exploited as propaganda for sectarian ends. James Joyce as a young man suffered identical torments and described them in language of surpassing beauty and gravity. Joyce was in the bosom of the Church yet found no consolation there, whereas Merton yearned towards that bosom as the only place of comfort.

Mr Merton acknowledges a deep debt to Joyce. Plainly he is right in doing so, even though he has turned Joyce upside down. Joyce was brought up in fear of his body which, after the missionary preacher's celebrated description of Hell, culminated in abject self-loathing. He restored himself through the catharsis of his art. *Ulysses* is a sort of violent purge for Catholic theology; if it failed to settle him, it is because it was excessive. (I cannot understand those very sophisticated people who draw attention to the essential Catholicity of Joyce, unless they give to Catholicism a far wider meaning than it could ever be granted by the Church of Rome. It seems to me as over-ingenious as Mr Patrick Kavanagh's attempt to equate Protestantism with Communism.)

Thomas Merton had a diametrically opposite upbringing. He had read *Ulysses* and all the more purgative Anglo-Saxon and French writers in his restless youth. Impressions, ideas, half-digested philosophies, had flowed through him but had not nourished him – Gide, Huxley, Plotinus, Crashawe, Chagall, all mixed up like a dog's dinner. He remained wretched and unappeased. Obviously he needed abstinence and a mild astringent but, like Naaman, he wanted some great thing. He went so far as to find the terrible demented missionary sermon of *The Portrait* edifying and stimulating. He liked its 'efficiency and solidity and drive'. In his large American way he wanted the biggest and strongest dose possible to cure him of his emotional surfeit. But even if it cured him such a remedy would have no universal validity. That is what is claimed for it.

But to revert to his sins, what were they? There are scenes in this book which threaten to culminate in orgies or at least in asterisks, but nothing happens except hangovers, some of these non-alcoholic. Once Merton throws a tin of maple syrup at a street lamp and someone is wound up in a Hindu monk's turban. He drinks sodas with the co-eds and goes on a trip down the Rhine with Spinoza and two immoral novels. He reads Gorki and endlessly he plays Duke Ellington on the portable vic and St Louis Blues on the piano. There are movies, movies, movies, till religion 'rinsed the grey pulp of the movies from his eyes'. Is it possible that these sins have been edited slightly so as to wear a universal character? Here is 'Mr Everybody' whose candour is always selective! He takes pleasure in manly avowals of those failings that are robust, high spirited or endearingly commonplace, but reserves for the General Confession what is squalid, mean and humiliating. Merton's silliest escapades are without sensuality. I do not find them commonplace, endearing or easily to be recognized with deep and genuine sensibility. When he had seen through Communism and was moving towards conversion he joined a Fraternity. He had to endure a week of initiation by torture and strange ritual. Then the initiates had to stuff themselves with bread and milk and wear a gold and enamel badge with their name engraved underneath. He wrote a book called *My Escape from the Nazis*. It was full, he says, of double talk and all kinds of fancy ideas that sounded like Franz Kafka. It does not appear that he had ever met any Nazis. The war was an ugly, exciting smear on news-pulp and celluloid. I don't think he ever tried to grasp what it was about.

He has not dismisssed rival philosophies without giving them each a trial. He pulls a plum out of every pie before he picks the winner. They are all horrid but one. Among the American Episcopalians there is Mr Riley; he talks about literature, politics and music instead of religion; he tries a too personal approach and is suspected of doubts about the Incarnation. In the Church of England he finds the Oakham chaplain, a rowing blue, who said that by 'charity' St Paul meant 'being a gentleman'. Typical of the Quakers was the lady who at a meeting produced a snapshot of the Lion of Lucerne to exemplify the Swiss love of independence. The Mormons fare no better.

Needless to say he becomes a Communist, for it is now almost obligatory for the ultimately pure-in-heart to have seen Communism from the inside and rejected it. He found his Communist associates earnest, bewildered, inconsistent, chattering bourgeois just like himself, and in addition they didn't serve drinks.

Then, of course, he took up psycho-analysis. The way he arrived at weary disillusionment with this still embryonic science is truly remarkable. In a chapter called 'The Harrowing of Hell', he tells how at the age of seventeen he met a black book called *The Outline of Modern Knowledge* which 'went into some details of psycho-analytical fortune-telling by the inspection of faeces, which I still preserved enough sense to laugh at at that time'. Later, this sense of humour deserted him and he got from the library all the psychological books of Freud, Jung and Adler and studied 'with all the application my hangovers allowed me, the mysteries of sex-repression'. *Then he psycho-analyses himself.* The shocking results were to him conclusive. 'If ever I had gone crazy I think psycho-analysis would have been the one thing chiefly responsible for it.' His argument appears to be that the Demon-Drink played only a secondary part in this sad story. If he hadn't been half-tight he would not have so far forgotten himself as to study, apply and finally expose this new and recondite branch of learning. *In vino veritas.*

As a child I read a horrifying story by E. Nesbit about some dummies made of newspaper who came alive. Thomas Merton's philosophy fills me with the same horror. It is without reality or humanity and yet it is alive and threatening. His Hell is a technicolor Hell, his Sin and his Expiation have no more authority than big black and white captions or headlines in churchy type. And yet the creatures of his mind, like those of Mrs Nesbit's story, have a species of invulnerability just because they are bodiless.

I do not mean that Merton is deliberately trying to impose on us. There are dreams, illusions, visions, which are the common property of all mankind, Christian and pagan. Their beauty and power lie in their iridescence, their elusiveness, their infinite variety; they have neither colour nor shape and cannot be located in time or place. Grasp them too firmly and try to skewer them or label them and they vanish away. Thomas Merton thinks he has them all pigeon-holed in the sacristy, but in fact there is nothing there, nothing but the print of his own clutching fingers.

Who has not felt at some time that there is a divinity that shapes our ends, that through misery and wrong God or Providence is working for Good? I had not realized before how this noble conception could be turned to nonsense by misappropriation. It is true that Frank Buchman, seeing God everywhere, thanked God for Hitler, and that Archbishop Stepinac saw the finger of God in the arrival of the Nazis and the bandit Pavelitch wrote 'A domino factum est istud et est mirabile in oculis nostris'. Protestants too are skilled in reading into history a divine justification for their prejudices. But Merton carries this habit beyond crime into lunacy. Of his literary tastes he writes, 'I think my love for William Blake has something in it of God's grace.' Of his first Mass, 'God made it a very beautiful Sunday . . . It was the first time I had spent a sober Sunday in New York.' Of the Hindu monk, the one with the turban, after he had made a helpful remark, 'Very probably one of the reasons that God brought him from India was that he should say just that.'

Everyone has at times, whether from scrupulousness or vanity, entertained the idea that his slightest action may have undreamt of consequences for good or evil. Merton makes it ridiculous by exaggeration. When the war broke out, 'My sins have done this,' he exclaimed, 'Hitler is not the only one.' And later, 'If I had accepted the gift of sanctity that had been put into my hand when I stood by the font in November 1938, what might have happened to the world!' And again, 'My own sins were enough to have destroyed the whole of England and Germany.'

But all the evidence goes to show that Merton's peccadilloes were insignificant and peculiar to himself. His failure, if it must be called that, is personal and cannot be used, as he uses it, to symbolize the Failure of Our Civilization. Till his publishers abetted him, the range of his small obliquities was very restricted. Though the case is now altered, they could not then as he supposes have influenced the Third Reich.

Indeed I would guess that it is vanity, not self-disgust, that causes him to present his imperfections on a cosmic scale. When he confounds his own sins with the sins of the world and prostrates himself with a despairing 'Nostra Culpa!' he gains rather than loses on balance. He has confused the focus so that his own frailties become too small to be distinguishable. You cannot see a pimple through an observatory telescope.

His main fault, that he has allowed his judgment to be clouded by emotionalism, cannot usefully be called a sin and is not likely to be either revealed or healed in the confessional. It derives from his temperament and his upbringing and it is more probable that he will cure himself by reason and reflection than by further emotional self-abasement.

The Reformation had many aspects, good and bad. Its most precious legacy, perhaps, is our belief that authoritarianism in spiritual matters is an evil far greater than the disorders to which the abuse of private judgment has often led. When we read Thomas Merton's words, 'I was forced at last by my own intense misery to give up my own will,' or, 'I rejoice in the prospect of a life protected from heat and anguish by the voice of chastity', we find a greater tragedy in the renunciation of the right to choose his own path than in all the stupidities and excesses a mistaken choice may have caused. There is no human society to which a man can unreservedly surrender his conscience or his will or his passions. A society whose solidarity is based on subservience will itself be servile. It will make a God of Universality or Uniformity or Obedience and for their sake it will make terms with every earthly power, even the basest.

Protestants, particularly the liberal ones, are today frequently warned that it is through the gateway of their moral and doctrinal laxity that the totalitarian enemy will make its approach. Now and again the ball has to be thrown back. Dostoievsky once prophesied that the Vatican and Communism would one day come to terms. There is, in fact, a curious magnetism operating between these two poles. When leading Communists are converted they become not Protestants but Catholics. The freer climate of the reformed faiths is uncongenial to them.

Those who are familiar with the apocalyptic literature of Communism could often, in Merton's most passionate confessions of faith, substitute 'Stalin' or 'the Communist Party' for 'God' and yet not feel that an injustice had been done to his character. For example Merton was shocked when some Communists, who had pledged themseves to peace, deferred to Communist policy and volunteered to fight in Spain. Yet when the time came for Merton himself to try out his pacifist convictions (he had taken the same peace pledge as the Communists), he too deferred to a higher authority and was ready to betray them. He accepted with resignation the possibility that he would be conscripted before he was received into his monastery. 'If God wanted me to go into the army, that would be the better and happier thing for me to do.' He has allowed God to usurp the place of his conscience, but is there not some trickery here? Has he not used 'God' as a synonym for 'Chance' or the 'American War Office' so as to sanctify his moral capitulation? In the same way a devout Communist or Nazi will accept with resignation instructions that outrage his conscience. He will persuade himself that in some mystical way they have been transmitted from the Party or the Leader himself, whose fatherly eye is always watching the least of his flock and who is the guardian of all their consciences. These two points of view are equally repugnant to all those who believe that a man's conscience must always be in his own keeping.

This book has passages of great charm and the writer has a sensitive and lively mind. Even in his unregenerate days, it must have been hard to dislike him. He has had a great moving experience, it may be said. Is he not right, therefore, to try to share it with the world? Why should we regard him with alarm and distrust?

I think he gives the answer himself. 'When we are acting with the best intentions we may be doing tremendous moral harm.' Emotionalism, controlled and organized, has the force of dynamite, and we heretics cannot ignore the bombshell he throws at us from the stronghold of his new orthodoxy. Only a fool could be deaf to the challenge implicit in his gentlest, saddest ejaculations. 'Mother of God!' he exclaims in one wistful moment, 'when, on the night I left the island, which was once your England. . .' That is a cry from the heart, full of pathos and nostalgia. Should we not rush to console him? But something holds us back. No! We have heard that voice before, centuries ago. And it led to bloodshed and cruelty and the denial of Christ's law.

Merton has closed his eyes and his mind. He cannot share

our visions, he is incapable of reciprocity, so we cannot trust ourselves to him. Perhaps he is not alone to blame. In a sense we are all of us prisoners of some passionately held belief – Catholics, Quakers, Communists, Mormons, Episcopalians – the less impregnable our stronghold the more closely we must guard it. Fear makes us defiant. But there are many manifestations of truth and there is no conflict till we claim that we alone have received the only authentic revelation.

[1949]

11

REFLECTIONS ON ROYALTY

The Irish attitude towards monarchy is rather inscrutable. Of course we are a republic, but the implications of republicanism have never been worked out and when Mr de Valera looked up the word in the dictionary he was regarded as a very pedantic and straw-splitting person. There is no very strong feeling against kingship as such in Ireland. King Leopold of Belgium, for instance, always gets a very good press, and the Habsburgs are not regarded as the former oppressors of some small nations whose national distinctiveness is more striking than our own; solemn people think of it as a consolidating civilizing, christianizing force along the barbarian marches, and, on a lower level, films about Alt Wien and Schubert and waltzing countesses and aged, grief-stricken emperors are very well received. As for royal marriages and babies, I suppose the epicentre of emotional disturbance lies somewhere between Foxrock and Greystones, but even in the remote provinces there are tremors and heartbeats to be registered.

The English have interpreted this susceptibility of ours in different ways. Thackeray, who was a complicated sort of snob, had a talent for dissecting simpler varieties of snobbery. In Ireland he hunted them from the Castle, 'the pink and pride of snobbishness with its sham king and sham loyalty', down to Mrs Mulholligan, the grocer's lady whose Kingstown villa was called Mulholliganville, or Dan O'Connell, who as Lord Mayor was 'as pleased with his red gown and cocked hat as Queen Quasheeneaboo with a new curtain ring in her nose'. 'They are on their knees still', he said, 'before English fashion, these simple wild people, and indeed it is hard not to grin at some of their naive exhibitions.'

Dan O'Connell was, of course, a monarchist. The kneeling

posture seemed to Thackeray so congenitally characteristic of the Irish that it was safe to smile at it. There has been a revolution since then and intelligent English people often look back regretfully on the old days and see a seemly reverence where Thackeray saw vulgar obsequiousness. I think that Thackeray if he lived today might even argue like Christopher Hollis and Evelyn Waugh that Ireland is naturally royalist, and therefore imperialist.

'Had Ireland remained in the United Kingdom,' writes Mr Waugh, 'Dublin would today be one of the great religious capitals of the world to which Catholics from all over the British Empire resorted for education and leadership. . . The language of the Church is largely that of the court, her liturgy abounds in phrases which sound strange on republican and democratic lips,' and he quotes Bossuet, 'The King, Jesus Christ and the Church, God in three names.'

Mr Hollis, on the same tack, refers to Ireland as a 'profoundly inegalitarian country' and reminds us that Maynooth was formed as a royal college to train Catholic priests to support Church and state, and that 'there is no Catholic tradition in favour of a Republic' and that 'the Orange Lodges were against the Union, while the Catholic bishops were for it', and so on.

What are we to make of all these paradoxes? Is it really true, as Thackeray, sneering, and Waugh and Hollis, applauding, would maintain, that the language of courts or sham courts comes easily to us or that, as Hollis argues, Irish republicanism is in origin Protestant and Anglo-Irish.

I think they are all three very superior people despising us for our frailties till they see the way to manipulate them. Now that we are a republic it is surely no heresy to admire the republican virtues. They are neither predominantly Catholic nor Protestant, and there is nothing specially Christian about monarchy.

Must a republic be egalitarian? I don't know what egalitarianism means. It is so often being denounced that it is strange I have never met anyone who professed it. Even in Russia egalitarianism has been condemned for fifteen years as 'petit bourgeois'. To say that all men are equal seems meaningless. If anyone believes in these *a priori* human equations it is the champions of class distinction, of top drawers and bottom drawers and rows of intermediate ones, in fact the disciples of

Waugh and Hollis. Reflect on the word 'peer'! They put Lord X, who is wise and benevolent, in the same drawer as Lord Y, who is stupid and malicious, and there more or less till they die they stay in sour unprofitable propinquity. Very likely Y is so malicious because he never sank to the friendly level for which his inferior faculties marked him out. Ninety per cent of us stay more or less in the social drawers in which nature put us, even after revolution and exile. The nimble 10 per cent who climb from drawer to drawer delude themselves that their agility is normal, but it isn't. Far away, as in a prison cell, the Xs and Ys hear the lonely tappings of their spiritual peers muffled by the intervening drawers. Can one not say that in republican theory, authority, or its shadow, prestige, which should belong to the wise, ought not to pass from father to son, like stocks and shares or family portraits, and that every philosophy which supports hereditary transference ought to be suspect? This would rule out royalism.

That, of course, is not the English way of looking at things. Arthur Bryant interprets their standpoint better than anyone I know. He mixes sentimentality and smugness and common sense in a frothy drink that is nourishing enough and only healthily intoxicating. If we could choke it down without retching it would do us no harm, but can we? Of Princess Elizabeth's visit to Canada and USA he writes that 'the Princess has hit the bullseye in millions of living human hearts. . . through her ceaseless and tremendous journeyings through the heart of two great nations', with the result that she has made men 'a little more ready to work together for a high and common purpose than they were before'. 'They [the royal pair] have helped to awaken the mysterious sense of social brotherhood and communion which is the cement of political communities. . . It is doubtful', he says, 'whether any statesman or administrator has done more to effect this in the past decade. Monarchy', he goes on, 'speaks like the tower of a mediaeval cathedral to the heart of those who it sought in the interests of humanity to bind together.' (Don't criticize this sentence! It's natural for a tower to speak as if it were hurling a block of masonry at you.) Then he explains that appeals to the heart as well as to the head are necessary for political union.

You see there is great emphasis on the heart. But in fact how deeply are our hearts really touched by these demonstrations?

That is a question we must each answer for ourselves. Analyzing my own emotions (and I can well remember being a royalist), I am sure that my romantic thoughts about splendid, decorative, powerful people had nothing to do with my affections and that they were very average. Let me think back though. I can't honestly say that I remember Edward VII's first visit to Kilkenny, but it made a deep impression on me because I said something which made the monarch laugh. The only king I had ever heard of was Herod, so I was alarmed but then reassured, and said to my father, 'It's all right. I am over two and in trousers!' He told this to the Bishop, Dr Crozier, who passed it on to King Edward, who 'laughed heartily'. But I only got moderate gratification from this triumph, for by the time I was old enough not to be embarrassed by the story I was disillusioned by kings. This happened after King Edward and Queen Alexandra's second visit.

We were ready to be thrilled. Large pictures of them covered with medals and jewels were pasted up on the nursery walls and we were to watch the procession to the Castle from the bow window which Mr Carew, the dentist in High Street, put at the disposal of his patients. There were Venetian masts on John's bridge and a huge banner across from Duggan's Monster House to the Tholsel inscribed 'God Bless Our Sporting Monarch!' There was much loyal cheering and everything was magnificent except the monarch and his wife, who bowled past in dreary black outdoor clothes bearing no resemblance to the glorious figures in the nursery. They had totally missed the bullseye in my living human heart, nor did I wish to work together for a high and common purpose with anyone. They weren't grand enough. After that I took my pleasure listening to the mishaps rather than the triumphs of the royal visit; how a peeress had dropped her emeralds down the WC and the feudal plumbing of the Castle had to be half dismantled before they could be recovered, how Sir Hercules Langrishe had stuck out his stomach and strutted down the picture gallery bowing right and left, pretending he was the king, just before the doors opened to admit the royal pair, who found everybody red in the face and smothering giggles. There were many stories like that to delight us. And even then we were aware that some people were jealous because the wrong people had been invited; pompous people had been made more pompous and sentimental people more sentimental, and there was a patriotic grievance that all the decorations had been hired from Leeds and a yet more patriotic grievance that there were any decorations at all.

Later on it was possible to rationalize my disillusionment. One learnt that there is a machinery for organizing enthusiasm. When Oliver Cromwell died, for example, his son Richard was proclaimed in Kilkenny 'amid greater jubilation', writes the chronicler, 'than was witnessed at the proclamation of any former ruler'. And he adds significantly that abundance of beer was provided for the common people at Croker's Cross. Well, if a Cromwell got all those cheers then, applause is fairly cheap. We believe we have outgrown this old-fashioned association of loyalty and liquor, but of course there is a much more elaborate machinery nowadays for arousing and guiding our emotions. And when it breaks down the crash is proportionately greater. It is hard to feel properly sorry for that fairly benevolent royal couple who went to Sarajevo in 1914 with the sole object of hitting bullseyes in human hearts, and who met a more realistic marksman there. Europe is still quivering from that disastrous attempt to coax into being a sentiment which did not exist.

Yet of course there is a strong argument for kings. There are social emotions which crave a focus, and where there are no kings there are dictators and film stars. I believe myself that fifty candles are gayer than a fifty-candle-power headlight, and the multitude of dowdy little German courts which still flickered faintly under Kaiser William may, like the light left on in back rooms, have dimmed very slightly the blaze of glory switched on in the sanctuary for the Führer. But to skip such an argument implies that we are scared of the currents of loyalty and devotion which humans generate among themselves in community and that our only safety is to canalize them so that they do as little harm as possible. In a republic, surely, devotion and loyalty should be used to warm and illuminate the small communities in which they are produced. There is no need for this complicated process of concentration and diffusion on which a constitutional monarchy depends.

Dublin booksellers have reported that *A King's Story: The Memoir of H.R.H. The Duke of Windsor* is one of their best-sellers, but reviewers have approached it with some embarrassment. Many royalists regard it as 'in bad taste' since it robs monarchy of some of its magic and its mystery; austere republicans also deplore it since it invests an unimportant love affair with a spurious glamour. But the Duke is anything but an exhibitionist; in his preface he acknowledges the assistance of some twenty-five fellow scribes, and plainly a great many beaters were needed to round up a shy and fugitive talent. The face that now looks at us through the bars of discretion and propriety and synthetic secretarial prose is a sad and hunted one and by no means complacent. If posterity continues to be interested in kings I think that Edward VIII will appear as one of the most attractive and honourable of them. He had from the start a low opinion of his capacities, his brain was no more than average (or, in the courtly pre-abdication parlance of *The Times*, 'men, not books, were his library') but he had what is rarer than brains, a dislike of humbug, of pretension and emotional falsity, and a determination to give expression as best he could to this antipathy. But he had neither guile nor common sense. Was it monarchy in general or just himself he distrusted? I think he scarcely asked himself this difficult question. He was humiliated by having to associate as a superior with men who were abler than he was, and knew it, but made a pretence of deferring to him. Their insistence that in virtue of his kingship he was a link, an emblem and all the rest, was a painful reminder that in virtue of himself he was very little indeed. The Archbishop of Canterbury had declared in the House of Lords that future historians would look to the King's speeches to learn the best that can be said about the industrial, social and commercial life of his generation, but he looked bored and displeased when the Head of the Church talked about the clergy. Mr Baldwin too paid him public compliments about the universal good-will that he had caused by his travels, but when the King decided to visit the distressed areas and when he was reported as saying 'Something must be done', the Prime Minister warned him against giving the oppostion a cue for suggesting that the government was not doing all that was possible.

In fact in a modern state there is less and less room for the privileged individual who says in a warm-hearted way what ought to be done but has no power to do it. It is easy to silence him by saying that everything is now so complex that he cannot possibly grasp all the facts, that he will only be misquoted and exploited. A king's duty is to show himself and to be shown things. This King's clergy and his ministers shooed him off their preserves by telling him he was a superb salesman. But his salesmen did not want him to encroach on their craft either. They too just wanted to be boosted. The King tried to 'throw the prestige of the Crown's solicitude round the workaday matters of commerce' (surely all the twenty-five scribes were at his elbow when he wrote that), but with the zeal of an amateur he bought up in South America a bag full of the trumpery jewels with which the Czechs were coaxing the dollars from the Argentine ladies. He showed them as an incentive to competition to some Birmingham jewellers and was severely snubbed. In their sphere, they were better aristocrats than he was.

If he could have been complacent he would have been happy. It is not true to say that it is no fun to be a king. George V collecting stamps and shooting pheasants better than anyone else, debating whether the clergy should be allowed moustaches, grieving that the American ambassador should insist on wearing trousers instead of knee breeches at the Queen's reception, was a contented as well as an honoured figure. So too was Uncle Arthur the Duke of Connaught, who knew all about badges and buttons and was merciless on those who wore sword slings of white leather when the occasion demanded gold lace. In fact rows of happy monarchs survived till 1918, splendidly upholstered dynastic figures bowing gracefully from spring seats to the cheering crowds that lined the carriage route. They did what their ancestors had done before them, but used prestige instead of battle-axes, popularizing new field sports and pullovers when they were well, new operations and health resorts when they were ill, thawing the sharp edges of innovation with the warm glow of tradition. But after 1918 the real changes began. The Western peoples forgot that monarchy could ever be an agency of oppression or beneficence, it had become a machine for public entertainment which they themselves could manipulate. They required to know about them as they knew about film stars and tennis champions, and they wanted both spontaneity and state. Royalty was expected to be intriguingly differentfromeveryoneelse and yet reassuringly the same.

A great change in tempo occurred when the horse, that slow dignified servant of state, capitulated before the new mass enthusiasms. In France George V's mount had shied at all the cheering and the King had broken his pelvis. In Canada his son had been dragged from his horse and passed from hand to hand.

These spontaneous welcomes proved in the end to be as monotonous as the old artificial ceremonies, and no more exciting. In Australia the King's hand was pressed till it was black and blue and every night his equerries had to bathe their trodden toes in mustard baths. There was no rest for the wearied brain, the dragging feet. He felt, he said, like an imperial souvenir, a lucky talisman, so irrepressible was the desire to prod and touch. In Western Australia an astute politician who wished to please his constituents made the royal train stop at every station night and day and roused the King from his bed to greet the crowds on the platform. The royal party could not conceal their satisfaction when the train slipped off its rails and their tormentor was pinned upside down lamenting in the lavatory.

But the kings and their peoples were equally responsible for this turbulent new relationship. The more self-critical princes were sickened with the smell of ermine and moth-balls, with formality and pomp. The King wanted, like a Caliph in the Arabian Nights, to 'know his people'. Instead he met convoys of doves with their wing-tips coloured red white and blue. In India he complained that his only contact with the people was by means of 'distant waves of the hand to murmurous crowds', and in Australia that he never got to know any place really well, so closely were his movements organized. In Nepal it gave him little satisfaction to know that 10,000 labourers had been working for six weeks to prepare roads and camps for his shooting expedition. Once in a Yorkshire coal-mining village the King was received with a sullen silence instead of the cheers to which he was accustomed. He records this objectively as an interesting, almost a welcome phenomenon, as if for once he was walking backstage of his own drama.

The most interesting pages in the book deal with Mr Baldwin's attempt to save the monarchy from the King's destructive logic. Probably the twenty-five scribes have pared away some of the asperity of the King's argument and we shall never know quite how bluntly he charged Premier and Primate with hypocrisy for punishing him for the intention of honourable marriage. Would they, more than their predecessors, have taken his throne away had he simply made her his mistress?

The Premier asked himself down to the Fort for an interview. He left his suitcase in the hall and the suitcase with its confident

implications roused a gust of royal anger. If kings are now symbols only, at least he could make a symbolic gesture, the ghost
of a once formidable displeasure. If he could not send Baldwin
to the Tower at least he could send his suitcase back to his car.
And the suitcase became the symbol of an unpardonable
encroachment, for Mr Baldwin thought the King was intending
'to store up homely touches' for his speech about the abdication.
The King was to be pushed with fatherly pats down an easy
slope to exile. Baldwin, in a cloud of tobacco smoke and
measured bonhomie, so ready to be understanding and to waive
ceremony before he was asked, so determined to have his own
way, was invincible. The King hadn't a chance.

It was a personal but not a national tragedy. There is little
evidence that as a king he would have been sagacious or even
sensible. It was as though he used all his energy and independence of judgment in the sphere of his emotions. In politics his
views were often commonplace or impulsive and were usually
wisely overruled. For example he had the idea in 1935 that a
group from the British Legion should go to Germany to shake
hands with their former adversaries, but obviously these semi-
official hand-shaking expeditions were an insult to the victims
of German militarism and only strengthened the Nazi belief that
the British would allow Germany a free hand in the east. He
shared also the official Anglo-Indian view that Gandhi was a
'ludicrous', although sinister, figure. Like Baldwin he cold-
shouldered the Emperor of Abyssinia so as to avoid 'throwing
Mussolini into the arms of Hitler'. He deplored the Coronation
oath which was the justification of his dynasty before history.
He repeated hackneyed sneers about the League of Nations and
the Treaty of Versailles.

What could he do on his own that wasn't harmful? He excused
the Beefeaters from wearing beards; defying tradition he syn-
chronized the Sandringham clocks with Greenwich; he decreed
that on his coins his left-hand profile, the comely one, not the
right, as custom dictated, should be stamped. He chose his
amusements and his clothes with care, noting, for instance, that
polo and top hats had become symbols of predatory capitalism,
but he was always a person never a puppet, though he found
plenty of puppets in high places. When he drove with the Premier of Australia they had a hat-box with them. It held a battered
democratic Homburg which the Premier exchanged for his top-

hat when they passed through his constituency. The King himself was more often reproached for being too relaxed than for being too grand. He was reprimanded once by a high civil servant for walking to the Palace with an umbrella. It was so difficult to be aloof and mysterious and at the same time a jolly good fellow that in the end the King decided just to be himself. Perhaps his most kingly achievement was that he made it plain that the survival of monarchy is only of secondary importance; more vital is the sanctity of personal relations with which no politician has the right to tamper. This aristocratic assertion cost him his throne.

After reading Thackeray and Hollis and Waugh, it is strange to turn to Wolfe Tone, who is surely the first founder of the Irish Republic. He said that royalty and aristocracy were odious to the Irish people. He was over-simplifying, of course. Powerful people, whether their power is based on hereditary privilege or private wealth or political authority, enjoy an equal admiration everywhere. The magnetism of merit is relatively weak. It does not appear to be strengthened by revolution. Probably candour, the candour of the small child who gave an accurate account of the emperor's new clothes, is a better guarantee of democracy than dynamite. It was the personal tragedy of the last Emperor of India but one that he himself had something of that childlike candour.

[1952]

12

NURSERIES OF WRITING

A journal such as *The Bell* can spare only a proportion of its pages for exclusively literary contributions, and these pages must serve two diametrically opposite ends. Literature is a source of entertainment and inspiration, but it is also a means of self-expression, self-criticism, self-adjustment. In Ireland it is this second function which tends to get ignored.

We have plenty of libraries and periodicals, native and foreign, we have the wireless and the cinema. An Aran islander can, by turning a knob, have the illusion that Mr V. S. Pritchett is standing by his turf fire talking about D. H. Lawrence. In fact there is a surfeit of creative and critical activity of all kinds ready to buzz in our ears or flicker before our eyes and much of it is so competent that the day is approaching when only the very innocent or the very thick-skinned or those with an indomitable urge to be writers will feel justified in exposing their thoughts and feelings in print.

There are two or three admirable journals in Ireland whose aim is to give to their readers a sifting of the best that is produced at home or abroad. But in letters, as in agriculture, we are more significant as producers than as consumers. We don't really know how to cook cabbage but we can grow it to perfection. We are very unsophisticated readers but we have produced with no visible effort two or three of the great literary geniuses of modern Europe. That is to say, our minds are adapted to literary creation just as our soil is to the fruits of the earth, but in neither case is the trade balance always in our favour. Two years ago our shops were filled with Dutch and Italian fruit, while our own rotted in the orchards because we did not know how to pack it and market it. I suspect that there is literary talent rotting unharvested in just the same way all over Ireland, and a journal like *The Bell* ought to do something about it. Who else will?

What can be done? The usual remedies proposed are negative. 'Ban something!' 'Tax something!' We think of these cargoes of Sunday papers; but to me these are the symptoms of our disease, not its cause. We use this imported literature as a drug, when its real value is as a stimulant. And don't let us think only about the nonsense that is imported! You can incapacitate yourself with champagne as surely as with porter. Much of the literature that is imported from abroad is immeasurably more subtle and polished than our own because it is the interpretation of a society, or section of society, more cultivated, more skilled in self-analysis than ours. We shall learn much as connoisseurs of this literature but, as addicts, we shall forfeit all that we have learnt. And we shall, in addition, play into the hands of the book-banners and book-burners, who, in their hatred of origin-ality, are always ready to call up vulgar prejudices and xenophobia against the creative arts.

Take one or two of the great writers, Stendhal or Proust, for example. A pineapple is more exquisite than a plum, and Stend-hal and Proust are far greater than any living Irish writer. But a tinned pineapple is not better than a small sweet greengage from our own garden wall. Of course there is a small and sophis-ticated Proustean enclave here as in every nation, but to most of us the Proustean world is immensely alien. We can only take our Proust tinned. I am thinking least of all of translation difficul-ties, far more of the utterly different social and intellectual climate in which the immortal *A la Recherche du Temps Perdu* matured. So I believe that an Irish journal should, without a shadow of disrespect to the tinned food, give its first attention to the simpler fare we produce at home.

Concentrating on home produce, we ought to consider how it can be increased, improved, handled, distributed. And when we look at foreign countries, it might often be with a rather pre-datory gaze. What is worth taking home to adapt or imitate?

Self-expression is a matter of hygiene as well as of artistic creation. All over Ireland there are people who want for a moment to stand outside their small but complex world and examine it critically or appreciatively. And there is little relief in talk with other inhibited people in the same small world. The conversations and polemics of a small town fall to the ground like the seeds of a plant on a windless day. If they germinate, they are overshadowed by the parent stock or jostled into sterility by the other seedlings. They need a small puff of wind to disperse them; that is to say some print (but not too much print at first) is necessary for their dissemination. And there is no print to spare for this essential work of self-expression.

Let us accept then that writing is a necessary function, not a divine and uncertain gift from the gods. Every small community breeds its own critics, panegyrists, analysts, poets, just as it breeds its own postmen and carpenters and grows its own apples. And something is wrong with society when the apples rot under the trees, and barbarism raises its head uncriticized in our towns because the able pens that might assail it are unused or diverted to some trivial or secondary work elsewhere.

Every day a tide of articles and poems comes in from the country, congests the desks of city editors for a week, and then goes back home again, often unread. There is something tragic about this ebb and flow. It is horrible to have an article returned; it should be horrible to return it. In our repressed and inarticulate land every mouse of talent should have its crumb of wood pulp. It is not as if there was any shortage of pulp. Every year whole forests from Canada and Scandinavia pass through our provincial printing presses. But none of it is any use to the man who has some personal comment to make on the lunatic world in which we live. We are told that the climate is changing through deforestation simply that some tired hacks should write about Patent Pills or Shocking Tragedies or Disgraceful Scenes at Corporation Meetings. But suppose for a moment that some reflective citizen wanted to analyze the Disgraceful Scene or some honourable local chemist chose to send a chemical report on the pills or some man of feeling wanted to touch our hearts instead of just to titivate us agreeably with details of the Shocking Tragedy, would there be even half a paragraph at his disposal? I was going to answer this question rhetorically, 'No, not one!' but it would be more truthful to say, 'I don't know'. You see the provincial press has lost all its reputation as a vehicle for serious thought and if the paragraph was offered, it would usually be refused. I was once sent some poems to criticize by a poetess in the Midlands. They were of average merit, and I said, 'Don't abandon them! Send them to the ——— Herald (the local paper), you'll be doing something to raise the standard there anyway.' The lady was bitterly offended. It seemed to her

the ultimate desecration for her poor poems to be printed locally.
She said she'd sooner burn them, and perhaps she did.

Where and who are the potential writers? To some people
writing is as necessary as breathing, to others it is a rare but
irrepressible act like a sneeze. These two classes usually force
themselves into print. But the defaulters almost all belong to the
third class, a very large one. They are the 'educated' people
whose critical sense runs counter to their creative flow, and they
are the bane and tragedy of Irish life. You can call them the
'Might-have-beens' or else the 'Damned-if-I'll-let-others-be-if-
I'm-not.' They are a scornful, shoulder-shrugging tribe, as stern
with others as they are with themselves. They won't just sit comfortably in the manger themselves, they are on their feet the
whole time snapping at the skinny nags who venture to
approach the hay.

Now these people ought to be writing. I would go so far as
to say that even if they wrote badly, they still ought to be
printed. They would learn then to be kindlier, more constructive
critics of others. They might come to see that writing *is* a form
of self-expression, not of self-exhibition. Great writing is not the
antithesis of inferior writing, it is its climax, the peak of the
pyramid. I have never heard of a genius trumpeting in vacuo.
Always around him, protecting him and giving him confidence,
there is a multitude of articulate ordinary people expressing their
thoughts according to their limitations.

Then of course there are the mute, inglorious Miltons, stifled
by economic oppression, but I doubt if they are as numerous as
in the days of Gray's 'Elegy'. I suspect that many of these inglorious Miltons are no longer mute. The social pressure probably
catches them at a different angle. Maybe they are writing quite
remuneratively about those Pills and Scenes and Tragedies. A
psychological not an economic revolution is required to rescue
them from under this mountain of nonsense.

All this is very well known and universally admitted. There
is no need to elaborate. The question is: 'What is to be done?'
Very little directly. But can we urge that the burden of responsibility to the Irish writer be shared as widely as possible?
Couldn't we start a search for other airholes through which our
suffocating Irish talents could come up to breathe?

Firstly, we could keep track of articles, poems, stories of merit
or promise which we could not print, and grouping them region-

ally we might issue from time to time an album or anthology for each county. Perhaps *The Bell* could ask some skilled writer from that county, resident or émigré, to edit it. Almost every Irish county has witnessed the rise and fall of these seasonal collections. They have always been worth the effort, and if they had the backing of a Dublin journal they might prove more enduring.

But there is another way. Dublin monthlies have a high mortality rate (even *The Bell* went into retirement for a couple of years), but provincial papers – and there must be some fifty of them all over Ireland – continue for generations.* They can't die because though we can do without masterpieces in verse or prose, we must have somewhere to advertise Rhode Island Reds and Hair-Perms and Upland Hay, Blue Bangor Slates and Cook Generals. We must know about the hurley match and the pig market and Miss Morrissey's wedding. These country papers have strong and spreading roots. They are ideal stocks on which to graft a twig or two from a less hardy but equally valuable tree. And country editors are often men of vision who would gladly co-operate. Standish O'Grady of *The Kilkenny Moderator* was neither the first nor the last to make the experiment.

In a word, *The Bell* might come to some arrangement with a county paper, offering now and again to fill a page with edited local material. It might offer to organize a review column using as far as possible local critics. No publisher will bother to send books for review to a single obscure provincial paper, but if four or five were grouped together and the reviewing was carefully organized, the books and the critics might be forthcoming.

Does this sound a patronizing policy. . . a Dublin magazine attempting to interfere in the concerns of the provinces? The intention is just the reverse. How much provincial talent has Dublin swallowed up without a thank-you or passed on to London or New York? Now the time has surely come for Dublin to disgorge a little so that the provinces can receive back something of what they once gave. Can *The Bell* help in this task and could there be a finer one?

[1951]

---

* *The Bell*, of which Hubert Butler was Books Editor under Peadar O'Donnell, ceased publication in December 1954. See the author's essay '*The Bell*: An Anglo-Irish View' in *Escape from the Anthill* (1986).

13

SAINTS, SCHOLARS AND CIVIL SERVANTS

Every now and then small books on local antiquities are published in the provinces, reviewed enthusiastically in the local press, and bought conscientiously by the local clergy and intelligentsia. They make no impact on Dublin scholarship, no one reads them there or pays them the more valuable tribute of seriously criticizing them. They are not usually very good and yet they have a charm and an authenticity that is their own. The writers have visited what they describe again and again, they have scrubbed old tomb slabs with bunches of wild carrot, barked their shins climbing locked gates and waited patiently while the village antiquary fetches some treasure for their inspection and pricing. It is perhaps a Chinese calendar found by his brother after the earthquake of San Francisco. However austere the writer's intentions, he seldom manages altogether to exclude the traces of the sunlight and the fields and long desultory conversations in farmyards. Here he is vague and skimpy because it began to rain, here there is excess of detail because he wanted to stretch to its uttermost some hawthorn-scented evening.

These books were once lush and gossiping. Now they are rather prim and scared, as though some official of the Board of Works was watching with ironic smile. They do not digress very much now and that is a pity because it is in digressions that we provincials have the advantage. A Dublin guess as to who built the Giant's Grave is as good as ours, but only we know who stole the Corporation mace. In one respect the books have not changed at all: there are plenty of misprints. Mr O'Kelly's book* on the place-names of Co. Kilkenny belongs to the new 'austere'

* Eoghan Ó Ceallaigh, *Place-names of Co. Kilkenny* (Kilkenny People 1954).

school of country lore. Mr Brandon's* is at a slight tangent to it, but they both illustrate so well the obstacles in the path of those who study the Irish past that they can be considered together.

Mr O'Kelly is an accomplished Irish scholar and, in a small way, he has done for Kilkenny what Canon Power did for Waterford. Expanded and improved, this book might rival Power's in importance. But first of all every Kilkenny person should buy it, read it and, most urgent of all, criticize it and send their criticisms to Mr O'Kelly. Even those who are not Irish scholars are entitled to comment, for Mr O'Kelly, like many other topographers, has had to wrestle with that demon of unreality which the Gaelic League begat upon the Post Office. I wish, for instance, he could have liberated the citizens of Bennettsbridge from that Civil Service conceit, Baile Ui Cheochain, by which their village has been rechristened, for it has been known as Bennettsbridge or Pons Sancti Benedicti since the fourteenth century. Though the new address may recall a forgotten townland, no local person has ever used it or even heard of it. Even the Ormonde Deeds do not record it. How did we come by it? Often I've wondered whether it has not some origin like the Slovene mountain which is mapped 'No-thank-you-I-don't-smoke'. The Italian cartographer from Milan was in a hurry. He had waved his cigarette case enquiringly at the mountain and had been misunderstood by the natives.

Local history is bedevilled by these metropolitan intrusions. Irish place-names are a slow indigenous growth. Many of them come and go with the tribes and families that cultivated the fields. As they fade they carry a little history away from everyday speech, but a sediment remains in the printed record. What can be stupider than to falsify this record?

For example, did the lips of man ever utter Mr O'Kelly's phrase 'Garran an Chraimirigh'? Did they not always say 'Cramersgrove'? Or just 'Cramers' or 'the Grove'? Two generations ago the Miss Cramer-Roberts were known to many. I have photographs of them. Their tennis-racquets had very long handles and there were buttons all down the front of their black bodices. They would have looked at you in blank amazement if

---

* Rev. E. A. Brandon, M.A., *To Whom We Dedicated* (Dundalgan Press, W. Tempest Ltd 1954).

you had talked to them about Garran an Chraimirigh. They were harmless people: they ought to be allowed the luxury of knowing best about their own name. For a similar reason Wallslough should not be called Loch an Fhaltaigh. It derives from the Norman family of De Valle. They may have been aliens but they came to Ireland before the potato. Ought not the same courtesy to be extended to them as is shown to 'Kerr's Pink' and even 'British Queen'? A generation ago local Irish scholars such as Canon Carrigan, the historian of Ossory, would never have made these mistakes.

As one explores more ancient names the need for unprejudiced commonsense becomes more and more apparent. Mr O'Kelly's pages, like those of every similar book in Ireland, are peppered with the names of saints whose hallowed, featureless figures are used to stop the gaps in our knowledge of the past, gaps through which the salubrious breeze of free inquiry might otherwise be blowing. On page 54 three of these saints, of whom history has no record, follow one after the other: St Lamraighe of Killamery, St Sheallacham of Kiltallaghan, St Teresa of Kiltrassy. Now the first two of these saints Mr O'Kelly has invented and the third he has imported from Spain. Canon Carrigan gives no authority for any of them. Killamery derives from the Lamraighe tribe, which is also to be traced in Munster and in Monaghan.

Mr Brandon's little book concerns the saints, principally Irish, to whom the Irish Protestant churches are dedicated. It appeared first in instalments in the *Church of Ireland Gazette*. It was an excellent idea but badly executed. Such a book cannot easily be written if one has not caught some infection from Dr Plummer's scholarship, Father Shearman's enthusiasm or Canon O'Hanlon's gigantic industry. It is true that Plummir (*sic*) is listed tersely just after F. (*sic*) Gibbon's *Decline and Fall* (two [*sic*] volumes), but one looks as vainly for the learned credulity of Plummer as for the learned scepticism of Gibbon. This is very depressing because the book makes its appearance with some pomp, a foreword by a bishop and another by a lord, and acknowledgments to a dozen Church dignitaries.

The decline in Irish book-production is so acute that now, as with an infants' class, the critic has first of all to give marks for tidiness before approaching the question of knowledge. Mr Brandon and his printers start at the very bottom of the class.

From the National Muesum (*sic*) on the first page to Wedon, alias Weedon, Northamptonshire, and St Ethelbreada, alias St Etheldreda of Ely on the last, the printers have added on every page a philological puzzle of their own to all those that the student of hagiography must encounter. The *Gazette* is an admirable paper, but those who know it will conjecture sadly that this tornado of misprints originated in Middle Abbey Street rather than in Dundalk. For did not the *Gazette* recently publish an excellent article in which simultaneous homage was paid to W. B. Yeates, the poet, and J. B. Yates, the painter?

I have calculated that between them and their printers, Mr O'Kelly and Mr Brandon have in a single year added seven or eight new saints to the calendar. Does not this floodlight one of the methods by which in even less literate centuries the hosts of Heaven were recruited? The Irish saints, over six thousand of them, live in a seldom-traversed reserve into which, for some generations now, no unsurpliced scholar had ventured very far. One hundred and fifty years ago the clergy themselves were more enterprising. Ledwich, a canon of St Canice's, Kilkenny, dared to say that the Irish saints mostly never existed. He said that St Coemgen was a mountain, St Senan a river, and St Domangart was just Co. Down. 'Let the impious and foolish tales of ignorant and superstitious ecclesiastics warn us of that miserable degradation of the human mind, which alone could give them currency and credit.' And, 'to believe that a barbarous people, naked and ignorant as American Indians, should have preserved the pedigree of St Kevin is too much for the most stupid credulity.' This is very rude as well as unjust and Ledwich made it worse by exhorting the 'Hibernians' that their hearts 'must overflow with gratitude to the Author of all Blessings' because of the 'fostering care of Britain,' which had led them to polite manners. It is refreshing, none the less, to hear a scholar say just what he thinks, even when candour is easy, as it was for Ledwich in 1804. National consciousness cannot have been as sensitive then as it later became, for John, Earl of Upper Ossory, of the royal line of Ossory kings, accepted the dedication of Ledwich's book. Nor did any rumour of Tithe wars or Disestablishment disturb the peace of Aghaboe Rectory in those pre-Victorian days.

I do not think that his outburst did any harm. It provoked a long and lively discussion and out of the commotion several of the great figures of Victorian scholarship emerged, Petrie, O'Donovan, O'Curry, Graves, some of them 'Ascendancy Irish,' some native. The new archaeology was more neighbourly as well as more cautious than the old.

Though Ledwich's valuable essay on the history of Kilkenny had certainly paved the way for the Kilkenny Archaeological Society, that Society, which for nearly a hundred years exercised a great influence on the study of the Irish past, was swayed much more by Petrie, a Protestant champion of the Irish saints, than by Ledwich; as the century went on, less and less was said against St Kevin and his fellows and, as the Anglo-Irish and their Church began to feel the draught of doom, a reticence which had originated in courtesy continued in discretion.

For the middle years of the *Journal of the Royal Society of Antiquaries of Ireland*, as this Kilkenny organ was later to call itself, the Irish saints became the unchallenged property of Father Shearman, a delightful writer to whom the saints and their complicated family ramifications were as real as his own parishioners. His work is of lasting value, for, even if the people, places and events, which he co-ordinates so ingeniously, belong not to this world but to fairyland, the texture of his argument is sound, his learning and industry beyond praise.

The Prince Consort was invited to be Patron of the Society and he sent £25. By many delicate adjustments the harmony of the Society was maintained. I am sure that no one was so crude as to say, 'You be nice about our Royal Family and we'll be nice about your Saints,' but the scandal of Ledwich was never repeated and in one of Father Shearman's genealogical trees it can be seen that both St Mochop of Kilchop and St Aedhan the Leper were distant cousins of Queen Victoria.

All that is long ago. Reading Mr Brandon's book I felt convinced that the reaction against Ledwich had now gone far enough and that the movement for the rehabilitation of the Celtic saints, which had begun in chivalry, had ended in sterility. It is not only that Ledwich wrote much better than his more orthodox successors, but his ideas acted like leaven even on those who disagreed with him, while Mr Brandon's little book could only have been published in a society in which the last bubble of intellectual ferment had long ago died down.

One would not wish a return to the rolling periods of Ledwich, but Mr Brandon's periods wobble so at the joints that it is often a miracle that they reach the end of a paragraph without a collapse: 'It is to be regretted that the church has not used the name of this saint more widespread,' or 'His chief claim to fame is due to the mentioning of him by St Augustine.'

Sometimes he risks a conjecture of his own. 'He (St Fethlimidh) was known as 'the Small,' which seems to imply that he was a person of diminutive proportions,' but he is not often so daring. His only aim seems to be to prove that we are no upstart garrison Church, or, as he puts it, that 'the historicity of our church is constantly emphasized by our dedications.' At no point does he show any of that concern, which Ledwich expressed so tactlessly, for the 'human mind' and its possible degradation by believing things that are not true, and yet if his Church and mine has claims for survival in Ireland, is not that concern for truth one of the strongest?

He is very careless, though accuracy is surely an important element of Truth, even when you give it an ecclesiastical capital. The Synod of Drumceatt, which he spells differently in different places, was not held in Co. Meath but near Limavady. No saint was ever called St Molna or St Finntian Munnu and St Laserian was not called Lamliss, though he had a cave at Lamlash on the Isle of Arran. What does Mr Brandon mean by saying that 'St Ibor, an obscure fifth-century saint, probably had Danish origins'? The Danes were not in Ireland in the fifth century. To say that St Moling was also called St Tighmulling is like saying that Mr Brandon is also called Mr Celbridge-Rectory.

But it is poor fun critizing Mr Brandon like this, for his book is far better than no book. No Irishman who is sensitive to the numinous quality of our civilization can afford to ignore the Irish saints. Mr Brandon can reflect that if he wrote a book in a more sceptical vein, he would have to meet a volley of abuse greater than Ledwich ever encountered.

But why should it be undermining to our morals or bruising to our national pride if one were to argue that the Irish saints were many of them the tribal gods of a gentle and intelligent people, whose racial origins retreat so far into history that to use national terms for them, Celt, Iberian, Gaulish, would not be easy? I was brought up in the diocese of St Canice, but the less I believed in him the more I was fascinated by him. He covered five Irish counties and as many Scottish and Welsh ones with his churches and miracles. He left his crozier in Iona, the little toe of his right foot in North Italy, and, standing on one leg, was fed by seagulls in the Gower Peninsula. He is a link between the mediaeval world and one that is immemorially old. Those who treat him as a monastic fiction are as wrong as Cardinal Moran, who saw him in his own image as a busy Irish prelate with widespread diocesan responsibilites. The Lives of the Irish saints reflect an ingenious innocence, a primaeval charity, that links them with Greek legend and the beginnings of poetry. For example, when St Ailbe, travelling in Italy, resurrected two horses and their groom who had been killed by lions, he took pity on the hungry, disappointed carnivores and arranged for a suitable meal (an 'aptum prandium') to come down from Heaven for them on a cloud.

St Coemgen was not, I am sure, as Ledwich maintained, a mountain, but St Senan has undoubtedly a very queer relationship with the Shannon, as though the same tribe had left its name with saint and river. And Coemgen's pedigree is quite as odd as Ledwich declared. He is said to have got his name because he was beautiful, 'caem.' But his father was Caemlug, his grandfather Caemfid, his mother Caemell, his brothers Caeman and Nathcaem, his sisters were similarly called and they were almost all of them saints. Though there are several lives of Coemgen we are told nothing more convincing about him than that he gathered apples off willow trees and that a bird nested in his outstretched hand. Surely his life requires a more cold-blooded Ledwichian analysis than that given him by (say) Mr Liam Price in his learned and excellent surveys of County Wicklow.

The only really repulsive saint in Mr Brandon's collection is not Irish but Norse, and has, alas, some claims to 'historicity.' St Olaf the Holy, also called St Olaf the Fat, who has a church in Waterford, is a figure from Belsen. At his orders those who rejected the Gospel had their hands or feet cut off, their eyes gouged out, were crucified or strangled. Mr Brandon is very terse about him and even the charitable Canon O'Hanlon is at loss to account for these excesses 'in so just and humane a king.' 'A zealot in his endeavours to establish Christianity,' he declares, 'Olaf seems often to have wanted prudence.' In his case it is a relief to learn that his toe-nails grew for thirty-six years after his death, that there was in Norway an annual ceremony of cutting them, and that when his unbelieving brother had him burnt alive (one may ask how did he have toe-nails if he was burnt alive), a dragon issued from his ashes and destroyed the brother. These anecdotes are reassuring because they permit us to be sceptical of what without them might be plausible. There is hope that St Olaf was quite an ordinary man like the rest of us and that his 'imprudences' as well as his virtues have been exaggerated.

Since archaeology became a state-supported profession, first audacity went and then integrity, and there is today in Ireland no room for any but the pundit and the puppet, and a curious parasitical entente has been established between them. I have heard distinguished scholars discoursing at Glendalough and Clonmacnoise, evading the central issues and revealing their real thoughts only in giggling asides. There is the same falsity in this as in the pseudo-democratic brogue which Victorian noblemen used for the gardener or the joviality of head-mistresses on Parents' Day. Only the stupid are deceived but it is to them that this homage is paid.

Professional scholars will be indulgent to Mr Brandon because he does not seriously challenge their authority, but let some Ledwich of our meagre days, shorn of his imperial arrogance, raise his head from a country rectory to write a serious but sceptical investigation of Coemgen and there would be a sally from all the fortresses of learning. What a brandishing there would be of monophthongs and cranial indices and marginal glosses! The wretched Ledwich junior would fly for his life and only the most experienced student of academic footnotes would be able to detect that the scholars in their hearts had sympathy for the heresies that had been uttered but resented that the diplomatic truce should be breached by an outsider.

If you turn to the country publications of a hundred years ago and compare them with those of today, you will be stunned by the utter decay of that lively and daring spirit of inquiry which once gave rise to the Kilkenny Archaeological Society and was nourished by it for many years. Where did it go to and what are the inhibitions that prevent its return? The first stage in their detection is to recognize that they exist. As the scholar bends over his manuscript, a shadow falls on his page, and then a second shadow and a third. Who is it that has tiptoed behind him? Is it the Minister of Finance, calculating the cost of university chairs and the grants for excavation? Is it the President of the Gaelic League or the Secretary of the Tourist Board, watching over our cultural and spiritual exports and imports? Is it St Olaf brandishing his imprudent crozier? Is it . . .?

But the shadows fall so thick and fast on my own page that I cannot see to write. I shall write no more.

[1954]

14

ZHIVAGO'S CREATOR

I

To those with some acquaintance with Russian literature, Pasternak has been a well-known name for thirty or forty years, but not till the publication of *Dr Zhivago* did his fame extend beyond a very small circle of initates. It was easy for the Russians to say that the award of the Nobel Prize was a political act and to be sceptical when it was explained that it was his entire work that was being crowned at Stockholm, and not *Dr Zhivago* alone. And in fact it may have been admiration not for his literary works but for his courage and integrity, it may have been indignation at the way he was treated, that brought him the prize. Pasternak is not a typical Nobel Prize winner. Two of these three books show him to have been far more like James Joyce, whom the adjudicators ignored, than like Pearl Buck, whom they crowned.

These works,* except for the autobiography, which is recent (1954) and rather stilted and slow, as though a grasshopper were trying to walk, are very hard to read and as much in need of glossaries and commentaries as *Finnegans Wake*. While Joyce dismembered language, Pasternak tried to dismember experience. The pattern of their work shines out (as in a kaleidoscope) from a swirl of fragments. Yet in one way they are in startling contrast. Joyce, in his early work, was a social and spiritual rebel and he wrote as lucidly as Ibsen, whom he revered. It was when he rejected the society that he satirized that he began to tunnel like a care-free beaver beneath the foundations of speech and the

---

* Boris Pasternak, *The Last Summer*, Introduction by George Reavey; *Prose and Poems of Pasternak*, Introduction by J. M. Cohen; *An Essay in Autobiography*, Introduction by Edward Crankshaw (all London 1959).

fragile conventions of human behaviour.

Pasternak followed a contrary course. It is as an elderly man that he comes out of his tunnel. He writes with indignation and faith. Forgetful of his old preoccupation with the winding ways of thought and feeling, he writes simply what he thought and felt.

In his new mood he dismisses his old one more curtly than we can: 'I would not lift a finger to rescue more than a quarter of my writings from oblivion. . . I dislike my style up to 1940. . . I dislike the disintegrating forms, the impoverished thought and the littered and uneven language of those days.' He complains that his ear had been vitiated by 'our verbal whirligigs and the twisting and chopping of all familiar things'. He and his friends 'were then so tongue-tied that we could only be original despite ourselves and make a virtue of our inarticulateness'. He condemns 'the affected manner, the besetting sin of those days', in which his early autobiography, *Safe Conduct* (here published by Benn) was written.

Pasternak was the child of Imagism and Symbolism, period names for the artist's perennial revolt against the Philistine acquiescence in commonplace values. Associating these values with the bourgeoisie, one could easily become a revolutionary and join in the Fascist or Communist assault upon the bourgeois and his cosy conventions. But this special cosiness, which the artist scorns, does not appear to be politically conditioned. It survives social revolution, and many of these literary rebels suffered a shattering disillusionment. While in America Pound found refuge in a mad-house; in Russia Mayakovsky, Yesenin, Fadayev, Tsvetayeva, all killed themselves long before Stalin's purges had begun.

Pasternak had not committed himself so deeply. He was the type of fellow-traveller whom left and right condemn as a parlour-pink, and in Russia the pinks seem to have kept their colour, their principles, their dignity, much better than the reds, the whites, the blacks, the browns. Pasternak in his disillusionment had only to throw overboard the idiom of literary rebellion. Yet that idiom was a stage in his literary development and these early books, which illustrate it, cannot be ignored as he would wish us to do.

Only a very devoted coterie could read the prose of these first two books with pleasure. Pasternak's individual vision is smothered with 'individualism,' with tropes, metaphors, conceits. Yet we often meet laboured anticipations of those graceful images, which decorate and only occasionally obstruct the narrative of *Dr Zhivago*. Did he perhaps in the end owe something to Soviet Russia, that harsh step-mother to the imaginative writer? Lucidity was perhaps born of suffering. His early prose certainly suggests that some mighty inscrutable masterpiece was on the way, had not Lenin intercepted it, some portentous Russian version of *Finnegans Wake*, which a generation of foreign translators would have prowled around despairingly.

Observe in these books his obsession with trains. A volume of verse was called *On Early Trains*, and there is hardly a story without its train. They were to culminate in that magnificent train journey in *Dr Zhivago*, unsurpassed in literature; but these early Imagist-Futurist trains were cherished for the tricks they played on vision. They moved through the world of confused senses and drowsy children. Or rather *they* did not move, the landscape did, as it does for trains at fun-fairs – but very pretentiously. Tunnels are mountains that creep over the carriages, a terminus is a reef that leaps on a train and extinguishes it. 'A little later the rushing embankment was suddenly held in check by the brakes. . . . The stations flew away to the end of the train like stone butterflies.' On a journey through the Alps the train does actually move, but very oddly: 'Overhanging jags leapt onto the train and, settling themselves on the carriage-roofs, called to each other, waving their legs, and abandoned themselves to the free ride.'

In those days he seems to have cultivated his individual vision by looking at things upside-down or back to front; if it helped him later to resist the iron conformities of the Soviets, the discipline may have been a good one.

A story called, rather oddly, 'The Childhood of Luvers,' is an epitome of all the merits and defects of the early Pasternak. Zhenia Luvers is a small girl, and for an adult to see the world through her unsophisticated, non-rational mind, many constrictions and contortions are necessary. Often he succeeds: 'One of the metal globes on the bed gleamed like a single bead. The other was extinguished because a garment had been thrown over it. Zhenia screwed up her eyes, the bead moved away from the floor and swam towards the wardrobe.'

More often, the wheels of imagery turn, the words fly off in a shower of sparks, but nothing happens. Whose fault is this – ours, Zhenia's, Pasternak's, the translator's? Here is Zhenia looking at a small back-street: 'It shone like something in a dream, brilliantly and minutely illuminated and noiseless, as though the sun, wearing glasses, was scrabbling in the chickweed.' Pasternak, as he peers sympathetically over Zhenia's shoulder, and gropes for images, has completely blotted out the little girl.

The coterie which the early Pasternak fascinated vanished without a trace; so did the bourgeoisie, which he shocked and mystified. He wrote no prose for twenty years. Then he wrote with something of the economy and lucidity of a man crying for help. The problems of speech and sensibility to which he had dedicated his youth and middle age seemed secondary. Things had happened to himself and to the craft of letters, which had to be told. It is not always easy for a complicated man to express himself with simplicity, but in *Dr Zhivago* this difficult *tour de force* was almost achieved.

II

Not long ago a successful Soviet author explained to me that the position of the unorthodox writer in Russia was not so bad as one had heard. 'You can't stop a man writing a book,' he said; 'if it can't be published now, well, he'll put it in a drawer, and, if it is good, some day it will be printed.' Headmasters, advising their pupils with literary ambitions not to 'coddle their talents' but to go into the civil service, normally argue in this way too: 'If the right stuff is in you, it will come out, however unsympathetic the environment.' In fact they visualize literary genius as an explosive natural force, which nothing can repress. Judging by *Dr Zhivago* their optimism is only half justified.* Here is a sublime masterpiece that has been kept for ten or twenty years in a drawer. It has all the marks of irrepressible genius but it also has grave blemishes, which suggest that while it is not easy to neutralize creative gifts, they can be damaged and distorted

*Boris Pasternak, *Dr Zhivago*, translated by Max Hayward and Manya Harari (London 1958).

by public indifference or hostility.

Dr Zhivago is a work of great beauty and consummate integrity but it should have been many books, not one. The thoughts and experiences of a lifetime have been crammed into an elderly man's first novel (for Boris Pasternak was born in 1890). Though in general the narrative flows freely, the track seems often to be choked with an accumulation of feelings, descriptions and observations which should have found expression decades ago. The digressions have the air of inhibited short stories and towards the end of the book new characters make brief hasty appearances like customers before closing time. Yet as a story of the Russian Revolution and its impact on a few strong personalities, it can have no equal. Yury Zhivago belonged, like most of his friends, to the prosperous intelligentsia, which sympathised with the Revolution and tried to preserve intact and untarnished through the years of disillusionment and terror that vision of equity and justice which had inspired the early revolutionaries. Some succeeded better than others, but they all betrayed their principles more easily than they betrayed their friends, and politics are seldom more than a stormy background to the drama of personal relations. The friends meet and re-meet in Moscow, on long train-journeys, in Siberian woods and villages. Some had become zealots, others vagabonds or opportunists, others were guilt-tormented slaves, idealizing their own bondage. Zhivago himself clung to his personal independence with a tenacity beyond his powers, losing his health and seeing his wits grow dull and his heart cold, but retaining his integrity.

Pasternak is, of course, primarily a poet and an overflow of poetic sensibility which should have found its proper channel seems to have flooded some pages with obscure symbolism. There are uncanny coincidences, justified forebodings and in casual episodes a hint of 'deeper significances'. For the most part the novel moves on a clear sunlit Chekhovian plane but these sudden plunges into the twilight of Dostoievsky tilt the story needlessly towards unreality.

Dr Zhivago was accepted for publication in Russia during that brief thaw which ended with the Hungarian revolt and its suppression. Its rejection was a great disaster for Russia and for the West, for its publication would have made it difficult for us to taunt the Russians with their harshness towards their internal critics. That the thaw was a very real one, many pages of this book give evidence. For Zhivago the Revolution had been 'like God come down to earth from heaven', yet a few years later, he was saying:

Those who inspired the revolution aren't at home in anything except change and turmoil. . . . For them transition periods, worlds in the making, are an end in themselves. . . . Yet Man is born to live, not to prepare for life. Life itself is such a breathtakingly serious thing! Why substitute this childish harlequinade of adolescent fantasies, these schoolboy escapades? . . . Revolutions are made by fanatical men of action with one-track minds, who are narrow-minded to the point of genius. They overturn the old order in a few hours or days and for decades thereafter, for centuries, the spirit of narrowness, which led to the upheaval, is worshipped as holy. . . . There is nothing more self-centred and further from the facts than Marxism.

Yet in his contempt for 'the slinking bourgeois breed', Zhivago was at one with the revolutionaries. It seemed to him that their boasted 'habit of independent thought' was a mere by-product of their leisure and their privileges and that, when these were lost, their moral fibre collapsed too.

If another thaw were to come and more manuscripts were to be taken from their drawers we might find that Russia in its essentials had changed very little. Though winter alters the outward face of everything, when spring returns even small and delicate things are seen to have survived. One had thought that the childlike candour and freshness of Russian literature, its spontaneity and subtlety, were gone for ever, yet here they all are again.

The translators do their work well. Pasternak uses homely images, which easily in translation sound crude or comic; yet though something is lost much of eternal Russia remains. The thick black ice is chunky like the bottoms of broken beer bottles. The starry sky throws a pale blue flicker like the flame of methylated spirit over the black earth. The aspens have the scent of fresh toilet water and pale thin hollyhocks gaze into the distance over the fences like women in their night shifts, whom the heat indoors has driven out for a breath of air.

As in the old Russia the writer still has power to undermine pomposity with humour and irony and to tame the vast distances with detailed and intimate sketches of the things nearby.

[1959]

Endnote   On 18 February 1959 Hubert Butler chaired a meeting of a literary society in University College, Dublin, when the topic for discussion was *Dr Zhivago* and the award of the Nobel Prize for Literature to Boris Pasternak. He had already reviewed the novel in *The Irish Times* (second section above) and was shortly to discuss Pasternak's earlier prose (first section).

The topic, even by the exacting standards of Ireland in the 1950s, was uncontroversial. Introducing the discussion, Butler spoke for about ten minutes and stressed Pasternak's links with the pre-revolutionary intelligentsia and his affinity to Chekhov in certain regards:

> Chekhov had to compromise with his conscience many times, but when he saw an opportunity of making an effective protest, he did so. For example, he resigned from the academy when Gorki was ejected for political reasons; and at the time of the Dreyfus case in France he quarrelled with the reactionary and anti-Semite paper which published his stories, even though this meant quarrelling with his bread and butter. . . I think that Pasternak may have acted as he did in refusing the Nobel Prize fully alive to what would follow, and in no way surprised. He seems to have Chekhov's unfrightened realism and he may be finding what has happened more entertaining than alarming. He has lived as an honoured figure behind the iron curtain for the greater part of his life. He knows all about it. Now that he has punctured quite a large hole in it, he is probably quite pleased with himself and would be puzzled by our sympathy.

This sympathy was not echoed universally. Immediately after the debate a notice appeared throughout the College above the name of the Registrar, J. J. Hogan, intimating in capital letters that 'NO PERSON NOT A MEMBER OF THE COLLEGE MAY BE INVITED TO TAKE PART IN OR BE PRESENT AT ANY MEETING OF A COLLEGE SOCIETY WITHOUT THE PERMISSION OF THE PRESIDENT'. At the time Butler felt that this retrospective rebuke had been caused not by his discussion of Pasternak – 'which was innocuous' – but by his attitude towards the Compulsory Conversion Campaign in Croatia (see 'The Sub-Prefect Should Have Held His Tongue', *Escape from the Anthill*, pp. 270 ff.). In fact, several notable figures were *personae non gratae* in UCD during these years, and the Pasternak debate was neither a major nor an isolated incident. (*Ed.*)

15

ON LOVING BULLS

Coming from Algeçiras the traveller will see on the main Casemates Gate of Gibraltar two big painted notices. Awed by all he has heard of the defences of the Rock he will presume it is some warning about Security, Passports, Prohibited Areas. But he will be wrong. One notice is in Spanish, the other in English. In both the public is notified that any case of cruelty to animals is to be reported immediately to the local secretary of the RSPCA, Mr P. H. Barnett. In fact it is a gesture of defiance at the great peninsula behind, in which for centuries millions of men and animals have jostled in affectionate but brutal intimacy of which the English disapprove. The Rock has been a pulpit as well as a fortress and the Spanish, in English eyes, are very cruel to animals. Is this true?

Gerald Brenan, in one of his books, has maintained the opposite. The Spaniards, he says, are singularly tender hearted. To put an old companion cat, dog, donkey, 'out of his pain' in the English way seems to the Spaniard sheer murder; useless or moribund animals are, therefore, abandoned or thrown over cliffs so that they may pay their debt to nature at their own time and in their own way. Certainly to judge by all the birds that twitter in cages all over Spain (I counted thirteen cages hanging in a row outside the Customs House on the Rock itself) the Spaniards are passionate birdlovers. They love eating roast partridge, yet the humblest will deny himself this pleasure in order to have two sleek partridges hanging on either side of his front door in dome-shaped cages about the size of small tea-cosies. They love their dogs and hate to be separated from them. When they take their produce to market, they will tie them by a rope to the tail-board of their cart. The patient little dog trots behind mile after mile along the macadamized road to town. Twice we saw big collies riding on the carriers of bicycles and you often see dogs slithering about on the curved tops of vans. The dogs pay a high price for this intimacy with their masters but often they will put their paws on the table-cloth and unreproved take what they fancy from their master's plate. It is a different system to ours. Perhaps in their way the Spaniards even love bulls.

For half a generation now the English have wearied of their own complex humanitarianism and are often envious of the unorganized sensibilities of less fortunate people. On the bullfight question the more sophisticated have all veered towards Hemingway and away from Mr P. H. Barnett. It would be interesting to take a vote at cocktail-time in the lounge of the Hotel Reina Christina at Algeçiras. Though you could almost read the Gibralter RSPCA notice through the telescope in the garden, I think you would find that 70 per cent of the Anglo-Saxons had been to bullfights and 75 per cent approved of them. One need not count the handful of romantics to whom every aspect of an Illfare State is glamorous and who recall that the middle-class Spanish Republic would probably have ended by suppressing the corridas. To quite normal people the bullfights are acceptable, because they are Spanish, traditional, indigenous; they demand courage and skill and grace; they help us shed our insular prejudices. There are some who say it is like the ballet. There are more pretentious ones who say that tauromachy is a revival of ritual magic and symbolizes the mystical kinship which the old Iberian hunter felt with his prey. Even Sacheverell Sitwell, who, in his sensitive book about Spain, says that he cannot 'condone' bullfighting, is fascinated by its ceremonial trappings. Naturally by the time he has done justice to the spangled suits, the plumed hats, the infinite artistry, he has condoned bullfighting twenty times over.

I think the Anglo-Saxons would all revert to their out-of-date scruples, if, instead of going to the great bullfights, they visited the small village celebrations from which the fashionable corridas developed. By chance we met one in Benecassim near Tarragona. It was St Anthony's Day, which is sacred to animals, and along the road we saw horses being dressed up for processions, dogs being blessed and many charming sights. In Benecassim a whole street was barricaded at either end by upturned carts, planks, bedsteads. It was all very gay. On the wrought-iron balconies the women and children were standing among their geranium pots. Where there were no flowers they had decorated the rails with coloured rugs and counterpanes. All the men and boys were in the street with sticks and stones. After a while a door opened at the other end of the street and a very small young bull put out his head and withdrew it again. A little later, urgently propelled from behind, he plunged into the street. He stood surprised and uncertain, looking at the crowds. Suddenly a shower of bricks and stones fell round him and he trotted back in alarm to his doorway but it was closed. Everybody was in high good humour and the more the bull charged the more they were pleased. There was a certain sportsmanship about it for no one threw stones who was not in the bull-ring, but it was not very daring to be there. For the purpose of subsequent boasting we climbed into it ourselves for a moment. It was not at all like a ballet or a mystical communion; all we saw was a number of happy animated boys and men throwing stones at a bull. We asked a motherly old lady beside us why they had a bullfight on St Anthony's Day. She replied with smiling sweetness that had it not been for St Anthony's patronage 'the little animals' would never have got to Heaven.

This was the raw material of a bullfight and the finished product, which we later saw at Malaga, was only a sophisticated urban embellishment. The spectacle in the vast crowded bull-ring was brilliant. The bull charged about with ten or twelve little flags fluttering on the banderillas that sagged from his torn neck-muscles. The matador, gorgeous in green and gold, skipped with unbelievable nimbleness and daring in front of the bull, varying his blows with caresses on the soft nose and deft little side-kicks on the jaws. Yes, perhaps it *was* like a ballet. It was as natural as a cat playing with a mouse. There was the same exquisite feline grace, superb timing, sportsmanship (the cat always allows the mouse to think it can get away) and on a deeper plane there was perhaps that mystical communion between the slayer and the slain. The art of the cat usually neutralizes our sympathy for the anguish of the mouse and I did not find it a disgusting performance. The audience was far too intent on technical excellence, on Double Veronicas in Reverse and other virtuosities, to be sadistic. 'Matelo!' 'Kill it!' they shouted, when one bull, with blood pouring from its lung, responded too half-heartedly to the matador's provocation. There was grave dignity in the climax, when the bull, like a general at last surrendering his sword, ponderously knelt down first on one knee and then on the other. Then a functionary in a matter-of-fact white coat finished him off, the horses raced in, the corpse was dragged away, the golden sand was raked till it was smooth, the president said something from his box and the matador danced round the ring waving an ear or a tail or whatever his prowess had earned.

One bull jumped the barriers and started to gore two attendants, who were led limping away. I was surprised to find myself regretting that the bull had not tossed them both into the ring with a magnificent sweep of his horns, for those who in Rome think as the Romans think, invariably think it to excess. Committed to the detached appreciation of beautiful gestures, where does one stop? I decided that for myself it would be best in future to stop at the entrance gate with Mr Barnett and the RSPCA in dowdy old-fashioned disapproval. And I regretted that the Sitwells and their kind had led the way in.

It is to be doubted whether the bullfighters really have that robust Iberian ancestry that the afficionados claim for them, though there is a fine early mosaic of men struggling with a bull at Sagonto. They belong much more to the decadence of imperial Rome. At the Roman city of Merida in Estramadura there is a huge amphitheatre in which you can still see the sluices and channels through which the water was conducted for shipwreck scenes. A favourite entertainment was to launch a toy ship on the miniature sea, man it with a crew of wild beasts and Christians and allow it to sink. The Romans were a highly developed people and in this spectacle there was much to please the eye of the artist and delight the connoisseur of technical innovations. There was sportsmanship in it too. The Christians were given swords and those who pleased the audience by their resistance would, of course, be fished out of the water and allowed to compete at the next spectacle. There would certainly be among the spectators a cultivated colonial called Situvellaunus. He would talk with such knowledge and charm about stage-sets and navigation and costumes and traditional ceremonies and Numidian lions that the ordinary person would feel shy of disparaging an entertainment which Situvellaunus found edifying. Only some very crude provincial would venture to suggest that it was tough on the Christians.

The arguments which justify bullfighting are all of the double-edged kind, which the ordinary person cannot handle without danger. If Waterloo was really won on the playing fields of Eton, there is a case for saying that the Spanish civil war, in which such unheard of cruelties were committed on both sides, was won (or lost) in the improvised bull-ring at Benecassim.

[1964]

PART THREE
EUROPE AT WAR

16

THALBURG REVISITED

Most of us are surrounded by pleasant, respectable well-educated people and we think we know them. In fact they are the enigma of the century and very little effort has been made to discover why a little pressure, rightly applied will turn us all into a pack of terrified and self-deceiving morons and bullies. Books have been published about the rise of the Nazis in Brunswick and in Schleswig-Holstein but only W. S. Allen, in his account of the little town of Thalburg between 1930 and 1935, has made a serious effort to solve the enigma. His book*, like all conscientious documentaries, is a little too full of facts, dates and references to be easily digestible by the casual reader, and it is a misfortune that it was not compiled twenty years earlier, when there would have been more people to interview and the mechanism of self-justification with its tactful silences and overflowing waste-paper baskets was not working so smoothly. In those garrulous chaotic days Mr Allen might not have been obliged to give fictitious names to the town and its principal citizens.

Thalburg is a charming little north German town, about the size of Kilkenny. It had a moat and cobbled streets and some mediaeval half-timbered houses and a great sixteenth-century Lutheran church. There were residential suburbs with lawns and shrubberies and a nice view across the river to the wooded hills. It has twenty-three religious and charitable societies, two soccer clubs, three gymnasiums, twenty-one sports clubs, eight choral societies, five shooting societies, a gardeners' club, three daily newspapers, a lecture society and a museum society, a town band, two cinemas and a public library. Living in a castle nearby, it had a baron with icy but excellent manners. In fact I

* William Sheridan, *The Nazi Seizure of Power* (London 1966).

171

cannot think of any Irish town of ten thousand inhabitants with so many pretensions to civilization.

They were all, of course, Christians, except for one hundred and twenty Jews and a handful of free-thinkers, and apart from 6 per cent Catholics, they were Lutherans. Because of the town's importance on the railroad, a third of its citizens were civil servants, averagely well-educated, but being dependent on official-dom for their jobs and promotions, inclined to be discreet.

Mr Allen can see only one or two serious defects in this admirable little community. Though religious distinctions counted for little, class distinctions were important. That explains the multitude of clubs. You were obliged to sing or shoot or drink beer in working-class clubs, or middle-class clubs, or upper-middle-class clubs. And probably the Baron had to do them all alone.

Then there was a rather tense nationalism, some of it sensible enough like the gardeners' society's crusade for German vegetables and the housewives' club's attack on Americanized department stores. There were twenty-four ex-soldiers' clubs and much parading and declaiming. Wreaths were always being laid on memorials and heroes' graves, and when Field Marshal von Mackensen came to visit his old friend the Baron, there was a splendid reception at the station and a guard of honour marched through flag-decked streets behind the Baron's limousine all the way to his estate.

In 1930 all twenty-four clubs banded together to ask the Prussian Minister of Education to ban *All Quiet on the Western Front* from the school libraries. When anything went wrong, like the collapse of the local bank, the patriots blamed it on the Treaty of Versailles or the Social Democratic Party (the SDP), the official scapegoats for the Armistice, or on Bolshevism, or godlessness. Yet, in fact Thalburg was by no means a revolutionary town; the Communists had lately polled only 5 per cent of the votes, whereas the SDP had 45 per cent. The SDP was reformist-socialist and controlling the government in coalition with the Catholic Centre Party, they naturally feared a revolution. It was largely Lutheran and was regarded by the Communists as their principal enemy. The Rightists called the coalition 'A league between Rome and the Reds!' This was a clever gibe, for the Centre and the SDP were irresistible in combination.

Mr Allen's contention is that Nazism was not a megalopolitan disease only but that it had roots also in the countryside and the provincial towns. And if the country soil had not been well prepared by local agents the movement could never have expanded and flourished.

He deals excellently with economic and social causes, the lost war and its after-effects of social change, inflation and unemployment. But men have lost wars before without social and intellectual suicide, and it is Mr Allen's study of the personalities of Thalburg that is so deeply interesting.

Every neighbourhood has frustrated intellectuals who espouse some silly-clever cause in order to lever themselves above suffocating commonplaces. If it is an anti-intellectual cause, they are sure of allies. Walter Timmerlah, the first Nazi in Thalburg, seems to have been one of these unfortunates. He owned the leading book-store and made it the intellectual centre for the town, where he often entertained poets and writers. He was a gentle and kindly man, who sang in the choir at the Lutheran church. He had taught in South America, and returning from his travels was shocked by the post-war havoc of his native town. Soon other agreeable people joined him. There was August Tiere, a school-teacher, Trautmann, the Director of the Girls' Lyceum, the two county court judges, a hotel-owner, and the Baron. The Baron was a public-spirited person who kept his estates going with the help of a small pension for war-wounds.

But the most valuable recruits to the Nazi cause were the two Lutheran pastors. They were as deeply concerned about godlessness as the Baron was about Bolshevistic expropriations, and their training and his had given them claims to culture, while isolating them from its contemporary manifestations. From their crumbling but sound-proof citadels, it was easier to talk than to listen. Allen says, 'The problem of Nazism was primarily a problem of perception.' If so, the clergy and the landlords and the social élite perceived nothing. They set in motion the machinery which ground to powder all the fine things they talked about, neighbourliness, charity, social responsibility, and intellectual freedom. They did this quite unconsciously and with no subsequent awareness or regrets.

Many pastors had been campaigning for Hitler long before he came to power, for though hostility to any independent faith was implicit in National Socialism from the beginning, it was not explicit for those who were ready to be deceived, and the Nazis were expert at handling them. On the eve of the 1930 elections a Lutheran minister from Berlin addressed a great meeting in Thalburg, and told them that the Nazis were neither economic extremists nor anti-religious radicals. This reassured the waverers, and the following day the Nazis increased their votes fifteenfold. A quarter of the citizens were now Nazi, so they decided to intervene more actively in the affairs of the Church.

Their opportunity came three weeks later, when there was to be an election to the Thalburg Council of Church Elders. The Lutheran members of the SDP, resenting the reactionary politics of the Elders, decided to run candidates of their own. The Elders were outraged and, blind to their own political partisanship, declared that the SDP was trying to drag 'the hatred and agitation of partisan politics even into church'. Promptly the Nazis came to the aid of the Elders, bringing down from Berlin a Lutheran pastor who was a Nazi Deputy in the Reichstag. He addressed the largest audience they had ever mustered in Thalburg and told them that the Marxists (and by that he meant the SDP) were 'the Murderers of the German People and in the pay of the Enemy', and that the Nazi movement, like the German army, represented all Germany.

On the next day the voting for the Elders' Council took place. Many of the SDP stayed away, some perhaps as a genuine gesture of godlessness, some because they were stung by the challenge that they were introducing politics into religion. There was only a quarter of their usual vote. The Nazis, more realistic, brought four times as many as usual to the polls. The Führerprinzip makes it easier for the godless to exploit the godly for their mutual advantage. Though the SDP was the biggest political party in Thalburg and 90 per cent of them were Lutheran, not one of their candidates was elected to the Council.

No doubt the socialists should have tried to counteract the Nazi pastor with a socialist one. But it was an SDP dogma that 'religion is a private matter'. The Nazis on the other hand claimed, like the clergy, that it was allied to 'Deutschtum' and concerned the whole German people. And behind the scenes they were preparing their own pan-German religion, basing it on *Blut und Boden* and the ancient Teutonic mythology.

The socialists were irritated and, since religion should be 'a private matter', they proposed to the City Council that the town subsidies to the Lutheran Church should be curtailed.

This was very untimely for just then they should have been able to count on Lutheran support against the Nazi teaching, which was infiltrating into the schools. The SDP paper, the *Volksblatt*, revealed that August Tiere wrote Nazi slogans on the blackboard, that another teacher had wandered round the streets drunk after midnight shouting Heil Hitler! and that a third gave the Nazi salute in class and encouraged his pupils to wear swastikas on school outings. However, the bourgeoisie decided to overlook all this and to concentrate on the socialist enemy. Just at that time a new School Advisory Committee was due to be elected. The bourgeoisie made out a list of candidates, all of them Nazi sympathizers. They decided to purge not the Nazis but the socialists from the schools.

To clinch the matter, yet another Lutheran minister, who was a Nazi Deputy in the Reichstag, came down and addressed a mass-meeting in Thalburg. He urged the Church to support the Nazis and said that the whole German army was behind Hitler; he demanded that the SDP be outlawed in Germany. The next week there was a Hitler Youth Conference in the town with parades and banners and sports, and on the day before the election another pastor addressed a huge audience on the subject of the School Advisory Council. He told them that Liberalism and Socialism were poisoning the youth, that Protestantism and German Folkdom were inseparable, and that in the National Socialist Movement 'Christianity will celebrate its resurrection'. The meeting closed with the scurrilous Nazi song the 'Horst Wessel Lied'.

In the battle of the School Council a resounding victory over the SDP was won and the following day, headed by three bands and 1200 SA men, the Nazis marched off to celebrate in the forest the old German pagan festival of the summer solstice.

1932 was the last year of democracy in Germany but only the SDP seems to have been aware of what was impending. Yet they miscalculated. They thought that there would be be a Nazi *putsch*, which would have to be violently resisted. The Nazi strategy, which was quasi-legal, quasi-religious, quasi-conservative, took them by surprise. The SDP was destroyed piecemeal in unspectacular engagements. The leaders were first levered out of their positions of authority and influence and then inconspicuously moved to the quarries and the concentration camps.

The Lutheran ministers continued indefatigable in their support of the Nazis. In the last months a pastor came down from Hanover to warn the Church convention against the godlessness of the SDP, and a Thalburg colleague told them that the SDP was the chief force behind 'atheism and free-thinkerdom'. The Baron was there too and he adjured all the clergy present to join in the struggle against Bolshevism. Finally the Nazis gathered an audience of 'preachers, Church elders, teachers and school committee men' in one of the town's hotels and a pastor told them that German Christianity had received its death blow from the Weimar constitution and that only the Nazis could restore 'the God-fearing man'. At the end of his lecture another pastor challenged him. 'The Nazi racial programme', he said, 'will lead to idolatry and mass-hatred.' This is the only anti-Nazi statement that Mr Allen had collected in Thalburg from a Lutheran minister; he was vigorously opposed and the Nazi pastor warmly applauded.

All this Christian support had to be rewarded and encouraged and, as the Third Reich came in sight, there was a period of feverish Nazi church-going. One day all the SA, the SS and the Hitler Jugend went *en masse* to pray. And when at the end of January 1933 Adolf Hitler became Chancellor, 200 SA men paraded to church in uniform to give thanks. There was more celebration when Hitler achieved his electoral victory in the Reichstag and a sermon from Pastor Muenchmeyer on the theme, 'What a transposition through Divine Disposition.' But the supreme occasion in Thalburg was Hitler's birthday on 20 April 1933. The church was decorated with swastikas and the prayers of all the Thalburgers invoked for their Führer. A day of non-stop processions and gaiety followed, to wind up with a ceremonial burning of 'filth literature' in the market place and the unveiling of a memorial to a very dim Nazi hero called Schlageter. When the dedication was over, the pastor adjured them all to be worthy of Schlageter and of Adolf Hitler and led off with a hymn.

How long was it before the clergy and their parishioners came to their senses? Probably never. The approach of the war and the danger to Germany must have swept most of them away from their misgivings on a wave of irreproachable enthusiasm. The loyalty which they might have witheld from Hitler they could not refuse to the Fatherland and the two loyalties had been inextricably interwoven. Yet, there were still a few years when the more self-critical had time to reflect. No sooner were the Nazis firmly in the saddle in Thalburg than they started a campaign 'to revitalize the Church', in other words, to force its members to join the semi-pagan 'German Christian' movement. The two pastors of the big Church, who probably did not yet grasp what it was all about, supported the movement. Did they read an article in the Thalburg Beobachter applying to Hitler the verse (Romans 11.36), 'For of Him and through Him and unto Him are all things. To Him be the Glory for ever. Amen?' And if so, did it disturb them? Possibly, for though every member of the Council of Elders was a Nazi, all the same the German Christian movement never flourished.

Very slowly the Protestant resistance began. It was six years too late and all their positions of strength had been abandoned and they were tongue-tied by compulsory patriotism. Yet they redeemed themselves a little by their growing unpopularity. In a couple of years Kurt Aergeyz, the local Nazi boss, started an anti-religious campaign with the object of making Thalburg the first town in Germany with no church-goers. The Hitler Jugend pelted the crucifix on the town church with snowballs and broke up confirmation classes. A detective was planted in the church doorway taking down names and making notes on the sermon. Was anything provocative ever said? There is no record of this, but it was felt that even to attend church was a gesture of defiance and this gesture was freely made. The respectable first Nazis, 'the idealists', were edging out of the movement or being edged, and Walter Timmerlah, a Nazi no longer, sang more assiduously then ever in the church choir.

Anti-Semitism had never been popular in Thalburg. Everybody knew the local Jews, and even in the schools their children were not teased. When the Jewish banker, Braun, died in 1937, sixty Thalburger businessmen, though they had been warned not to do this, attended his funeral. A year later, when Jewish homes and shops were being ransacked, though none risked his skin on their behalf, some Thalburgers protested. Only the County Agricultural Society had supported the official boycott of Jewish businesses, but local sympathy was not of much practical use to the Jews. Stunned by what had happened elsewhere the Jews avoided their friends so as not to embarrass them and passed on to them some of their own panic. When the Jews were already suffering unbearably, the local paper reported that the chairman of the Thalburg synagogue had sent off a telegram to all the consuls and ambassadors in England, France, America and Poland to say that it was a lie that Jews were being persecuted in Germany. Possibly the telegram was not a Nazi fraud. Everybody else thought it wise to conciliate the Nazis, so perhaps the Jews thought this too. They disappeared inconspicuously from Thalburg with few explosions of hatred and only two suicides.

Curiously enough, the Baron seems to have been the only respectable anti-Semite in Thalburg, maybe because in his remote splendours he had never become socially involved with Jews. After the first meeting of the new Nazified County Council in 1933, he had proposed that all county contracts be taken away from the Jews, that the Jews be expelled from the Old People's Homes and deprived of all other county services. We are always being told that the German aristocracy had been redeemed by their snobbery and had nothing but scorn for the vulgar dreams of the Austrian house-painter. In fact the Nazi corruption was as classless and creedless in its choice of victims as the Black Death.

Apart from force and fear, it was Nazi efficiency that attracted most disciples to the cause. This was so superb as to suggest that true goodness is inevitably haphazard and bungling and that democracy, if it is to make concessions to the infinite diversity of man, is bound to be shifting and precarious. Aergeyz, the Nazi dictator of Thalburg, was a genius who made no concessions at all. From the August evening in 1933, when he was found in Broad Street trying to beat to death a prostrate and bleeding Social Democrat, to that other day in 1945, when he posted the local militia along the country roads and bade them fight to the death, while he himself drove away to the mountains in his Mercedes with two blondes and some cases of schnapps, his judgment was flawless. For fourteen years he dominated the little town, making it a model of its kind. He followed the Nazi recipe, which was first to create chaos and then, by suppressing it dictatorially, to win the support of all peace-loving citizens.

Unity of a kind brings prosperity of a kind, and Aergeyz made the town rich. He reduced unemployment by forcing the businessmen to employ more workers than they needed. To provide all the new uniforms the clothes factory had to employ seventeen new workers. He forced the middle-classes to have

178

stew every Sunday and to give what they saved by this humble fare to the poor. He enlisted all the cultured souls in Thalburg in his campaign to induce tourists to visit it. This was easy enough for cultured people can always persuade themselves that when they lend grace to tyranny, they are not abetting it but humanizing it. They turned the old moat into a beautiful park with ponds for swans and in the forest hundreds of workers were taken on to build an open-air theatre for Nazi cere-monies. It was called the Holy Place (for Aergeyz was edging them all by easy stages towards German Christianity). He got the museum director to put up sixty historical tablets along the town walls. One of his ideas (or was he just appropriating some-one else's?), the Christmas tree in the market square ('so that everyone should be able to enjoy one'), was later adopted all over Europe. In such ways he brought in one year (1936) 60,000 tourists to the town. The inspiration for all this came, of course, from Dr Goëbbels, under whose astute patronage more tourists came to Germany than ever before or since in German history, bringing back to their own countries the good news of the reno-vation of Germany and the peaceful intentions of the Führer.

Dr Kurt Schumacher, an SDP deputy, said in the Reichstag that the Nazis made their appeal to whatever was most swinish in man. This is unfair to the swine as well as to the dupes of the Nazis. For swine are not cruel and malicious, they are merely greedy and stupid. It was mainly the revived economy of Ger-many that brought the 'good Germans', the clergy, the nobility, the farmers, and, from outside Germany, the tourists, to the pig-trough, grunting and perceiving nothing.

As for the Catholic Church in Thalburg, small as it was, it had at the start put up a better resistance than the Lutherans. The priest swiftly got into trouble with the Nazis by urging his parishioners to vote for the Centre (Catholic) Party and, in the year of Hitler's victory, the Catholic Young Men's Society was suppressed and its property confiscated. Soon the Centre Party was dissolved too and the Concordat signed. When this hap-pened, the Catholics also were assimilated and a couple of years later we can read in the Catholic Grade School annual report that the headmaster had brought pictures of the Führer to be hung in every classroom and racial tables and genetic laws to be framed upon the walls.

While he was still a Nazi, Timmerlah had complained of Kurt

Aergeyz to the Nazi Gauleitung in a detailed indictment of thirty-one counts, ending up Heil Hitler! They were extremely basic and a more perceptive man would have seen them as small sins, the legitimate offspring of his own large ones. For example:

Aergeyz had given the job of supplying garden chairs and beer mugs for the brewery to his brother, though another ironmonger had offered them at a lower price.

He had given his father-in-law the contract to supply boots for the Labour Service Camp.

Though at the bonfire of Filth Literature he had raged against the Jews, he went on seeing his sister, who was married to a Jewish lawyer.

He had struck down the venerable Party Comrade P—— and threatened to beat him round the market square with a dog-whip.

He set the Nazi officials to spy on each other, threatened to transfer the Nazi teacher, August Tiere, to East Prussia, and to organize a boycott of another disobedient Nazi's tavern.

He protected the Leader of the Women's Group, though she had used Party funds for the purchase of stockings.

He told lies, and would not allow a proper auditing of the accounts.

Timmerlah's last series of charges was headed: 'He is not a true National Socialist.'

The Gauleitung acknowledged his indictment and Aergeyz was officially reprimanded. He was not, however, removed. For Aergeyz was, in fact, a true Nazi and just the kind that was wanted.

Allen thinks that social resentment was the passion that fuelled Aergeyz's boundless energy. The Nazi movement had given him the opportunity to avenge himself on those who had patronized him in the past. That explains his vindictiveness against the 'idealistic' Nazis, the teachers and the lawyers, and his rage against the Church, the citadel of the town's respectability, though it had been so immensely co-operative.

Were there any anti-Nazi heroes in Thalburg? A great many were purged and others kept quiet or argued like von Altberg, the County Prefect, that 'he could do more good within the party than if he were outside and powerless'. Such people would be slow to remember those who were less diplomatic; all the same we know of an elderly teacher who refused to join the Nazi Teachers' League. She was an old maid who had boxed Kurt Aergeyz's ear when he was a little boy. She said the whole thing was 'nonsense' and she refused to have anything to do with it.

And she got away with this.

In fact, of course, nonsense is always nonsense and when sensible men acquiesce in it, it turns into something monstrous and cruel.

Another mistake which the 'good Germans' made was to think that there can be a political way of ironing out the inequalities (the least of which are money and class) which alienate men from each other. Only individual men can do this, though the Churches, as protectors of the individual soul, could help them. But the clergy had a way of seeing 'the Hand of God' in outbreaks of public nonsense, whose origins are hard to perceive and trace. As interpreters of God, they feel they have a divine commission and, in sanctifying nonsense, they squander the prestige which honest and perceptive men have accumulated for them through the centuries.

[1967]

17

CARL VON OSSIETZKY

Many of the greatest martyrs and saints of modern times will never have their biographies written or their centenaries celebrated. Nobody knows when or how they died. Their lives are often a complex web of insignificant detail which few would have the patience to unravel. Often they have struggled in solitude against mass movements and it is inevitable that the mass media, through which we now obtain the most of our information, should ignore them.

Lately I found a grimy old pamphlet dating from the first years of Hitler. It is called 'The Case of Carl von Ossietzky' and it was the work of fifteen eminent English writers. It is an appeal to the Nobel Peace Prize Committee on behalf of Ossietzky, who was at that time in a German prison.

They wrote: 'We have all tried to do something for the cause of peace, but he has done more than any of us. He has done most of all living men to deserve this acknowledgment from his fellow-men.'Because of these efforts Ossietzky did get his Nobel Prize in 1935, but a year or two later he died reclaiming marshland in Esterwegen prison camp. Nobody really knows about his death.

Why does nobody care either? Germans of the East and the West are now combing history for evidence that they resisted Hitler but Ossietzky and his friends are seldom mentioned. Very few people talk of the large and honourable resistance to Hitler, which was extinguished before the war began, before Auschwitz was thought of, and which left the German opposition leaderless. The reason for this silence is clear. History is written by survivors and most of those who survived till 1939 had had to make many moral and political adjustments in order to do so. Inevitably they have encouraged us to believe that the best martyrs are diplomatists who balance one tyranny against another and choose (provisionally of course) the least repugnant. Ossietzky, who did not want any tyranny at all, does not fit comfortably into this picture, and so he is honoured neither in the East nor the West. There is much competition to be numbered among those brave Germans who tried to murder Hitler because he was losing the war, but Ossietzky, who opposed Hitler because he was Hitler, and war because it was war, has been almost totally forgotten.

His fifteen sponsors seem rather out-of-date figures too, Aldous Huxley, Gilbert Murray, Rose Macaulay, Norman Angell, Gerald Heard, Bertrand Russell, J. B. Priestley, Leonard and Virginia Woolf to name a few. They all had this in common with Ossietzky: they hated the Organization Man, the mechanical dummy who does what he is told. And they believed he could be resisted. Nowadays most writers either belong to an organization themselves or else believe that the world created by the Organization Man is so obscene and ludicrous that they can only laugh at it, the bitter laughter of the defeated, of Joyce and Beckett, Albee and Genet and a hundred such others, and with a certain sad satisfaction reflect that this world is a Vale of Tears anyway and we should turn our minds to the next.

Ossietzky was different. He was the son of a Hamburg merchant and had fought with average ability and less than average enthusiasm in the First World War. Even then he had realized where German militarism was tending. As soon as he was demobilized he started a weekly in Hamburg whose aims he describes thus: 'We who are supporters of peace have a duty and a task to point out over and over again that there is nothing heroic in war but that it brings terror and misery to mankind.'

As a result of the German military collapse, there had been a great cultural revival with which the names of Einstein, Thomas and Heinrich Mann, Arnold Zweig, Gropius, Max Reinhardt, Hindemith and Bruno Walter are associated. There was springtime in the air and for a few years all Europe looked to Berlin as it had once looked to Weimar. To Berlin Ossietzky went. He started there the *Nie Wieder Krieg* movement and became editor of the *Weltbühne*. Till the day of his last arrest it was the principal literary organ of resistance, first to the reviving German militarism and then to Hitler.

Weltbühne had been called *Schaubühne* before the war, and was an organ of the theatre. It was connected with a firm that published children's books, *Emil and the Detectives*, translations of *Dr Doolittle* and so on. But soon it was clear that the independence of the actor, the writer, the artist, was about to be threatened and that the *Weltbühne*, the world-stage, required them. The paper changed its name and its character. It became militantly anti-militarist and earned the hatred of the General Staff. For Ossietzky claimed with good reason that some of the generals were lending support to the Black Reichswehr, a secret society, directed against German democracy and defending itself by what were known as the *vehme* murders. He revealed that German commercial aviation was being used as a screen for military activities. He opposed the granting of naturalization papers to Hitler. He attacked those, who, under Nazi pressure, had banned the famous anti-war film, 'All Quiet on the Western Front'. 'Today', he wrote, 'German fascism has slain a film. Tomorrow it will be something else. . . Soon only one tune will be permitted, and every one of our steps will be carefully measured.'

Ossietzky was not forced into resistance by violence like the Jews, nor by political theory like the Communists. Rudolf Olden, his friend and lawyer, who was editor of the *Berliner Tageblatt*, explained him as a *Bürger*, a civilian defending the rights of civilians.

The generals were handling Hitler very gently, for they believed they could use him and had no notion how soon they would be his puppets. Ossietzky, who saw clearly what was happening, had to be silenced. In an action for slander the generals secured his arrest and imprisonment. Yet till Hitler came, a *Bürger* could still count on some justice. Over 42,000 Germans signed an appeal for his release, a brave thing to do for it was only three weeks before Hitler came to power. When for a brief period General Echleicher took over the government Ossietzky was released.

But soon the flames of the burning Reichstag lit up unmistakeably the shape of the future. His colleagues on the *Weltbühne* escaped abroad and Ossietzky's friends urged him to think of his small daughter and to follow them. But he had written: 'The man who is opposing the Government of his own country and who goes across the border, speaks with a hollow voice.'

He refused to leave. The writers of my old pamphlet recall

how Socrates was urged by Crito to fly to Thessaly while there was time; it was a duty to his friends, to his family, and Socrates had answered: 'The principles, which I have hitherto honoured and revered, I still honour.'

The day after the Reichstag fire Ossietzky was taken to Spandau Prison and thence to Sonnenburg concentration camp. After that there were a few rumours from fellow-prisoners who escaped of beatings and torture but nothing definite. We know more about Socrates.

Since Ossietzky was the principal leader of the German resistance to Hitler, why is his name so seldom mentioned when the whole German people is being charged with complicity in Hitler's crimes? I've suggested the reason already. It is because Ossietzky and his 42,000 supporters, who were eliminated with him, were absolutists. Hitler to them was an absolute evil, whereas to most of their contemporaries inside and outside Germany, he was only a relative evil. Effective German resistance collapsed with Ossietzky, for only relativists were left. Not only in Germany but all over Europe, millions of intelligent people believed that Hitler could be 'handled', used effectively against the Communists and then, when his work was done, discarded. One must recall that while Ossietzky was in Sonnenburg, the British Ambassador was shooting elk with General Göring, and Ribbentrop was an honoured guest with Lord Londonderry in Co. Down.

The ghost of the relativist delusion still haunts us, corrupting history as it once corrupted politics. When it is finally accepted that Hitler was wholly evil and Stalin's most effective ally, Ossietzky and the thousands who died with him will be remembered again. They were the men who would have saved us – had we supported them – not only from Hitler, but from Stalin as well.

[1964]

18

THE CHILDREN OF DRANCY

Lately I was comparing three versions of the story of the Children of Drancy and it occurred to me that we mostly have more detailed information, more curiosity, about remote and now irrelevant events like the murder of the two little Princes in the Tower in the summer of 1483 or the death of 123 English people in the Black Hole of Calcutta on 19 June 1756. Two of the writers I consulted said it was in July, a third said it was in August 1942 that the 4051 children were sent off to be killed in Poland from the transit camp at Drancy north of Paris. Were they French Jews or foreigners? Were they girls or boys? It is usually said boys, but suburban residents on the outskirts of Paris who heard them wailing at night say they were little girls, and there is a story of a bleeding ear torn by a harried police inspector as he removed an earring.

They spent four days without food at the Vélodrôme d'Hiver (the winter cycle-racing stadium) before their mothers were taken from them, then they were loaded three or four hundred at a time into cattle trains at the Gare d'Austerlitz and taken to Auschwitz. It was related at Nuremberg that an order came from Berlin that deportees from Vichy France should be mingled discreetly with the children to make them look like family groups. Was this done? It is not as though dubious legend has grown up around these children as it has around King Herod's far smaller enterprise in Bethlehem. The facts are bleak and few. It should not be hard to find more and to iron out discrepancies. But no one seems interested.

I believe we are bored because the scale is so large that the children seem to belong to sociology and statistics. We cannot visualize them reading Babar books, having their teeth straightened, arranging dolls' tea parties. Their sufferings are too great and protracted to be imagined, and the range of human sympathy is narrowly restricted.

Had four or five children only been killed and burnt, and had it happened outside the booking office at the Gare d'Austerlitz, we would have responded emotionally and probably their names and their fate would have been carved on a marble tablet like that which commemorates the victims of the Black Hole outside the Post Office in Calcutta. And the names of their murderers would be remembered for ever. But to kill and burn 4051 children after transporting them to Poland was a huge co-operative endeavour, in which thousands of French and German policemen, typists, railway officials, gas-fitters and electricians were engaged. It was composite villainy, and when you try to break it down there are no villains, just functionaries as neutral and characterless as the clusters of ink blobs of which a press photograph is composed. The officials who handled the children were, we are told, deeply affected. Even the Vichy Commissioner for Jewish Affairs, Louis Darquier, who deported Jews in their thousands from France, had suggested that the children be transferred to a French orphanage, but he did nothing about it. Though Pierre Laval, the French Premier, was enthusiastic about the deportation of all foreign Jews, even those under sixteen, neither he nor Pétain realized that they were not going to be 'settled' in the East but killed there.

Even at the peak of the organizational pyramid one finds duty, routine, idealism of a kind more often than sadism as the motive power; in the interests of a more glorious future the tender impulses had to be suppressed. At the Jerusalem trial even the most hostile witnesses failed to prove that Eichmann, an exemplary husband and father, had ever been guilty of wanton cruelty. These people were really what they claimed to be, idealists, whose seedy ideals would never have germinated and pullulated in any other century but ours.

However confident we may be of the facts, there are irreconcilable divergences when we come to their interpretation. 'Too much science,' say some. 'Too much literary scorn for science,' say others. François Mauriac, who was in Paris at the time, wrote some twenty years later:

Nothing I had seen during those sombre years of the Occupation had left so deep a mark on me as those trainloads of Jewish children standing at the Gare d'Austerlitz. Yet I did not even see them myself. My wife described them to me, her voice still filled with horror. At that time we knew nothing of Nazi methods of extermination. And who could have imagined them? Yet the way these lambs had been torn from their mothers in itself exceeded anything we had so far thought possible. I believe that on that day I touched upon the mystery of iniquity whose revelation was to mark the end of one era and the beginning of another. The dream which Western man conceived in the eighteenth century, whose dawn he thought he saw in 1789, and which, until 2 August, 1914, had grown stronger with the process of enlightenment and the discoveries of science – this dream vanished finally for me before those trainloads of little children. And yet I was still thousands of miles away from thinking that they were to be fuel for the gas chamber and crematorium.

Yet even at the time few thought like that. It is easier to forget about the Children of Drancy than to liberate ourselves from the increasing control that science has over our lives. The year after Mauriac wrote what I have quoted, Charles Snow delivered at Cambridge his famous lecture on 'The Two Cultures' in which he claimed that the traditional culture of the past, and science, the culture of the future, should make peace with one another. Charles Snow, a novelist himself, addressed his lecture mainly to the 'traditional' man of letters, scolding him for being ignorant of elementary scientific knowledge like molecular biology and the Second Law of Thermodynamics.

He quoted with approval someone he referred to as 'a distinguished scientist':

Why do most writers take on social opinions which would have been thought uncivilized at the time of the Plantagenets? Wasn't that true of most of the famous writers of the twentieth century – Yeats, Pound, Wyndham Lewis – nine out of ten of those who have dominated literary sensitivity in our time? Weren't they not only politically silly, but politically wicked? Didn't the influence of all they represent bring Auschwitz that much nearer?'

Snow scolds Ruskin, William Morris, Thoreau, Emerson and D. H. Lawrence for their rebellion against the Age of Science: 'They tried various fancies, which were not in effect more than screams of horror.'

I dislike quoting Snow when he talks nonsense or endorses other people's nonsense (when I was younger I enjoyed his novels and in 1941 wrote a rave review of *The Masters* in *The*

Bell). As an Irishman, who knew Yeats, I can only gasp when the great Irish poet is linked with Auschwitz.

Snow's lecture caused tremendous interest. It was published and many times reprinted. There was a three-week long correspondence in *The Spectator*, most of it favourable to Snow. He was thinking on popular lines. When he wrote his novels he was Charles Snow, then he became Sir Charles, and finally Lord Snow.

Only F. R. Leavis, Professor of English Literature at Cambridge, reacted violently. He delivered and later printed a lecture furiously attacking Snow, denouncing him as few leading writers have been denounced before. He too was printed in *The Spectator* and there was much comment, most of it hostile.

Snow [writes Leavis] takes inertly the characteristic and disastrous confusion of the civilization he is trying to instruct.

He is intellectually as undistinguished as it is possible to be.

He thinks he has literary culture and scientific culture. In fact he has neither.

He rides on an advancing swell of cliché without a glimmer of what creative literature is or what it signifies.

Who will assert that the average member of a modern society is more fully human or alive than an Indian peasant?

As a novelist he doesn't exist. He can't be said to know what a novel is.

Leavis is an ardent champion of D. H. Lawrence, and, possibly, compared to Lawrence, Snow as a novelist is negligible.

Leavis mentions the Indian because Snow had a detailed plan for rescuing the poorer peoples of the world by means of a scientific revolution. He thought, for instance, that the USA and Britain should educate ten or twenty-thousand scientific specialists 'to the level of Part 1 Natural Science or Mechanized Science Tripos' and send them to India, Africa and South-East Asia to help industrialize the inhabitants and lever them out of their pre-scientific stagnation.

How could Snow fail to see that the transportation of six million Jews to the camps was, like the atom bomb, among the most sensational of science's achievements and that, in the international field, science is more often used as an instrument of hatred than of neighbourly love. Think of the export of arms to Iran and to the Contras in Nicaragua, and indeed of the great build-up of armaments all over the globe.

He was surely driven to entertain these visions, more fantastic than the dreams of William Morris, by his knowledge that science was in fact irresistible and had enormous potentialities for good and evil, which only the men of traditional culture, if they accepted it and understood it a little, might be able to control. If they know a little about genetics, for example, they might be able to monitor and arrest the appalling experiments of the geneticists, which now only religious leaders with the wisdom and authority of the pre-scientific centuries behind them can forbid. They might have persuaded the Americans to industrialize Vietnam (if the Vietnamese wanted to be industrialized) rather than devastate it. But at present the average man of letters knows nothing of science and most scientists are culturally illiterate. Snow says that the average scientist, when one tries to probe what books he'd read, would modestly confess, 'Well, I've tried a bit of Dickens.' Snow himself must have guessed that the gulf between the Two Cultures is unbridgeable.

Has any decade seen so much sophisticated science-promoted violence as the Eighties? All over the world, in small countries and large ones, men who could not invent a pop-gun themselves have access to the newest and most lethal weapons. In Ireland the IRA get their arms from Libya and pay for them by kidnapping the owners of supermarkets (the ransom is always paid and then lied about). Where do the Libyans get their arms from? Who knows? A brisk trade goes on all round the world and the great powers are helpless to end it.

For Mauriac, the eighteenth-century dream of a future enlightened by the discoveries of science had died at Drancy. In England Aldous Huxley and George Orwell had earlier predicted all sorts of horrors. In his book *The Revolt of the Masses* (1932) the Spaniard Ortega Y. Gasset had analyzed what was happening much more accurately: 'Technicism, in combination with liberal democracy, had engendered the Mass Man. . . Modern science has handed over the command of public life to the intellectually commonplace.' Observe the calibre of the world leaders of 1987.

Snow would have none of this. 'The scientific edifice of the physical world is in its intellectual depth, complexity and articulation the most beautiful and wonderful work of the mind of man.' In fact beauty is in the eye of the beholder. A primrose by the river's brim is just as likely to dazzle it as the structure of the haemoglobin molecule. All nature can be seen as beautiful.

According to Snow let the Two Cultures but unite and educate those twenty-thousand Mechanical Science Tripos men and the gap between the rich and the poor will be bridged, overpopulation checked and atomic war averted.

Most thinking men stand midway between the despair of Orwell and Mauriac from which only the grace of God can rescue us and the twenty-thousand Tripos men, but believe that God and the Tripos men are slowly converging. Though they might express themselves differently, they would concur with the prayer which Major Cooper, the heroic astronaut, composed on his seventeenth orbit round the earth; it ends:

Help us in future space endeavours to show the world that democracy really can compete and still is able to do things in a big way and is able to do research development and conduct new scientific and technical programmes.

Be with all our families. Give us guidance and encouragement and let them know that everything will be okay. We ask in Thy name. Amen.

Though the joint session of Congress to which this prayer was read approved of it, a Hindu about to be industrialized might complain that life is more complex than Major Cooper and Charles Snow believed. A certain intellectual simplicity is the price that has to be paid for irrigation and tractors and freedom from famine and disease. An idea that has to travel far by modern means and circulate freely among alien people must, like an air passenger's luggage, be very meagre indeed.

In spite of that, most men would sooner believe in the healing powers of scientific research and technology than accept François Mauriac's counsel of despair.

But the true answer of the scientific optimist to Mauriac will not, I think, be found by Major Cooper in outer space or by those twenty-thousand Tripos men. Should one not consider the question of size and whether we really have 'to do things in a big way'?

Anti-Semitism, the idea which killed the Children of Drancy, was small and old and had existed for centuries in small pockets all over Europe. If humane ideals had been cultivated as assiduously as technical ones it would long ago have died without issue in some Lithuanian village. But science gave it wings and swept it by aeroplane and wireless and octuple rotary machines all over Europe and even lodged it in Paris, the cultural capital.

No one likes thinking on these lines. Yet observe how even pity can become helpless and sometimes destructive when it is divorced from deep personal concern and becomes a public matter. Public pity forms committees, sends tinned meat, secures entry visas, but the beating of its collective heart can be heard from miles away and it is easily eluded. Those in charge of the children eluded it by taking them to Auschwitz. It was to dodge public pity that the children were torn from their mothers and travelled alone or with doomed strangers. The mothers, when their future first became known, preferring death for their children to the lonely fate they foresaw for them, had started to throw them down from the tops of buildings. They would have continued to do this from the railway carriage windows and the dead or dying bodies might have roused some dormant committee into action in France or Germany or Poland.

Something similar was happening in Free Europe. As the funds of the refugee committees swelled, the price of liberty for a Jew went higher and higher. The compassion of the Allies, turned into cash, could be used against them. In 1944 Allied pity could have saved a million Jews in return for 100,000 trucks, but the trucks would have been used against Russia and so divided the Allies and resuscitated the latent anti-Semitism of the Russians. Looking at the matter in the large way it was better even for Jewry as a whole that a further million Jews should die.

Because of these complexities the Children of Drancy will always remain shadowy figures, and as nursery symbols of the vast cruelty of the world we shall go on using Herod and the little princes and the Black Hole. These stories are educative because they are about wicked men who can be punished or at least reviled, and not about that Faceless and Mysterious Collective Iniquity against which we are powerless. It is not a satisfactory choice, all the same, because historians now think that Herod never massacred the Innocents and that Richard Crookback never smothered the princes and that Suraja Dowlah thought the Black Hole was properly ventilated, whereas no one denies what happened to the Children of Drancy.

It is because we do things in the big way that the Wicked Man has now become so elusive and almost an abstraction. The chain of responsibility lengthens every day; we can think of it as an immense row of Part 1 Science Tripos graduates holding hands across the earth and linking together the triumphs of civilization to a depth of savage misery which the Aztecs, because they never discovered the wheel, could not inflict upon their victims. Snow mentions with approval a prototype of these Tripos men, a Prussian called Siemens, a pioneer in electrical engineering over a hundred years ago. I prepared this paper by the light of electricity that was brought from the great dam at Ardnacrusha on the river Shannon by Messrs Siemens a generation ago; each bulb had 'Siemens, made in Germany' printed on it. In this way Siemens helped to modernize Ireland, but Ireland was only one link in a long chain. In November 1932 Karl von Siemens used his wealth and influence to bring Hitler to power and later his firm installed the electricity at Auschwitz, where of course it was not used just for reading lamps and making toast. There too, as at Lublin, Siemens set up factories for the employment of slave labour, while for their factory at Berlin Haselhaorst they bought seven hundred women from the SS at Ravensbruck at four to six marks a head. The directors of Siemens were on the American list of German industrialists to be prosecuted at Nuremberg, but probably they were all humane and agreeable men belonging to the upper, beneficent end of the long chain; anyway, the charges against them were dropped. On the other hand, Ezra Pound, who had, on his own responsibility and not as a link in a chain, given much foolish praise to the Fascists, was punished and arraigned. Yet he had never killed or enslaved anybody.

It will always be so. A mischievous poet is like a thorn in the finger. He can be pulled out. But the mischief that results from a concentration of Tripos men is like disseminated sclerosis. And that is another reason why we talk so little about the Children of Drancy.

Charles Snow was surely right when he said that most literary intellectuals are 'natural Luddites'. I think he meant that they continue to worry when worry is useless. Ruskin, Morris, Thoreau, Lawrence, all repudiated the new world to which engineer Siemens was devoting his genius, but even a century ago it was hard already to contract out while now it is all but impossible. Should I read by candlelight because the firm that gave me electricity illuminated also the last agony of the Children of Drancy? I don't think so. I am less frightened of science than I am of that doctrine of the Mystery of Iniquity, which is to many the only consolation left now that there is no traffic on the road to Brook Farm, and New Harmony is sealed off. The Mystery of Iniquity has its roots in despair, but wickedness would no longer be mysterious if the chains of responsibility were shorter and science, which lengthened those chains, must be forced to go into reverse and shorten them.

Fortunately there are still small communities where the Wicked Man is not yet woven so scientifically into the fabric of society that he cannot be extracted without stopping the trains and fusing the electric light. It is not a coincidence that two small countries, Denmark and Bulgaria, stemmed the flow to Auschwitz better than any of their more powerful neighbours on the continent. Apart from size the two countries have nothing in common. The Bulgars are primitive, the Danes a highly sophisticated people. They are no doubt individually as wicked as the rest of us, but wickedness still has a name and an address and a face. When the rumour, a false one, went round Sofia that the government intended to deport its Jews, the citizens demonstrated outside the Palace and blocked the roads to the railway station. In Denmark on the night of 1 October 1943, when the Jews heard they were to be rounded up, each family knew which Danish family was prepared to hide them. Very few were caught. At the Gare d'Austerlitz the Children of Drancy were surrounded by the most civilized and humane people in Europe, but they were scarcely less isolated and abandoned than when they queued up naked for their 'shower-bath' in the Polish forest.

But I must answer the charge made by Snow's scientist that W. B. Yeats 'brought Auschwitz nearer', because by focussing his mind on distant horizons Snow failed to see what was under his nose. Yeats deliberately chose the small community, moving his heart and his body and as much as he could of his mind from London to Ireland, his birthplace. For him and a dozen other well-known Irish writers Ireland had been a larger Brook Farm, a refuge whose walls were built not by some transcendental theory but by history and geography. For a few years our most parochial period became also our most creative. If there was in Yeats a Fascist streak it derived from his disillusionment with the drab unheroic Ireland in which the dreams of the visionaries of 1916 had ended. He complained that 'men of letters lived like outlaws in their own country'. When he saw that Irish Fascism promised to be as drab and demagogic as Irish democracy, he rapidly back-pedalled and rewrote the song he had composed for the Blue Shirts, making it so fantastic that no political party could sing it. He led the campaign against the Irish censorship and in everything he did and said he was a champion of intellectual and moral and social freedom.

In all this he was an isolated figure and even in Ireland the range of his influence was very small. But in my opinion personal and parochial efforts like his did form a real obstruction on the road to Auschwitz, whereas its traffic was never once interrupted by conventional weapons.

The courage of the astronauts, the talents of the twenty-thousand Tripos men are needed, but they must break down, link by link, those long chains of atomized guilt with which the Children of Drancy were strangled.

Postscript

The Children of Drancy were not totally forgotten in France. On 5 November 1978 a programme on the last days of Marshal Pétain was to be screened. It was abruptly withdrawn and a film on the Renaissance Pope Clement VII was substituted. The reason was that there had been a remarkable national re-examination of conscience in France due to an interview published in *L'Express* with the eighty-year-old Darquier, the Vichy Government's Commissioner for Jewish Affairs, whom I have mentioned already. Despite the kindly intentions towards the Children of Drancy with which he has been credited, he had deported 75,721 French Jews to German concentration camps, including the Children. He was so virulent an anti-Semite that even the Germans were surprised by his zeal. He escaped to Spain and was condemned to death in his absence but this was soon forgotten. After a pause he changed his name to d'Arquier de Pellepoix and, an elegant figure with a monocle, he became a welcome guest in the cocktail circles of Franco's Spain. It was here that the enterprising correspondent of *L'Express* contacted him thirty-three years after the war was over. He was a sick man crippled by hardening of the arteries, but he still enjoyed the protection of many leading figures, military and political, and he met the correspondent's enquiries with amused condescension. The six million concentration camp deaths, he declared, were a Jewish invention. 'They were all of them exported to new homes in Central Europe,' he said. 'The only victims of the Auschwitz gas-ovens', he added, 'were fleas.' (I suppose he meant that their clothes were fumigated in preparation for their new life.) He refused to look at the photographs of the piles of gas-chamber victims. 'Jewish fakes!' he exclaimed.

The whole of France was moved by the new revelations. President Giscard d'Estaing and Prime Minister Barre warned about the treatment of their Nazi past on the television screen and the press. Simone Veil, the Minister of Health, was profoundly stirred. She had been deported to Auschwitz with her family at the age of fourteen.

'It is the first time since the war,' she said in the National Assembly, 'that anyone has dared to go so far.' There were pictures of Auschwitz and the other death camps shown on television and in the press. There was a clamour to have Darquier extradited. There was much indignation that French television refused to acquire the American series 'Holocaust'. 'Too expensive,' one network said, and an artist Marek Halter opened a fund for private donations to contribute to the cost.

Then the public prosecutor, acting on orders from the Minister of Justice, opened a new case against Darquier for 'defence of war-crimes and incitement to racial hatred'. But Spain has never extradited political offenders to France and time had run out under the twenty-year Statute of Limitations.

[1968/78]

19

THE KAGRAN GRUPPE

I believe one of the happiest times of my life was when I was working for the Austrian Jews in Vienna in 1938-9. It is strange to be happy when others are miserable, but all the people at the Freundeszentrum in the Singerstrasse were cheerful too. The reason surely is that we have always known of the immense unhappiness that all humanity has to suffer. We read of it in the newspapers and hear it on the radio but can do nothing about it.

Most people tied to a single job or profession die without exercising more than a tenth of their capacities. In the Singerstrasse for many months all my faculties were engaged and I exercised an intimate control over the lives of a great many people, and I believe I helped them.

Hitler brought into the world misery such as no man had previously conceived possible. It had to be combated. The British were slow to observe this. The Irish never did. As late as 1936 Lloyd George went to Germany and told Hitler he was the greatest German of his age. London's society hostesses flocked round Ribbentrop and received invitations to the Olympic Games which, thanks to Goëbbels, were a huge success. Predictably, the poor silly Duke and Duchess of Windsor visited the Führer.

The mood in Ireland was one of ignorant indifference. It was expressed in the Dàil in 1943 by a very pious Catholic, Oliver Flanagan. 'There is one thing', he said 'that the Germans did and that was to rout the Jews out of their country.' He added that we should rout them out of Ireland: 'They crucified our Saviour 1900 years ago and they have been crucifying us every day of the week.' No one contradicted him.

But I was as Irish as Oliver Flanagan and I was determined

that Jewish refugees should come to Ireland. At the time of the Anschluss the Quakers were settled in the Freundeszentrum in Vienna and through Friends' House in London I got permission to join them. The Freundeszentrum was a former nobleman's palace in the Singerstrasse and when I got there, together with a charming and energetic young Quaker called Mary Campbell, I was put in charge of the Kagran Gruppe, a group of Viennese Jews who had banded together for collective emigration.

My first few weeks at the Freundeszentrum were spent at a desk filling in hundreds of 'bogen', or emigration forms, for the crowds of applicants who turned up. After the usual questions about age, religion, profession, married or single, the women were asked, 'Can you cook, wash, scrub, knit?' The men had a corresponding questionnaire. Almost all the questions were answered in the affirmative. At the bottom one added one's comment. I do not know what happened to the stacks and stacks of bogen. Probably they were forwarded to the Friends' House in Euston Road and carefully filed. What would we have done if some instinct had told us of Auschwitz? Why was I the only non-Quaker there?

I think now it was obtuse of us not to have anticipated Auschwitz. I had walked along the Prater Strasse to the Prater, the great Viennese Park where bands played and stalls sold ice-cream and coffee. The street must have had a great many Jewish shopkeepers in it, because all the way down there were broken windows in front of looted shops with VERHOLUNG NACH DACHAU ('Gone for a rest-cure to Dachau') scrawled over the surviving panes, and the air was full of the mindless hatred which war, that fosters all our basest passions, would inevitably make murderous.

I speak German and French so I was shortly sent to the Conference on the problem of the German Jews at Evian, by the Lake of Geneva. The League of Nations had at last got to work and it was attended by representatives of all the countries in Europe and America. Vague gestures of goodwill were made. I talked to the two delegates from Ireland, or rather from the Irish Embassies in Paris and Berne. One remarked, 'Didn't we suffer like this in the Penal Days and nobody came to our help.'

When I got back I visited all the embassies to get visas for the emigrating Jews. There was a kindly official at the Mexican embassy who would sign an entry visa for anyone who asked.

Even though it might fail to get them into Mexico it would get them out of Austria. So many applicants arrived that he had to get his wife and family in to help him.

One day I visited the Peruvian embassy. It was a splendid building with a large map of Peru painted on the staircase. I entered a spacious room with well-filled bookcases and handsome furniture. At the far end was a small figure seated at a large desk. I assumed he was the Peruvian ambassador, though in fact it was probably the consul. After the Anschluss the ambassadors had all been transferred to Stuttgart or Berlin. I appealed to him to persuade his government to admit Viennese Jews. He looked at me doubtfully and then said: 'I was wondering if you could help me. You see, I too am a Jew and want to get out as soon as possible. I've just written a letter to Churchill. Do you think that a good idea?' 'It would be much better to write to Emma Cadbury,' I replied. He bowed but looked too proud to be interested.

At this time the Bolivian consulate was one of the most thronged in Vienna. The report had got round that land was being given to agriculturalists on favourable terms, and that engineers and craftsmen were required. Of the many that applied only a very few were accepted. In the autumn a group of about 200 Jews were urged to prepare immediately for the journey. While the relief organizations hurriedly helped with the official formalities, they themselves sold their possessions with desperate haste for whatever they could get for them. They kept only the barest necessities for the journey and such goods as they could carry in their trunks to their new home. A few days before the boat was due to sail they were informed that there had been a misunderstanding between the Gestapo and the Bolivian Consulate. No visas would be given for Bolivia and the expedition could not set off. The 200 settlers, now without homes or property, had to wander round the streets looking for hospitality from their friends.

At Eichmann's trial in Jerusalem in 1961 it emerged that he personally was responsible for providing the field in which the Kagran Gruppe was trained. When he was in Vienna emissaries from Palestine had approached him for help in the illegal immigration of Jews into British-ruled Palestine. 'He was polite,' they said, 'and even provided a farm and facilities for setting up vocational training camps for prospective immigrants. On one

199

occasion he expelled a group of nuns from a convent to provide a training camp for young Jews.'

Eichmann, like other Nazis in the early days, was sympathetic to Zionism and this lasted till 7th November 1938 when Ernst von Rath, the Third Secretary of the German embassy in Paris, ironically an anti-Nazi, was murdered by a 17-year-old Jewish youth Herschel Grynzpan, whose family had been deported to Poland. This led to Krystallnacht in November 1938, when all the synagogues in Berlin went up in flames, 7500 Jewish shop-windows were smashed and 20,000 Jews were taken off to concentration camps. This increased the tension in Vienna and ever more people joined the Kagran Gruppe.

I found a letter of that time describing the desperate atmosphere to my wife:

There was a meeting yesterday of the leading Jews. I was very much moved by their courage and seriousness and idealism and innocence, as it seemed to me. They spent about twenty minutes deciding whether they should take their mahogany sideboards and bamboo hat-racks by ship or not and describing them. They have to go first to Sweden (that is to say if anything comes of the scheme at all and they can raise £14,000) and then after they've had their 'umschulung' training in agriculture there, they go off to somewhere like Paraguay, or, if they are lucky to Colombia, where there is some sort of community settlement already. I said that even shipping furniture from Belgrade to Dubrovnik, as we had done, was far dearer than selling it and then buying new stuff. They looked shocked and I realized I had said something hurtful and callous about their homes, and that to many its furniture was an intimate part of their lives. They had grown up with it and it was full of memories. This was 'Papa's chair and this was Mutti's' and the more stuck in their ways and the more entrenched they are, the more terribly touching it is. However, I'm glad they did decide to bring only the most cherished pieces. This afternoon when I was alone the Controller of Foreign Currency in the biggest bank but one – quite a swell with an almost complete set of gold teeth – pleaded to be allowed to join the camp with his wife and go out with them. He produced an armful of testimonials, but how could he be any use there?

But the real time for seeing people is between nine and one thirty. I see about ten and by the time one has reached the tenth one is utterly drained of sympathy and ideas and resourcefulness. I just gaze at them and put a new nib in the pen and rearrange the papers on the desk. In some cases it's just a matter of advice, how to find the address of a relation in Cairo or Cincinnati or something like that. There is a tremendous drive on now to Aryanize all the gemeindehauser (blocks of flats) and private houses along main streets where flags have to be hung on important occasions. As a result four people who came to me yesterday have had a notice to quit by August 1st and nowhere to go. They might get taken in as tenants by a Jewish landlord, but what are they to do with their furniture? Aryans who take Jewish lodgers also are liable to lose their flats. There was one old gentleman yesterday with an ear-trumpet in a state of mind about his flat. It belonged to his wife's daughter who was illegitimate and consequently happened to be Aryan, but he was terrified of disgracing her by living with her and was going to move out. Another couple had married Aryanized daughters who were very anxious to suport them, but for the same reason they were frightened of embroiling them and wanted to emigrate. There was an old officer with a testimonial from his General about his bravery at the battle of Przemysl.

It's such a relief when one comes on a really nasty one, as one does, e.g. a Feinkost Erzeuger (maker of delicatessen), with a horrible Aryan wife who wanted to know if the Friends' House in Philadelphia would get her an affidavit if she became a Quaker. Then there was a young police-officer, very well-educated, and a dark scared fanatical writer on a fashion paper, dozens and dozens of Beamter, Buchalter, Mechaniker, Techniker and chauffeurs and garage proprietors. There was one young Jew who had become a Nazi and hoped to become an honorary Aryan but wasn't accepted. And yesterday at the end two women and a little girl turned up. I was so fuddled by that time I can't remember what they wanted but they suddenly quite spontaneously and untheatrically all three began to snivel.

A plump dark-haired woman, a Nazi named Baronin Rikki von Appell, was always straying into the Friends' Centre. I think her job was to keep us under observation and she was particularly concerned about me as I was not a Quaker. She knew about Quakers and remembered the good work they had done in Vienna in 1920; theViennese werestarving so the Quakers among other projects imported 1500 cows from Holland, to provide milk.

But what was I up to, a non-Quaker? She was puzzled and asked me to join her and a friend on a boating trip on the Danube. We started from Klosterneuburg and I was enchanted with the unspoilt beauty, the water lilies and scarlet willows growing beside the river bank so close to a great city. Her friend was a thin fair-haired woman with a slight limp. She told me she had been engaged to be married, but because of her limp the Nazis, for genetic reasons, refused to allow it. She did not seem particularly resentful. I satisfied Rikki's curiosity by telling her that, like the Quakers, I had come out to help the Jews. She said the Jews were parasites who had speculated on the dwindling value of the Austrian crown after 1918. I did not accept this but was too ignorant to comment.

If I'd been a Quaker I would have said that the Quakers would help anyone who was suffering unjustly. The Quakers helped the Social Democrats when in 1934 Chancellor Dollfuss, a so-called Christian Socialist or Fascist, had crushed them. In Emma Cadbury's brilliant account of this period, *A Three-Day War and Its Aftermath*, she wrote that this civil conflict in Austria was one of the main causes of the Second World War. The Nazi take-over of Austria without opposition from England or France had made Czechoslovakia, now surrounded on three sides, an easy victim which the great powers would hesitate to defend.

Had it not been for the Three Days' War Austria would have been well able to defend itself against the Nazis. Democracy had been growing there as in Germany before the collapse of the two empires in 1918, and in Austria the Social Democrats (socialists) then became the dominant power in Vienna. Emma Cadbury describes all that they did for the workers' libraries, adult education, hospitals, clinics, and above all housing. Before the war 73 per cent of the people had been living in two rooms or less. In 1922, 60,000 houses were built with space for trees and grass and flowers. It was a superb achievement.

'Thus,' writes Emma Cadbury, 'life was made easier for the proletariat and Communism found no foothold in Vienna.' But the Social Democrats had their enemies. Chief among them were the Christian Socialists, who were strongly influenced by the Catholic Church. They were extremely hostile to Hitler but regarded the Social Democrats as enemies of the Church who were impoverishing the middle and upper classes by overtaxation. The Social Democrats were ready to co-operate in fighting Hitler but the Christian Socialists could not wait. On 12 February 1934, with the approval of Chancellor Dollfuss, the Austrian army with the help of the Heimwehr, the army of the Christian Socialists, and the police made an assault on the Social Democrats. They and their army, the Schutzbund, were no match for the forces allied against them. Nearly 2000 were killed and some 5000 wounded. Many were executed and imprisoned. The

Quakers were quickly on the scene distributing food with funds that came through the International Federation of Trade Unions.

The Austrian Nazis must have taken heart when they saw this great split in the ranks of their opponents. On 25 July 1934, a group of them broke into the Chancellery and shot Dollfuss. It was thought that this might lead to an immediate Nazi take-over. But Schuschnigg managed to forestall this move and thirteen of the assassins were hanged.

Schuschnigg was summoned to Berchtesgarten and was bullied into signing a capitulation; as he had hoped, President Miklas refused to endorse it. Then he decided to hold a plebiscite, appealing for Social-Democratic support, promising to free their members from prison. March 14th, 1938, was to be the Great Day.

The vote would certainly have gone against the Nazis, so on 12 March, Hitler strutted into Austria. He crossed the frontier at Braunau and received a riotous welcome near Linz, his birthplace. Cardinal Innitzer ordered all the church bells in Austria to be rung. Schuschnigg was thrown into prison in the Gestapo headquarters and later was transferred to Dachau.

It was some months after this that I came to Vienna.

Typical of many is the story of the first Austrians I brought to Ireland. Erwin Strunz, an 'Aryan' with a Jewish wife and two small children, had been a trade union secretary with promise of a career in parliament in the Social Democratic Party till Dollfuss took over the government and routed the socialists. The Strunzes had no friends abroad and with a small son and a new-born baby they could not cross on foot over the mountains into Switzerland.

Erwin was advised by his Jewish friend Dr Schonfeld, President of the Austrian Atheists Association, to visit the Quaker Centre in Vienna. He had called on many Labour leaders and ecclesiastics. None of them could help. Then he remembered the work the Quakers had done in starving Vienna in 1920. With a letter from Dr Schonfeld he visited Emma Cadbury at the Freundeszentrum. It was there I first met them at my desk and filled in their two bogen. Erwin told me he was an atheist and Lisl, who had big black eyes and a lively but firm expression, said to me, 'I will be a Mohammedan if it will help my children'. I entered them both as 'konfessionslos' (without Church), which in fact was the creed of very many Viennese Jews.

Emma Cadbury gave permission for 200 Kagraners to meet in the Quaker Centre and discuss their plans. They begged her to help them emigrate and form an agricultural co-operative overseas. Erwin and Lisl went early every morning with little Peter and all the others on the long tram journey to Kagran, a suburb on the left bank of the Danube. The group worked under the supervision of armed guards from the Gestapo who relished watching middle-aged Jews, many of them once rich sedentary businessmen, cutting trees, digging irrigation trenches, making a road; men who had never before held a shovel in their hands. They worked all the summer, while Emma Cadbury, Mary Campbell and I tried desperately to get entry permits for them to Peru, Bolivia, Rhodesia, Colombia, Canada. As I had already realized at Evian, nobody wanted them.

Erwin and his wife were in great danger. They slept every night in fear of the heavy knock at 5 a.m., the hour usually chosen by the Gestapo for the departure to Dachau. The Viennese Nazi Party thought there might be leader material in Erwin so the Party solicitor offered to arrange a divorce. He would be housed, temporarily, in the factory to avoid painful meetings with his ex-wife and children, and a blue-eyed Nazi woman had agreed to marry him. He was told he was lucky as she had a house of her own and some money. He would ultimately be transferred to the synthetic petrol factory at Dusseldorf and allotted a car, a monoplane and a villa. He could attend the university and later be drafted to the Party Leader School in Nuremberg. It was a dazzling offer so when he did not reply the Party grew suspicious. He hurriedly took sick-leave and simulated a nervous breakdown while still digging at Kagran. The Gruppe had seemed to be a way out of his difficulties, but now the future looked very menacing.

On 16th September 1938 he was rung up after midnight: 'Erwin. You have 48 hours to get out. Your arrest and deportation to Dachau has been decided.' He recognized the voice; it was a friend who had joined the Nazi Party but worked on behalf of the underground. (There were many such.) Erwin was thunderstruck, for though he had anticipated trouble he had not expected it so soon. He came to me next day in the Singerstrasse so hopeless and dispirited he could hardly speak. I finally found out what had happened and explained the situation to Emma

Cadbury. After a good deal of telephoning, somehow she obtained entry permits for England which arrived within two hours.

The Kagran Gruppe had set aside funds for the fares of emigrants which Hans Koch had entrusted to the treasurer, Viktor Strasser, and they were kept in a moneybox with two keys of which Koch had one, but when he went to get the fare for the Strunz' journey he found the box empty. Strasser had stolen it all. We were forced to apply, as often before, to the Gildemeester Fund. (Gildemeester was a Dutch philanthropist to whose outstanding generosity in these terrible times I have seldom seen any reference.) The Strunzes got off on the train to Ostend and I telephoned to Peggy, my wife, to meet them at Charing Cross. After they arrived in London, owing to the strain of recent weeks, Erwin had a genuine breakdown and Peggy took them all back to her mother's home at Annaghmakerrig in Co. Monaghan.

After my own departure from Vienna I went on trying to get accommodation for the Kagran Group in Ireland and England, but Mary Campbell, who had been in charge of it with me in Vienna, was drafted by the Quakers to other work and replaced by a woman who knew nothing of Vienna or Kagran and did not speak German, so the heart went out of the idea of group emigration. She simply selected those most easy to place. In this way she was able to dispose of Hecht, the Kagran bee-keeper, Kalan, one of the very few agriculturalists, and Weinberg, our butcher and his wife: she was delighted with herself for this achievement, particularly when she had her picture in the *Daily Mirror*.

We were left with a goldsmith, seven academics, a hairdresser, an umbrella maker, and many clerks, teachers and shopkeepers. It soon emerged that simply shelter and support in a friendly ambience was all that could be organized. This we achieved through the generosity of various private people in Ireland such as Arland Ussher in Cappagh, Co. Waterford, and Sir John Keane at Ardmore. I went to Bunnaton, a youth hostel in Donegal that was empty in the winter months. The parish priest, Fr O'Doherty, wanted to build a road from Bunnaton to Port Salon and hoped the refugees would help him. We also found places in England for three groups of Kagranners. Inevitably in Ireland the sectarian question arose and, I believe, our Irish

Refugee Committee was unwittingly to blame for this. Members of committees seem always to be chosen to represent different interests whereas they should only have one interest, in this case the defence of the persecuted.

The long peace was about to end and the fate of the Jews had not precipitated that 'saeva indignatio' in the rest of Europe that would have given encouragement to the many hundreds of thousands of non-Jewish Germans who hated Hitler and, in 1944, welcomed the rising against him. Thousands must have died fighting for a Fatherland that had betrayed them.

Lately I came across a newspaper report of 10 December 1938 which I had cut out at this time. It tells of a great meeting in the Mansion House, London, on behalf of the Jews. The Archbishop of Canterbury spoke of 'the systematic persecution without parallel even in the Middle Ages', and the 'incredible mental and moral torture' to which the Jews were being subjected. Cardinal Pacelli sent the following telegram:

The Holy Father's thoughts and feelings will be correctly interpreted by declaring he looks with humane and Christian approval on every effort to show charity and give effective assistance to all those who are innocent victims in these sad times of distress.

The tone of these two communications is very different. The Archbishop is explicit, the Cardinal is vague and general, but I do not think one can argue from this that the Englishman's heart was the warmer. It is the difference between the leader of a more or less homogeneous body and the head of a worldwide and heterogeneouscommunity of believers. The Pope had followers in every land, all the Archbishop's were in one. Our disappointment in Pius XII springs from the delusive hopes that have been placed in universalism, in ecumenism. Now we know that if Christendom were ever to speak with one official voice, it would be a mouse's squeak. There would be so many conflicting sympathies to reconcile that in the end silence might seem best.

Catholics claim the Pope was impotent and I believe that was so. For example it was said that the Pope saved 400,000 Jews in Hungary. But these Jews owed their lives principally to the fact that Roosevelt had followed up an ultimatum about the deportations with a tremendous bombardment of Budapest on 2nd July 1944.

As it happens, we were all wrong about the 400,000. It emerged at the Eichmann trial that he had defied all the neutral nations, Roosevelt and the Pope, and deported 1500 Hungarian Jews in mid-July, and in October the shortage of labour in Germany was so great that they asked for a further 100,000. Since trains were no longer running, they were obliged to walk. Of 800,000 Hungarian Jews, some 100,000 survived.

Some are surprised that people are not more impressed by the compliments paid to the Vatican by the Jewish leaders and the fact that the Rabbi of Rome even gave up his Jewish faith. But are the few who are dragged ashore entitled to give thanks on behalf of the millions who drowned? And is it not easy to undervalue the formidable social power of the community? The Jews were penniless refugees in foreign lands. Would many countries (Ireland for example) have accepted them readily if they had publicly claimed that the Pope or the Church had failed them in their hour of need? The Austrians who came to Ireland never even blamed Cardinal Innitzer, the Austrian Primate, who ordered all the church-bells in Austria to be rung when Hitler entered Austria to forestall the plebiscite. In reply to Cardinal Pacelli's cautious telegram, they themselves sent a very grateful one from Ireland to Rome. The Jews have reason to be apprehensive, even when a non-Jew like Hochhuth criticizes the Pope on their behalf. When *The Representative* was played in Paris, demonstrators leapt into the auditorium crying 'A bas les Juifs!'

It is clear that in times of stress parliaments and Churches are peculiarly subject to mass-pressure and one cannot expect too much from them. Nobody, whatever his faith, who had read the fulsome greeting from the leaders of the Evangelical Church in Austria to Hitler, 'the Tool in the hands of the Almighty' and 'the Fulfiller of the Divine Will for the Salvation of our People', could be confident that his own Church would have shown greater courage or foresight.

In the twentieth, as in the first century, we find the burden of Christianity borne by solitary and often anonymous individuals.

[1988]

PART FOUR
FAMILY

20

A FRAGMENT OF AUTOBIOGRAPHY

My father farmed about six hundred acres, half of them at Burnchurch farm near Bennettsbridge and half at Drumherin, some six miles north-east of Kilkenny City. From the time I was eight I used to bicycle with him to Drumherin where the two Phelan brothers, Johnnie, who was enormously fat, and Paddy, who was thin, were stewards. It is, I believe, the wild country where John Banim placed his story, 'Crohoore of the Billhook'. For a long way the road to Ballyfoyle was lined with tall beech trees soaring above the banks on which moss, eight inches deep, half smothered the primroses and ferns within it. There was a big lake on the farm, the Kilkenny reservoir, which my father had sold to the Corporation. He and Paddy and Johnnie went round the fields prodding the bullocks. Paddy had a stick which he dipped in cow dung and slapped on the back of those which were to go to the fair. My father must have hoped I would make some interested comment, but I was always thinking of something else and never did.

Burnchurch farm, where a third brother, Joe Phelan, was the steward, is only half a mile away from Maidenhall and is beside Burnchurch rectory which my great-grandfather had built for himself five miles from Burnchurch church. He was a portly pre-Disestablishment rector and a friend of the Bishop, who pressed on him a second parish, that of Trim in Co. Meath. He persuaded his son, Richard, who was at Balliol, to come home and be rector of Trim. Richard, whose memory I revere, was a distinguished archaeologist who lived out the rest of his life in Trim and published with the local printer a still valuable history of the town, republished in 1978 by the Meath Archaeological Society. He was married to Harriet, the liveliest of Maria Edgeworth's many half-sisters.

To his eldest son, James, my great-grandfather gave Priestown, the small family home near Dunboyne in Meath which had been Butler property since the time of Edward II. After his father's death, when the remarkable twelfth Baron Dunboyne had died, my great-uncle James was one of several distant cousins who claimed to succeed him. He failed. The twelfth Baron was the Roman Catholic Bishop of Cork and, sooner than be succeeded by remote Protestant relations, he had defied the Pope and married, hoping to rear a son whom he would bring up in the Catholic faith. But he had no son, and he got an appalling denunciation in Latin from Pius VI for 'living in foul concubinage with a heretic woman'.

Though we live in Kilkenny we are only distantly related to the Butlers of Ormonde who had lived in Kilkenny Castle since 1391. Since they are gone and their memory is fading, in 1967 I formed the Butler Society with the present Lord Dunboyne so that a large and once powerful family should not lose its place in history. I only rarely met my Priestown cousins but I had very many English cousins through my English grandmother. Till I went to school my father taught us maths, my grandmother taught us history and my mother taught us French and English and at the same time managed to run the dairy and keep ducks and hens. She used to send them, wrapped up in butter-paper, to relations in England, in particular to my cousin Alice Graves, who in return sent me the suits that her two sons, Cecil and Adrian, had out-grown. They were at school in Berkshire and I was appalled one day to learn that I was to follow them to Bigshotte Rayles. It was in the prep-school belt of the Home Counties, a land of pine trees and heather and chalk and golf courses.

It was so extraordinary to be dumped in this strange place that I thought my parents had given me away. My first few weeks I wandered round in a swoon and when anyone asked a question I gaped at them. When one day Miss Reeve, the headmaster's sister, took my temperature (two boys had measles and lived behind a flapping carbolic sheet) I bit the thermometer in half; she tried again and I bit the second one.

I have forgotten the names of thousands of former acquaintances but I remember the names and faces of all the boys at Bigshotte. I remember all the shrubs between the pavvy and the swimming-bath. Hundreds of episodes present themselves in heavy type. Everything else since is in italics. It is said of prep schools 'that they rub the corners off'. This agonizing process was applied to me, and it could not have been more painful and irreversible were it done with a pincers and a file. I was well fed and never beaten or much bullied. Indeed, I was the favourite pupil of Mr Reeve, the headmaster, and he cast a blight over one Easter holiday by coming to stay. He was an excellent teacher and, thanks to him, I got the top mathematical scholarship to Charterhouse.

My enthusiasm for mathematics started when I got to trigonometry and discovered there was an abstract world which ran parallel to the treacherous concrete one and could not be reached from it. I had stopped believing in Heaven and everything I had been told about it soon after I got to Bigshotte. (How could Mr Reeve or anyone else possibly know?) I was proud that, when the prayer-bell rang, I began my second prayer, the one my mother taught me, 'Lord God, if thou existest. . .'. Here in trigonometry was an escape route I could believe in.

Ronnie Huggard and I were to sit for scholarships to Charterhouse and when the other boys had drunk their cocoa and gone to bed Mr Reeve set us problems (he called them 'riders') to do in the empty classroom. It was wonderfully peaceful. We could hear Mr Reeve reading aloud to Miss Reeve on the Private Side, the flames flickering in the dying fire, Rex, the school dog, snoring, and upstairs Matron saying 'Lights out!' It was a magical hour. At half-term Ronnie and I went up to Charterhouse and some weeks later the news came that I had got my scholarship. There was a whole holiday to celebrate my victory and it was spent playing cricket, though I would much rather have spent it indoors doing riders with Ronnie. But Ronnie was weeping bitterly. He had yearned to go to Charterhouse but without a scholarship his father could not afford to send him.

Mr Reeve made me Head Boy early on. Since all I wanted was to get away this did not mean much to me. It was announced at Evening Prayers and this time I heard the sound of Bernie Cooper snuffling piteously behind me as we knelt. He had thought he was going to be Head Boy.

Years later an unpleasant idea occurred to me. Perhaps Mr Reeve favoured me not because he thought me interesting and clever but because Cousin Alice Graves was Sir Edward Grey's sister and he was English Foreign Secretary at the time. Their mother and my English grandmother were sisters. I only knew of him because Granny used to write him disapproving letters about his commitment to Home Rule.

About Charterhouse there is no need to say much as Robert Graves, who was a nephew of Cousin Alice, has said it all in *Goodbye To All That*. He reports a conversation he had with Nevill Barbour, who became a friend of mine at Oxford. It wouldn't be enough, they agreed, to dismiss the whole school and staff and start all over again. No. 'The school buildings were so impregnated with what was called the public school spirit, but what we felt as fundamental badness, that they would have to be demolished and the school rebuilt elsewhere and its name changed.'

At Charterhouse, except in class, there was no mixing between the houses and the scholars sat together at a small table in Upper Long. There were two other scholars at Verites but I found them both uncongenial and there was no escape from them. As for the masters, all the younger ones were at war and old ones were rescued from retirement to replace them. A. H. Tod, my dreadful one-eyed housemaster, must have been one of these.

My love affair with trigonometry ended during my first term, when in broad daylight Mr Tuckey, a Cambridge Wrangler, told us all about Functions in a crowded classroom in the Science Building. It was no longer numinous and mystical and I scarcely minded not understanding. Next term the headmaster Frank Fletcher (he was called Fifi and his wife Mimi) shifted me over to Greek. I caught up on it fairly quickly. Mr Dames Longworth, the fifth form master, was a tweedy Irish gentleman from Co. Westmeath. He swaggered about the room twirling his moustache and swaying his shoulders dramatically as he recited Greek iambics in a booming voice. 'Any old crocks for Studio?' he used to exclaim when the drawing master poked his head round the door to collect two pupils who were excused OTC (Officers' Training Corps) once a week. He was wealthy and had made himself irremovable by presenting the school with a racquets court. He and A. H. Tod had together compiled a famous book, *Tod and Longworth's Unseen Passages of Greek and Latin Translation*, which circulated round all the public schools of Britain. Tod's other distinction was that years before, drilling the OTC in Founder's Court, he had stepped back into the fountain. In the New Bugs exam at Verites every examinee was expected to know this.

As a housemaster Tod was a disaster. He was becoming senile and he never knew my name. Once he stopped me and said: 'Heh, Butler, send Butler to me!' My happiest day at Verites was when it caught fire and we had to toss all Tod's furniture and his collection of brass horse ornaments out of the window. I was the school swot and I sat in my study poring over Virgil and Homer but without real enjoyment, because Tod and Longworth seemed to lie between. I climbed very quickly to the top of the sixth and my mother was worried that I was not Head Boy or even a School Monitor. It was their privilege to stroll round Founder's Court, hands in pockets and coat swept behind them, in a special manner. I did not mind. As at Bigshotte, all I wanted was to be away.

At the end of the summer term in 1918 my moment came. I got all the five scholarships and prizes that were available in the classical sixth. Since my academic career ended disastrously and since they may still exist, I do not think it is boastful to give their names. I got the Talbot Scholarship and Medal for Greek, the Thackeray Prize for English Literature (Thackeray had been at Charterhouse), the Petilleau Prize for French and the top leaving scholarship. For many terms I had got the Form Prize, but as the war was on all prize money was given to the Red Cross and we got slips to stick into the books we already had and I think most of the money for the Petilleau Prize went to the Red Cross, too, because I was given *Princess Mary's Book of France*, which I had no use for, and there was no money for a second prize. When M. Petilleau, who lived in Godalming, heard this, he was very much distressed and went to his bookshelves and took down the complete works of Molière, bound in calf, and gave it as second prize. I was very good at Latin verse, which seems to me now the most futile of accomplishments and, on the strength of a translation of part of Shelley's *Adonais* into Lucretian hexameters, Fifi decided to send me up for the scholarship at Balliol, where he had been himself.

I failed but got the top scholarship at St John's. Fifi called me into his study to tell me. I was too old to cry like Ronnie Huggard but I had been humiliated and wanted to leave in a blaze of glory, so I did cry. Fifi patted me on the shoulder and said something about the Southern Irish temperament and that

I wanted to be 'aut Caesar aut nullus'. There were still two terms to put in before Oxford but I told my parents I was leaving. It was an unheard of thing as the war was over, but I got them to agree.

My mother had wanted me to go into the Foreign Office as she thought Edward Grey might take an interest in me but my father still hoped I might be a farmer, so it was agreed I should take an agricultural course at Reading University where Willie de Burgh, an Irishman, a cousin through the Greys, was Professor of Philosophy, and he and his family became life-long friends. Eric Dodds was lecturing there, too, a stage in his progress from teaching at Kilkenny College to being Regius Professor of Greek at Oxford. In his book *Missing Persons* he has written a charming account of de Burgh. I was happy and free for the first time. I learned no agriculture and I do not believe that the demobilized officers for whom the course was planned learnt any either. It had been hastily put together by experts on soil and pasture, book-keeping and the building of pig-sties and cow sheds (for this we started at the beginning with slides of Doric and Ionic columns), but the farm was some distance away and we only rarely cast a glance at cows and crops. Yet there was something conclusive about it. I had a younger brother, and nature clearly did not want me to be a farmer.

When I was fifteen I had passed through Dublin, still smoking after the Easter Rebellion, and I had decided I was an Irish Nationalist. This led to constant quarrelling with my family, which became worse when I found an ancient copy of *Robert Elsmere* by Mrs Humphry Ward at home and became a 'Free Thinker'. This was an exciting new phrase for me and I felt proud that unknown to myself I had been one at Bigshotte three years before and had never felt, like Elsmere, 'a castaway on a shoreless sea'. On the contrary, it had opened up to me the new abstract world of trigonometry and helped me to get my scholarship to Charterhouse. Elsmere's friend, Henry Grey, said to him consolingly: 'The parting with the Christian mythology is the rending asunder of bones and marrow. It means parting with half the confidence and joy of life. But have trust! Reason is God's like all the rest. Trust it. I trust Him. The leading strings of the past are dropping away from you; they are dropping from all the world.' I found this intoxicating, but who could I talk to about it? I had to go to Mr Tod with the two other scholars to

216

be prepared for confirmation. But how could I tell that dreadful old man in the armchair that the leading strings of the past had dropped away from me and that I did not wish to be confirmed? No I couldn't, not possibly, and so the Bishop of Winchester laid his hands on me and asked God that I should daily increase in the Holy Spirit more and more.

I consoled myself with the thought that when I got to Oxford all would be well again, but I found when I got there that Mrs Humphry Ward had become a sort of joke and nobody agonized about their doubts as Elsmere had done. Religion had become a subject, like Philosophy or Physics. You either took it or you didn't.

Yet in the lovely relaxed atmosphere I was no longer bored and I ceased to be a compulsive swot. Instead I was distracted by all that was new to hear and read and see.

There was still Plato and Thucydides and all the others, and Caesar and Virgil the third time round, but I could no longer concentrate. I never replaced my large Liddell & Scott's *Greek Lexicon*, which had got burnt in the Verites fire. For me only Lucretius survived the lecture-room and I still sometimes read him in an unscholarly way. It seems to me that if the atomic physicists who succeeded him two thousand years later had written in verse as he did, they would have seen that knowledge is only the beginning of wisdom. It is not safe in the hands of those who are not sensitive, as he was, to the beauty of the earth and the fragility of all we value.

I saw *John Bull's Other Island* and read *The Irish Statesman* and learnt about my own country, which I had previously only known from ground level. In the long vac. I met Sir Horace Plunkett and visited him at Kilteragh, the house he built for himself at Foxrock, which he had made a meeting place for all those who were interested in their country and, aided by his secretary, Gerald Heard, for all the leading writers of the day. It would be pointless to mention all the eminent people I met there as I was too inexperienced and shy to talk to them. Lennox Robinson took me to one of Yeats's evening parties and I went to AE's also, and a world unknown in Bennettsbridge opened up for me.

All my thoughts and hopes were about Ireland and I only got a second in Mods. But all the same two of the dons at St John's, Last and Costin, told me I was being considered for a Fellowship. I listened politely, with my mind elsewhere. I knew that

I would disappoint them in Greats.

Two years later I was back in Ireland with a bad degree, a third, or to be more precise no degree, because from what I took to be principle, but must have looked like pique, I refused to go through the ceremony. I cannot defend myself, as I gave offence to many who had nothing but good-will towards me.

My brother-in-law Tyrone Guthrie, who was at St John's with me, got a fourth but he had already found his vocation in the theatre and quickly recovered.

Cannot some alternative be found for exams in which ten people are bruised for every one who is exalted? One is not consulted when one's feet are put on the bottom rung of a ladder, and the higher you go the more painful the fall.

At home I found that the new world I had discovered was closing in again. The civil war had started, soon Kilteragh was to be burnt because Sir Horace was a senator, and AE was to die in England. Yet before this happened Plunkett urged me to join the County Libraries. He had used his influence with the Carnegie Trust to persuade it to start them in Ireland. To AE in the co-operative village the library was to have been the intellectual centre, while the creamery was the economic one. It was he who sent me to learn the trade in Ballymena, the headquarters of the Co. Antrim libraries. The organizing librarian in Dublin was Lennox Robinson, the playwright.

I have written about the libraries in *Irish Writing* of July 1949. They were a cultural bridge between north and south and I believe a great opportunity was lost in Ireland when, owing to an unhappy episode at the Dublin headquarters, their control, while they were still in embryo, was transferred to Dunfermline in Scotland.

This is how it happened. In August 1924 a short-lived periodical *To-morrow* published a story by Lennox Robinson called 'The Madonna of Slieve Dun', which the clerical members of the governing body considered blasphemous. They called for Robinson's resignation. The Carnegie Trust was informed and, unwilling to take sides in such a sensitive issue, they abolished the Central Organization in Dublin and resumed control from Dunfermline. From then on each County Library had to work on its own and the happy days, when all the librarians north and south of the border knew each other and visited each other and sought for advice in Dublin, were over. Till then writers had been in charge of all the County Libraries. There was Lennox Robinson and his assistant, Tom MacGreevy, a poet, in Dublin; Robert Wilson, a poet, in Co. Sligo, and Geoffrey Phibbs, a poet, and his wife, the artist Norah McGuinness, in Co. Wicklow; Frank O'Connor in Cork; Helen Roe, an archaeologist, in Co. Leix. Frank O'Connor has written of this period, his apprenticeship, in *My Father's Son*, first in Sligo and then in Wicklow with Geoffrey Phibbs, of whom he has given a delightful account.

I have always blamed Lennox Robinson for the break-up of our little community. His story was unimportant and sooner than take his stand for 'intellectual freedom', which is always at risk in Ireland, he should have resigned and so ensured that the Central Organization survived in Dublin. Soon after this I left the libraries.

Dublin had been in the past, and should be in the future, the cultural if not the political centre of Ireland.

I had a motor bicycle and through my years in the County Libraries I discovered the varied beauties of my country and the rich diversity of its people. Why is it that now we look at the beauty mainly as something we can sell to tourists, and the diversity of its people, their faith and their loyalties, not as an enrichment but a source of bitter antagonism?

I believe it was from AE that I learnt to be an Utopian. He recalled that it was in the small states of Greece, each scarcely bigger than an Irish county, that all our arts and sciences were first developed. What happened once can happen again and he saw the future of Ireland as a union of small co-operative communities. There is no trace of this now, but we have only to wait. The great metropolitan civilization, which has sucked all the vision and enterprise from the provinces, is already under threat. It has armed the ignorant and two embattled mouse-brained dinosaurs, one in the east, one in the west, confront each other. Will they both perish without progeny or will we find some way of liberating ourselves from our machines so that once more as men we can handle man-sized problems?

When my father died in 1941 I came home with my wife Peggy to live in Bennettsbridge. I brought home with me some refugees from Vienna, where after the Anschluss I had been working with the Quakers at the Freundeszentrum in Singerstrasse, and I soon found friends in Kilkenny. There was James Delehanty, who ran

The Kilkenny Magazine to which many later well-known writers contributed. There was the Kilkenny Archaeological Society, which with friends I revived in Kilkenny after a coma of fifty years. It is still thriving. There was also the Kilkenny Arts Society through which in 1952 we started the first Kilkenny Debate. It was on Partition. There were protests in Stormont and fury in Kilkenny and extra guards were drafted into the town. James Douglas, Secretary of the Unionist Council, and Colonel Topping, the Chief Whip, debated Partition with Sean MacBride and Eoin O'Mahony. Myles Dillon was in the Chair. That was the first of nine or ten peacefully contentious occasions. The debate on Neutrality with Basil Liddell Hart, the great military expert, and Brigadier Dorman O'Gowan would still be relevant today. I believe passionately in Irish neutrality, not an ignoble one as in Hitler's war, but one in which each citizen was on a war footing, a war for peace. Three Irishmen have thought in that direction: AE, Paddy Kavanagh and Bernard Shaw, and a plan for civil conscription has been sketched by AE in *The National Being*.

Then there was the Kilkenny Art Gallery Society, which after the death of the founder, George Pennefeather, fell on evil times. It had a new and splendid revival when Lord Ormonde gave Kilkenny Castle to the nation on 12 August 1967 and a spacious, well-planned art gallery was developed from the kitchen premises on the lower ground floor. My wife, Peggy, is its secretary.

I believe that it is in the first twenty-five years of our lives that our characters are shaped and our tastes are formed, and that the rest of our lives are spent either deploying our education, if we are at peace with it, or, if we are at war with it, making some compromise between what is congenital and what is acquired. I was at war with mine on an unremarkable battlefield and I have told in *Escape from the Anthill* whatever seems to have had slightly more interest than if, like satisfied people, I had had a nine-to-five life with a pension at sixty.

Like all my family I have loved growing things. My father was a skilled gardener and strawberries and seakale went in quantities to the Dublin market. He had a gardener and was able to draft extra help as well as manure from the farm, when he needed it. He planted espalier trees round the four quarters of the walled garden. It is over an acre and most of the espaliers are now gone except for a huge and prolific Bramley Seedling that has lost all but three of its eight arms. Till recently we were able to send in fruit and vegetables to the weekly Country Market, which, now that the creameries are gone, seems with its many branches to be the last trace of Plunkett's and AE's co-operative Ireland.

My greenhouses are now tumbling down and I use only a quarter of the garden; with reduced household and elderly appetites it is enough. But gardens, unlike houses, are easily restored and I see nothing final about this.

Can one write in the country far away from publishers and editors? It's difficult but not impossible. I published my first book, *Ten Thousand Saints* (1972), whose argument I still stand over, in Freshford, Co. Kilkenny; my present publisher lives at Gigginstown in Co. Westmeath; and I had a long connection with Irish and English journals till they mostly died, and also with Radio Éireann and the BBC Third Programme.

I take comfort from the fact that two centuries ago, Richard and Elizabeth Griffith, who lived here at Maidenhall, ran a flax mill on the river Nore and became well known writers in England in their day.

All culture was not then as now focussed on the capital, yet everything changes with incredible rapidity, and no one can predict what the future holds.

[1987]

221

21

AUNT HARRIET

When she got old and ill my grandmother grew frightened of being buried alive and she constantly asked for assurance that she would be given an autopsy. It was a persistent fear. 'She's going on about old Topsy again,' my mother said once, when coming out of her room. My mother was under great strain and I was no use to her.

I was at Oxford and found it a place of such abundance that Ireland and everyone in it, particularly my relations, were diminished. I was incessantly carping at them. In England we were nobody, while in Ireland, I maintained, if we gave it our first loyalty we could be somebody.

When Aunt Harriet, my father's sister, died, I went with my parents to keep Aunt Florence company at Lavistown. It is a small Georgian house with white Venetian blinds, built for the manager of the marble works by the founder William Colles. The marble works were still functioning in a desultory way just below Lavistown on the banks of the Nore. My father and mother slept in the big room over the dining-room where the coffin was laid on two chairs under the window. I slept in the small dressing-room off it.

Lavistown, which was four miles away from Maidenhall, was almost a second home to us; we were often there. I was very fond of Aunt Harriet, who superintended the cooking and the cook, Ellen, while Aunt Florence looked after the garden and the gardener, Donovan. We used to see more of Aunt Harriet because she had a bicycle, while Aunt Florence had to get Donovan to harness Maureen, the fat white pony. Aunt Harriet usually bicycled over with a cake in the basket on the handlebars and *The Christian Science Monitor* under it, for she was both a Christian Scientist and a Gaelic Leaguer. 'Well, chickabiddies!'

she exclaimed when she saw us. The cake she gave to my mother, *The Christian Science Monitor* to us children, ostensibly because of the Children's page, but I'm sure she thought some effluence of her faith might reach us through it. The stories were usually about dressed-up rabbits, mice, bluebottles; more moral than Beatrix Potter but less entertaining. Any message they contained was lost on us, but I was offended on Aunt Harriet's behalf when my mother said, 'Anyway, it's good thick paper; wonderful for packing eggs.'

My mother said Aunt Harriet became a Christian Scientist because a certain Dr Davis had failed to meet her under the clock on the platform at Kingsbridge Station in Dublin. She became a Gaelic Leaguer, I expect, because of the Cuffes who lived at Sheestown, a small house the other side of the Nore. Otway Cuffe was the brother and heir of the Earl of Desart, who lived at Desart Court about ten miles to the west. Mrs Cuffe was the daughter of a Cornish nobleman and they had thrown all their hereditary prestige, which in those days was considerable, into the Gaelic Revival, the development of a unique Irish civilization independent of politics. His sister-in-law, Lady Desart, had, as I have related in *Escape from the Anthill*, put her vast wealth largely at Otway Cuffe's disposal for the development of local industries. Though the bulk of the Unionists were sceptical, the Cuffes had many disciples. The Gaelic movement interested Aunt Harriet, while Aunt Florence was absorbed by home industries and craft work, and they had a large framed photograph of Otway Cuffe in the dining-room at Lavistown.

All this might seem irrelevant to the story I have to tell about Aunt Harriet. It is a very brief story but nothing at all if I do not convey the closeness I felt to that body in the box. Love? Affection? Admiration? I think absolute involvement is the right phrase. She must have suspected in me, when I was quite small, some germ of heterodoxy of the kind she had nursed in herself. One day, when I was playing on the gravel at Lavistown, I fell and scraped my leg. I pointed out to Aunt Harriet that it was bleeding. 'It's nothing,' she said and put a piece of stamp paper on it. I pulled it off the moment she was out of sight and never told my mother, who would have been angry; Christian Science was unpopular in those days because a co-religionist of Aunt Harriet's, Mrs Tighe of Woodstock, refused to have a doctor for her son and he died.

My two aunts went on sketching holidays every spring to Vernet les Bains but one summer Aunt Harriet went to Boston for some special celebration of Mary Baker Eddy, the great prophetess and heresiarch of Christian Science. My mother thought she might marry an elderly Christian Scientist there and feared for our prospects. We had always held that money that you inherit, unlike money that you earn, belongs to the family. We had forebears called Kingston who owned a shipyard in Cork and, when it closed, retained the ground rents of the buildings that went up on the quays beside the Lee. The ground rents passed on to their descendants, getting less and less with each genera-tion, together with some good miniatures of themselves in a blue velvet frame by Frederick Buck of Cork. We got the miniatures and my aunts the ground rents.

Aunt Harriet came back much invigorated from Boston. She had been also to the Niagara Falls. Mrs Eddy was dead at the time but she had seen her house and I think the cradle where she had been a baby. She had worshipped in the Mother Church of Christ Scientist and had not brought back a Christian Scientist husband. She would like to have told us more about Boston but everybody fidgetted uncomfortably when she started to talk of Mrs Eddy and asked her feverishly about the Niagara Falls.

Aunt Harriet was the strictest sort of Christian Scientist. She never admitted to any illness. She never went to a dentist but let her teeth fall out so that her cheeks contracted round three or four solitary tusks. This did nothing for her appearance. Aunt Florence had frequent small illnesses and many visits from the doctor. There must have been some snappishness between the sisters but we children never heard a word of it. We squabbled as much as most families do, but confronted by the outside world we were loyal to each other.

In those days, the Sinn Feiners were in the habit of visiting people, two by two and often by night, asking them for money for 'dependents of the Irish Republicans'. They went to Lavis-town one night and Aunt Harriet had looked out of her bedroom window and said reproachfully that she would give them nothing, that she had given up the Gaelic League when it had become political and when the Sinn Feiners had started a cam-paign of violence. After this little lecture they went away.

I told this to a friend of my own age who lived near by. 'I

don't wonder', she said, 'the Shinners got a shock and went off when Old Harriet poked her face out at them.' I took offence and told her she had no right to talk like that. She said pacifically: 'You should see my Aunt Eileen.'

I have left Aunt Harriet in her coffin a long way behind, but I am thinking of the memories she took with her; they were all unimportant but the past is a mosaic of tiny pieces, a fragment of a larger picture, Ireland in the twenties and the last days of the Anglo-Irish, and I will continue with more minutiae.

In the days before the War and the 1916 Rising, the more enlightened of the Anglo-Irish were trying desperately to identify themselves with Ireland. Aunt Harriet organized the first local Feis, an ancient festival of song and dance and miscellaneous junketting which centuries before took place at Tara. At the Kilkenny Feis there were competitions for Irish dancing and singing, lace-making, cake, jam, section honey and craft work. When it was all over Aunt Harriet was presented by the committee with a 'Tara' brooch, a richly ornamented safety pin with which the ancient Irish held their clothes together, mass produced from originals in the National Museum.

The Gaelic League was not 'political' in those days and even the British saw nothing against it. When Lady Aberdeen, Ireland's all but last Vice-Reine, came down to open our local concert hall, she defied the ridicule of the Anglo-Irish neighbours by dressing herself and the ladies of the party in emerald green with Tara brooches. She and her husband were very Scottish; he wore the Gordon tartan and they wrote a book called *We Twa*. They bred Aberdeen terriers and were Aberdonianly thrifty, and it was one of their aims to show how very Scottish one could be and yet loyal to the Crown. Why could not the Irish be the same? She entertained very little in the Vice-Regal Lodge, but started a campaign against tuberculosis with no political overtones, and motored all over Ireland trying with some success to introduce village nurses into every community.

Despite all this they were unpopular with both the more orthodox Gaels and ordinary Unionists; they were suspected of 'liberalism' which in Ireland was anathema to the traditional Unionist and one of our neighbours wrote a poem about them of which I can only remember one line: 'They cut the penny buns in half when Larkin came to tea.' (Larkin was a celebrated labour leader.)

The Cuffes and Aunt Florence and my mother all threw themselves into the crusade against tuberculosis (Aunt Harriet believed it was a delusion of the mind) and I think the Bennettsbridge village nurse was among the first in Ireland.

When Lord Aberdeen retired in 1915 he was made a Marquess and, conscious of his work for Ireland, he chose the title of Aberdeen and Tara, but the use of this most famous of all Irish placenames by a Scottish peer gave great offence. On leaving they sent photographs of themselves with an Aberdeen terrier beside them and one of the recipients wrote a letter which got great publicity: 'Thank you very much for the beautiful photograph of yourselves and your little dog Tara.' They changed Tara to Temair, which is a more ancient version of Tara but, as few knew this, no one objected.

Behind Lavistown is a big house, Leyrath, where Sir Charles Wheeler Cuffe, a distant relative of the Desarts, lived with his cousin Baroness Prochaska, an Austrianized Czech who was full of enthusiasm for home industries and handicrafts. She was very plain with projecting eyes and teeth and a gobbly Central European voice. I expect she knew the Czech language but only spoke it to her inferiors. She must have considered that the Anglo-Irish were a little like the Austro-Czechs, whose doom like theirs was only a few years away. She took up bee-keeping vigorously and prevailed on the County Council to appoint a Bee-Keeping Instructor. She had a row of hives at Leyrath with names like Peace, Love, Harmony. I don't know whether it was she or Otway Cuffe who was responsible for the Carpentry Instructor who travelled round the country villages. In Bennettsbridge he gave instruction to some twenty local boys in my father's barn once a week. I was taught with the other boys of my own age to make a small bracket on which to put a Holy Lamp. I was eight at the time and very class-conscious but had never learnt to say 'Please sir, can I leave the room?' And something awful happened that made the other boys titter and the Instructor pause to give me good advice. I thought of it with shame for months and months. This is the first time I've ever mentioned it.

The Baroness bought a horse-drawn coffee-van and got up every fair day at six a.m. and, joined sometimes by Aunt Florence, sometimes by Aunt Harriet or my elder sister, brought it to James's Green where the Kilkenny Fair was held. There they sold, very cheaply, tea, coffee and buns to the farmers, drovers and cattle-dealers. There was always a lot of money round the town on fair days, the pubs were crowded and there were men with plum-coloured faces walking unsteadily in the street. The coffee-van had an unacknowledged relevance to this. This went on for twenty years but the Baroness got ill and went to Auteven Cottage Hospital (this was one of Lady Desart's gifts to Kilkenny) and one day soon after that a lady, who was deputizing for her and had a less dominating character, was stopped, by order of the Corporation, and was not allowed in. The public-house keepers and other traders in Walkin Street, which led to the fair green, had put pressure on the Corporation. They claimed that they had a right to give drinks or proper breakfasts to drovers and that the coffee-van was depriving them of their livelihood. They said that the farmers were supporting the coffee-van because they were too mean to give their men the money for a proper breakfast.

Word of all this came to the Kilkenny Farmers' Union, an organization on which the Anglo-Irish landowners were well represented. A special meeting was held and they were all on the side of the Baroness and her coffee-van. And it was resolved that a message should be sent to her in hospital thanking her for her tireless work over the years and wishing her a speedy recovery. At the same time pressure was put on the Corporation to withdraw the veto on the coffee-van which the public-house keepers had forced them to make. The coffee-van continued as long as the Baroness lived but, when she died, it died with her.

I used to bicycle in with my father very early on the day of the Kilkenny Fair and we found the cattle from his two farms at Burnchurch and Drumherin waiting for us there, so it is not very difficult to revive all these memories, some of which are recorded in Aunt Florence's scrap book. It only slowly and sadly became apparent to my father that nature did not intend me to be a farmer. It was my younger brother, a small child then, who took over.

The Kilkenny Fair and the Kilkenny Farmers' Union ended long ago, as did the Instructors for Beekeeping and Carpentry, Lady Aberdeen's locally appointed nurse and her Women's National Health Association. I dare say they are not missed very much and have been replaced by something just as good, but some faculty of independent initiative, of overcoming apathy with an idea, has become rarer.

While Aunt Florence went to church in St Canice's Cathedral, Kilkenny, Aunt Harriet stayed at home praying and reading Mrs Eddy's *Science and Health with Key to the Scriptures*. Aunt Florence must have come back full of chat about the neighbours and their hats and the bishop's sermon. Did she have to suppress it all or did Aunt Harriet welcome this contact with the outside world?

I felt for her because at this time I was a very earnest Free Thinker, although I discovered at Oxford that my particular earnestness was twenty years out of date. I had the old nursery at the top of the house as my study and from there I could see my father and mother and two sisters setting off in the waggonette to Ennisnag church. I saw them turn down the avenue and eight minutes later I could see the top-hat of old Egan, the coachman (he sat on the box), appearing and disappearing and reappearing between the chestnut trees along the road and when it finally vanished I felt lonely but unyielding. Solitude was the price Aunt Harriet and I had to pay for our convictions. I did not change much but the world changed. In England people slipped out of faith and into indifference without mental or spiritual struggling. Earnest Rationalism like Lecky's and Bury's is the natural child of Irish Protestantism. It is the Catholic majority that keeps most of us defiantly Protestant.

Because of this, like a jelly that has stiffened inside its jelly-mould and slid out intact, I found myself accepting the Protestant ethos and bothering less about its dogma and mythology. We respect individualism and in particular 'the sacred right of private judgment', as Grattan called it at the Convention of Dungannon in 1782. In Ireland it has played the same part in the life of the Irish Protestant as Authority has in the life of the Irish Catholic. It is frequently under attack and I have always done my best to defend it.

What was Lavistown like in January 1925? The house is still there but it has changed and I have to resurrect it by conjecture and present experience, not memory. The aconites might have been just out under the shelter of the big cypress tree that fell down many years ago, and a few tight buds of snowdrops perhaps, but the mauve crocuses, the small ones that seeded themselves under all the deciduous trees that lined the path to the garden and the back avenue, would only just have poked above the leaf mould.

The pony Maureen would have been there but would Ellen the cook? The tennis court would have been there and properly mown, and not the flat shaggy rectangle that survives still beside so many Irish country houses, recalling the days before 1922 when there were often tennis parties at different houses six days a week.

I remember the inside of the house better. Aunt Florence took in *The Queen* and used to enjoy discussing with us the Social Problem page. Aunt Harriet had a row of Irish books and Dinneen's Irish dictionary, and when I was sixteen she gave me William James's *Varieties of Religious Experience*, which did not interest me very much because I was proud to have no religious experience. It wasn't until years later that I discovered she had left a yellow ribbon in a chapter called 'The Religion of Healthy Mindedness' with a subsection on 'Mind Cure.'

I must come back to that night of 25 January 1925. We had a quiet low-voiced supper in the drawing-room opposite to the dining-room in which Aunt Harriet lay, and then we went to bed. I went first because I was in the little dressing-room. It was only the second time I had been in a house with a dead person (Granny had died the year before) and I took a long time to go to sleep, thinking of Aunt Harriet and all the things that had happened and not happened between us. It was a long chronicle of trivialities, letters I had not answered, copies of the *Monitor* with marked passages that I had not acknowledged, little openings for thoughtful conversations which I had gently closed.

Perhaps Aunt Harriet had access to some peace of mind, some freedom from pain which she had spent her life trying to share with us. But it was very difficult to think like this. It was another hour before I slept and at about four I was roused by a tapping sound. It came from the room below. It is only because my elder relations are all dead and I am an old man now, soon to go into a box myself, that I can write like this. Perhaps I should not for I have nothing interesting to relate, only what happened in my mind, and that is discreditable but not exciting.

If I could have gone downstairs directly from my room I know

I would have, but to get down I had to go through my parents' room. They would certainly wake and I would put into their minds a horrifying thought, which it was my duty to confirm before expressing.

I spent the rest of the night wrestling with this problem even after the tapping had stopped. What worried me was the thought that in some supreme effort of faith she had half-conquered death, which like a wave in an ebbing tide had left her stranded half-alive on the foreshore.

I recalled Granny's fear of being buried alive. Would Aunt Harriet have woken up and not known whether she was already buried? And what could we do? Would I have to get Mr Lewis the undertaker? Where did he live? Was there a hammer and a chisel in the house?

I got up as soon as I could and as I passed through my parents' room my mother said to my father: 'Did you hear that rapping in the night? It must have been the knob of the blind cord tapping on the window pane. There was a bit of wind.' 'Yes, I expect so,' my father said indifferently. When I got down, all was quiet and the blind cord did have a knob at the end of it but the wind had stopped and I could not convince myself that my mother's explanation was the correct one. She had never believed in Aunt Harriet's faith healing. 'She could have saved herself with something quite simple like cascara,' she had said. I seldom think of that night now, though I once used often to do so. It was not a question of being right or wrong in what I thought. I had envisaged a possibility and at all costs I should have tested it. It was the first of ten or fifteen grave mistakes that I think over in the wakeful nights. I wrote a poem about them, and then found that Yeats had written some lines that were more apposite.

> Things said or done long years ago,
> Or things I did not do or say
> But thought that I might say or do,
> Weigh me down, and not a day
> But something is recalled,
> My conscience or my vanity appalled.

In the daylight, commonsense prevailed. Aunt Harriet was self-effacing and considerate. She would sooner have gone through the ordeal of death a second time than be resurrected in a blaze of newspaper publicity. Very quickly the night vision of hands battering helplessly at unyielding wood was submerged. Mr Lewis, the undertaker, arrived with the hearse and we took Aunt Florence with us to lunch at home and afterwards we met the hearse at Danesfort Cross and followed it to Burnchurch church, where my great-grandfather, once rector there, and all his family were buried. My mother said she had tried to find if there was some special Christian Science Burial Service and some special minister to perform it. Now it seems to me we did not try hard enough and that we should have urged her fellow believers to come down and do honour to their dead sister, who in a lonely way had been loyal to their principles.

Later still I felt that in view of the Cork ground rents it had been mean of us not to give my two aunts a tombstone to themselves. Instead we added their names as postscripts on the base of the tall cross put up to my Uncle Richard, who had caught cold and died after a tennis party in 1877 at the age of nineteen.

Forty years later, when I was in Boston, because of Aunt Harriet I went to the Mother Church of Christ Scientist and in a Christian Science Reading Room I found Mrs Eddy's *Science and Health with Key to the Scriptures*. I was astonished. Mrs Eddy took the offensive against philology.

'The dissection and definition of words', she wrote, 'aside from their metaphysical content is not scientific.' Extracting the 'metaphysical' content from the name Adam, she writes: 'Divide it in half and it reads A dam, as the obstacle which the serpent Sin would impose between Man and his Creator',and elsewhere she writes: 'Adam and his race are a dream of mortal mind because Cain went to live in the Land of Nod, the land of dreams and illusions.'

Was this the way Aunt Harriet and thousands of others reasoned?And yet I had to acknowledge that, as newspapers go, *The Christian Science Monitor* has many merits.

I learnt in Boston that Mary Baker Eddy had many enemies and critics there. One of them has related that some of the more ardent of her disciples thought she had conquered Death as well as Pain and that, when she proved to be mortal after all, one of them impersonated her and drove round Boston for several days in her well-known carriage till the faithful were ready to accept the truth.

Goodness often blossoms like roses on very rickety trellis-work, and beauty can grow out of nonsense. There are no grounds for supposing that one can live a life without pain and sadness, but is it wrong to believe that somehow, somewhere, this is possible?

Two years after Aunt Harriet, Aunt Florence eased herself out of life slowly and securely by many small illnesses. I got the Cork ground rents but after a few years the Post Office bought half the buildings on the site of the Kingston Shipyard and claimed to be exempt from ground rents. My two sisters got Lavistown. The gate lodge on the back avenue, where Donovan lived, belongs to my niece, who sold Lavistown to friends, who have made it a study centre. Students come there to learn about the flora and fauna of the Nore valley. The cows there produce special cheeses and the pigs special sausages. It is still a place where it is easier to believe in happiness than in pain.

[1987]

22

LITTLE K

PREFACE

I wrote this in 1967 under the impact of a tragedy that was still fresh in my mind. My opinions have not changed and, though more people share them, it has not become easier to express them. I have only once seen my grand-daughter and, as she lives the other side of the Atlantic, I am unlikely to see her again. She has passed from infancy to childhood, to adolescence, to maturity. Her body has changed but her mental age remains the same. She is one of nature's mistakes and left to herself nature might have taken her away, but though often disastrous experiments to improve on nature are made, we seldom trust her to do the best for us.

Yet there seems to have been an unexpected change of policy in the USA. Baby Jane Doe, the three-year-old child of Long Island parents, was born severely retarded with many physical handicaps. Spinal surgery would prolong her life but would not correct her retardation. Her parents, after consulting doctors, clergy and social workers, rejected the operation.

Thereupon a Vermont lawyer, a right-to-life activist, took the child's parents to court to force an operation. The Court of Appeal denounced his suit as offensive and supported Baby Jane's parents.

The Reagan administration then took up the cause but in June 1985 the Supreme Court rejected its appeal. There will be very few parents of such children who will not rejoice at the rebuff to the administration.

A further decision of the Supreme Court invalidated a 1982 Federal Rule which required that hospitals which received

Federal money should post up notices urging staff members to report any denial of treatment to handicapped new-born. On behalf of the majority in the Supreme Court, Justice Stevens declared that the reason why new-borns, such as Baby Jane Doe, do not always get special medical treatment is not because hospitals discriminate against them but because their families do not want them to have that treatment. Federal law, he held, does not require hospitals to treat handicapped children without parental consent or require parents to give it.

It was suggested that there should be hospital-based Infant Care Review Committees on which there should be clergy and community represenatives as well as legal and medical experts to review such cases. The *New York Times* ended its report succinctly: 'That puts the problem where it belongs: out of Big Brother's hands and into those of concerned committees.'

The Supreme Court has in this way many times proved itself to be the protector of the rights of the citizen against the state, the one against the many. The Reagan administration thrives on broad generalizations. Soviet Russia is an evil empire, Libya a terrorist state, Nicaragua a Communist threat to her neighbours. If we look at a very small map of the Earth and interpret it by the very big headlines in the daily press, this is quite a normal view of the world. But 99 per cent of its inhabitants live out of reach of the headlines; and their deepest feelings, their strongest convictions, are often incommunicable till someone appears like the parents of Baby Jane Doe with the will and the skill to articulate them and present them to the Supreme Court. It has often struck down callous and cruel decisions of the Reagan Justice Department, which, inspired perhaps by the Southern fundamentalists, tried to legislate in the spheres which the Founding Fathers held to be the province of private judgment.

I. LITTLE K

In order to treat this subject objectively I had thought of calling them A, B, C, D and E. C, D and E would be my three granddaughters, A and B their parents, but I find I cannot reach such heights of detachment and that I must call them by their true initials, J, D, C, S and K.

I do not see them very often for they live in America. C is five years old and rather serious. She does not say very much, preferring to nod for 'Yes' and shake her head for 'No', but the whole time she is remembering and judging. I have an idea that when she grows up she will reject a great deal that most people accept. I feel very close to her and wish I could be beside her when the times comes for her to make decisions. S, who is still only two, is very different. She accepts everything and everybody and flings herself laughing and chattering into the arms of those she knows. C and S both remember K, my youngest grand-daughter, of course, but there is always so much happening that they do not often ask about her. C liked to be photographed holding her but K went away when she was two months old and they will, I think, soon accept her absence as permanent. [So little happens to K that once at least I shall give her her real name, Katherine Synolda, 1987.]

On my way to see K this morning, I walked through the park at Yonkers and tried unsuccessfully to find the Doric temple from which you are supposed to see the broad sweep of the Hudson and the Palisades beyond. The park is laid out so as to make you forget that the largest city in the world stretches all around it. I walked down woodland paths, where wild copses of acacia and fir were choked and bent with their burdens of honeysuckle, and I came at last to a romantically ruined manor house with sagging roof and rotting window frames. The park is a place in which to relax, to tear yourself away from the complex and sophisticated problems of the city, where everything is pulled down before it has time to grow old, and plastic flowers outnumber real ones a hundredfold. So nature is allowed to half-strangle the shrubberies and tear the manor-house apart. But, in fact, you cannot walk very far without being reminded of the well-organized sorrows and joys of the city. At one end there is a Cardiac Centre and the jungle slides away from it deferentially towards the river; the rough paths compose themselves into gentle gradients suitable for wheeled chairs and cautiously shuffling heart cases. There is a smooth lawn with rectangular panels of salvia and petunia as neat and tended as temperature charts.

At the other merrier end of the park, the derelict manor house, embedded in kalmia and rhododendron, has a notice on it,

NO WEDDING PHOTOGRAPHS TO BE TAKEN HERE.

If you find relaxation here, it is by withdrawing and pretending; it is that fragile sort of peace which the gravely disturbed find in barbiturates.

East of the park and higher still above the Hudson is the long low white house where K lives. I met D there and together we went to her room. She is with ten other babies and she has her name on her cot. She has a sweet baby mouth and chin and large blue eyes and above it a high domed forehead, which would have been lovely too were it not for the sharp ridge that runs down it from her skull. She has, I am told, agenesis of the corpus callosum. That is to say the central part of her brain has not developed and, therefore, the optic nerve too is defective. The whites of those beautiful eyes are tinged with blue and she is all but blind.

'But look,' said a kind nurse, 'she blinks when I wave my hand. I think she can focus a little too.'

K did indeed blink, but it seemed to me that she just felt the draught of the nurse's hand.

D unclasped her hand, which was folded up like a bud, and showed me the palm.

'That's the Simian line going straight across. You meet it in mongols. But it's not a sure test, as she isn't a mongol. I showed it to an obstetrician and he just held up *his* hand at me. He has the Simian line too. All the other children here are mongols. Look at their lower eyelids! Look at the way their ears are set – very low!'

The nurse leant over and touched a small tin box attached to the cot and a tiny tinkle came from it.

'She loves her little musical box,' she said.

There was a pause while we watched for a sign that K was loving it but none came. The nurse closed it by saying, 'She never cries. She's so good.' (Later D told me that, when K was born, she did not cry, like other babies, but was unnaturally quiet.)

'Will she ever be able to walk?' I asked.

'Oh, why not? Of course!' she replied encouragingly.

'And talk?'

'Oh, I expect so. But you must ask the doctor.' She was embarrassed and broke off to greet a little boy who trotted into the room.

'Hello, Sammy! Back again?' and to us she said, 'Sammy is the brightest of our little mongols.'

I asked to see the older children and she took us into a sunny courtyard, where ten or twelve of them were playing. The swings were soaring up and down and a big ball was rolling about. A tall, almost handsome boy in a jersey with BEATLE printed on it rushed up to us jabbing his left shoulder and shouting something. It sounded like 'Resident! Resident!' 'No, we're not residents here,' D said, 'we're just here on a visit.' 'Resident! Whi How!' the boy bawled on, and we grasped that he was saying that he was the President of the United States. A girl of twenty with a broad blue band round her head, which was flopping from side to side, charged up to us. A swollen tongue stuck out of her mouth and she barked at us something we could not understand.

'Do they ever quarrel?' I asked the nurse.

'Oh, indeed they do!' she smiled at the innocence of my question. Then we went to the room of the totally unmanageable. 'Don't you come!' I said to D but he insisted on going with me. These children cannot be given toys, because they destroy them. Some were incontinent and some had limbs that were frenetically askew. Television was on non-stop. ('They love their television,' said the nurse.) Many of them had dreary commonplace delusions like the Beatle boy, taken from TV or secondhand from the newspapers. One or two had some droll hallucination which two months ago I would have found touching and even entertaining.

As we went down the passage we passed the open door of a small room and in it I saw a charming-looking woman with greying hair. Her husband was with her and they were talking to a young defective. ('He gets fits,' explained the nurse, 'that's why he has the black eye.') As the mother saw us she turned to the boy with a gay and loving laugh. He looked unresponsively back and I knew that her animation was directed at us rather than at him. She was telling us that she was ready to do her part in trying to lift the great curtain of sadness that hung over us all.

When we reached the hall two merry little girls dashed past us, with their parents behind. 'I know who you've come to see!' said the nurse, bending down to them. 'Yes, Lucy! Lucy!' they shouted and tore ahead. The nurse smiled at us as though to say: 'You see it's not all sadness. Children take it quite as a matter of course.'

But I think it is all sadness, unnecessary sadness, from which the world has piously averted its eyes. The realities are concealed from us by a labyrinth of platitude as specious and unnatural as the honeysuckle jungle at Yonkers. There is not a child in that large establishment whose parents have not at one time thought what they dare not articulate: 'I wish that my child would die!' And many, perhaps most, are still thinking it and secretly praying for it.

II. MME VANDEPUT AND THE NINE CATHOLICS

As we drove home D told me that one in ten of all the children in the USA is defective. I though he must be exaggerating but when I got back I turned to the appendix of the book about the trial at Liège of Suzanne Vandeput, who killed her armless 'Thalidomide baby'. The nine gently disapproving Catholic authors of this book, doctors and priests, give statistics of the mental defectives in France. They are about 7 per cent of the population. How many of these, I thought, can be as well cared for as our little K, surrounded from babyhood with toys and paint-boxes and swings, with practised smiles and laughter that is innocent or lovingly simulated?

The nine French Catholics are thinking of that too. Their book is learned, tender, imaginative. Not in one sentence do they denounce Suzanne; she was wrong, of course, they say, but they see her sin against a dark background of callousness, stupidity and smugness, and they recognize that science has transformed the human scene and totally changed the nature of our problems: 'The new drugs', writes Father Roy, 'can be as dangerous as they are salutary. The number of abnormal children is increasing; the doctors are opposing the process of natural selection by allowing beings to exist which are in no way human.'

They are aware that the support that Suzanne Vandeput received from press and public in Liège and beyond was not only sentimental and unreflecting but scholarly as well. Father Roy quotes with bafflement and sadness rather than horror two French doctors, Barrère and Lalou, who present a humanist point of view:

Our age has effected so many transformations on man that the moral problems raised can no longer be answered by the ancient formulae. It is almost a new reality that we must learn to accept and mankind will need many years to construct a new humanism founded on the new man. Euthanasia seems to be one of the keystones of this future edifice.

The fact that this is quoted without horror shows that the nine writers are aware how unresponsive we have mostly become to the ecclesiastical anathemas of the past. With the advent of totalitarian and nuclear war the old Christian tabus on killing have fallen into such confusion that one moral argument has now to support itself with ten practical ones. Most of their arguments are therefore addressed to the humane and far-sighted rather than to the devout.

(1) Only one writer, Father Roy, uses an argument that a sceptic or a Protestant might find offensive, for he links the euthanasia of the defective with divorce as a source of bad examples. Divorce, he says, is not only a disaster for the children of broken marriages but it also influences others to part, who without this way of escape might have 'risen above their selfishness' and 'attained to a richer marital understanding and love'. But a non-Catholic could argue that divorce has brought as much relief as tension, as much joy as sadness, and that this is no argument at all.

(2) Father Beirnaert SJ predicts 'personality disturbances' for the child, whom Mme Vandeput said she was going to bear in order to replace the armless child that she killed. It is right that we should reflect on such indirect psychological effects, but they are unpredictable. How can we judge their importance? One of the nine, Dr Eck, speaks frankly of the marriages that were broken because of a defective birth, and the jealousy that normal children, brothers and sisters, sometimes feel because of the special love which a good mother will sometimes give to her defective child. All these things may happen. But love and wisdom can sometimes solve these problems, sometimes must recognize that they are insoluble.

(3) Dr de Paillerets asks how can one decide that one malformation will justify infanticide, while another will not? How can we decide who will be unhappy, who not? Healthy people may be miserable and severely handicapped people may be cheerful.

(4) He asks how can we be sure that cures will not be discovered for defects that now seem irremediable?

(5) He says, if doctors, even in exceptional cases, were to become the auxiliaries of death rather than of life, would they not certainly lose the confidence of their patients? 'Without this confidence medicine cannot exist.' And he says that, since the time of Hippocrates in the fifth century BC, this 'unconditional respect for human life' has been obligatory. He quotes the Hippocratic oath, which all doctors are still obliged to swear.

(6) The sixth argument is very odd.

Infanticide [he says] puts a curb on the enthusiasm of those, who through their research contribute to the increase of our knowledge, and on the enthusiasm of those, who, devoting themselves to the care of the unfortunate children, now find that we are equivalently disowning them and regarding their work as unnecessary. Medicine needs support from all of us if it is to keep its essential dynamism.

It is possible that one day some instrument will be invented which will register human sympathy, warmth of feeling. Surely, if it was attached to Dr de Paillerets as he wrote this, it would register zero. How otherwise can he think of a parent's agony in connection with the progress of medicine and the nursing profession. It rouses instantly the suspicion that it may be in the interests of geriatrics and allied studies that men are sometimes forced by doctors to live on beyond their natural span.

(7) The seventh argument also betrays a curious professional egoism, disguised as modesty. Dr de Paillerets dreads the possibility of some kind of medical commission entrusted with the task of selecting infants for death. 'What a terrible temptation is this for us to accept such a right over the life and death of others.'

But what parents would ever grant to doctors such a right? It is right that only those who love the child and are close to it could claim and exercise. The doctors' function should be a minor one. It should be little more than that which, under pressure, the Catholic bishops of Nazi Germany permitted when they decreed that Catholic doctors and social workers could report to the authorities those afflicted with ills calling for sterilization, provided they did not at the same time order or authorize sterilization. The operation was performed in scorn rather than love, and permission was granted with casuistry, but it is not impossible to imagine that religious men and doctors could, without casuistry and without scorn, help a parent in a sad decision.

Most of these seven arguments deal with problems that we meet every day and that are solved rightly or wrongly according to our instincts and knowledge. There are stresses and strains in family life which we can palliate but seldom elude. A great sadness will produce other sadness whatever we do. It seems to me that when Dr de Paillerets considers these practical arguments against infanticide he has already despaired of defending the only absolutely compelling argument, which is that all killing is a mortal sin. He may have reflected that public opinion, like war, sometimes has the power to modify the most uncompromising dogma and that there was an absolute and peremptory quality about the support which the people of Liège gave to Mme Vandeput.

Palliatives

In our time there has been so much ecclesiastically condoned and sanctified killing that few clerics would nowadays have the effrontery to bring up again, without diffidence or qualification, that dishonoured and bamboozled old commandment, THOU SHALT NOT KILL. Father Roy condemns the doctor who simply repeats it and concerns himself not at all with the tragic situation of those who must cherish the helpless being which medical science has preserved for them. Left to herself nature would often have borne away the malformed child in a miscarriage or by some ordinary illness like measles to which, without inoculation, the often feeble defective child could have succumbed. The doctors feel a greater responsibility towards their profession than towards their patients. When a friend of mine with a defective child asked that it should not be inoculated he was told that he must not 'tie the hands of the doctor'.

The nine French priests and doctors are fully aware what a burden of responsibility they bear for what is happening. For the doctors save and prolong lives that are useless and unhappy and the priests mount guard over them with moral precepts. They urge upon their colleagues, in recompense, a devotion, a dedicated study, a depth of understanding, which is far beyond the reach of most men.

Dr de Paillerets writes of the meagre, badly supported

research which is being done on encephalopaths. In Paris it is often many years before the defective child can even be received into a specialized establishment. 'It is our duty as doctors', he writes, 'to expose this scandal. . . The Liège Trial has occured but the real trial is yet to come and, if we do not act in this matter, our place will be in the first row of the accused.'

And Father Roy, stressing the urgency, asks if we are prepared to postpone the laying down of new major roads till the specialized homes are provided. This question carries its own answer with it. No, we are not.

The nine Frenchmen also urge that the parents of the afflicted should form associations to discuss their common problems and share the burden. And Father Roy distinguishes between the 'pity', a negative, egoistic thing which men are ready to show, and the 'compassion' which is demanded of them and which forces them to share the sufferings of the afflicted and to act. He quotes Bernanos: 'Modern man has a hard heart and tender guts.' He weeps for the sufferings of others and winces at the thought of being involved in them.

Is there any likelihood that these generous ideals will ever be fulfilled? The next day, in search of enlightenment, I went uptown to see Dr S, the obstetrician who had delivered K. He confirmed what I had suspected. There is no reality in these dreams of Father Roy. Dr S is a kind and brilliant man but his talents have made him much sought after and there is no likelihood that he will ever desert his other patients in order to show more than perfunctory sympathy with the parents of defective children. Nor, as far as I know, has there been any 'dedicated study', any researches into the origin of K's misfortune, which might be helpful to others.

Then there is the question of parents' association. I learnt from one of the nurses in the home, where K is, that Dr S himself has a mongol child there. Yet he never told J or D about him, though he, as a doctor, frequently handling our problems both in his home and his profession, could have forwarded such an association more than anyone else. About this I do not feel I have any right to reproach him. We are all of us preternaturally sensitive about our defective children. For educated people they may represent a private anguish that is well nigh unshareable. This intense 'privatization' of our problem (to use an American word) belongs to the Age of Scientific Organization, as does the increase in the number of abnormal children. The bourgeois, for the most part, live in small labour-saving flats and it is usually obvious, if not obligatory, that the defective child should go to an institution where he can receive 'proper care'. Though it may well be that the parents think of their child every hour of the day, they do not have to talk about him or constantly plan for him. Only rarely will talking help them. About this I understand Dr S.

It was very different when I was a child. Our rector had a mongol daughter and the neighbours frequently took charge of her. (Father Roy would say that it was not half frequently enough.) She is looked after by her relations and I still see her sometimes, a woman of fifty. It is possible that our rare gestures of true 'compassion' were largely neutralized by our chattering 'pity'. But even such small efforts as we made would now be difficult and unwanted. The compassion which Father Roy demands is not compatible with professionalism. Doctors, nurses and social workers must take their courses, earn salaries, go where they are told, and so must the clergy. Their lives are too full, too controlled for them to have any time for that total imaginative involvement which is compassion. There is no reality in these dreams of Father Roy. The revolution in men's behaviour which he desires cannot happen in a scientifically organized society. The position which he is trying to defend is based upon moral precepts which have lost their validity. The relief which he promised will never come.

I asked Dr S what he thought of euthanasia and he said that Mme Vandeput was wholly wrong,. All life is better than all death. He was coming to believe that only in rare cases was even abortion justifiable.

'Are your objections religious?'

'If you mean am I a Catholic, the answer is no, but I believe in God.'

He was suprised that I should know about his little boy and he told me that he had often longed for him to die but he no longer did so. He had wondered too whether he had been wrong in sending him to an institution.

I did not ask him why he had not told J that he was a fellow-sufferer, as this might have comforted her a little. I now regret my shyness as I believe his answer would have shown that our attitude towards the defective is now one of absolute negation.

No trace remains of the old belief that they are in some way the special children of God.* They are just genetic mistakes which, since we cannot, like the Greeks, extinguish them, we must relegate to some place where they are no nuisance to society.

Dr S's God is different from mine. Churchmen are now ready to admit into their ranks those who reject all historical certainties and see God and his son Christ as constructions of the mind by which the human imagination tries to express its revelation of the divine. This revelation varies from man to man. To me God is the assurance that the world of men is not purposeless or evil and that we can trust ourselves to it and that, when old laws lose their significance, new ones will slowly shape themselves to take their place. As for Christ, he is the assurance that a man can learn when and how to free himself from the power of the law, however strongly it may be reinforced with venerable traditions and popular approval. The show bread may have to be eaten, the sabbath profaned, the prostitute exalted. 'GOD' is the promise that out of this disorder a better order will ultimately ensue.

III. NATURAL LAW AND THE GREEKS

My mention of the Greeks recalls to me that I have not answered one of the arguments (no. 6) used against Mme Vandeput. It is medical rather than religious but seems to suggest, as the clergy do, that there is some sort of Natural Law at issue, which we

* A friend of mine claims that this is untrue and that here in Ireland the Steiner movement is represented in the village communities at Duffcarrig and Ballaghtobin and other places. I have visited Ballaghtobin, which is in Co. Kilkenny, and know how dedicated men and women have devoted themselves to improving the lives of the handicapped adults. They think of the mentally defective as fellow individual spirits who have slipped sideways on the evolutionary ladder, but who command innate respect, dignity and potential. Some of the villagers among whom they live accept this and conclude that mongols, to whom in particular the movement addresses itself, are in the world to teach their busy 'sane' fellow travellers the true value of brotherhood, love, acceptance. Hence they view them as 'special' and inherit the children-of-God outlook. I appreciate but do not share this sentiment. (H.B. 1988)

neglect at our peril.

Dr de Paillerets quotes the Hippocratic oath which doctors have considered binding upon them since the fifth century BC.

I shall not give a homicidal drug to anyone, no matter who may ask me to do so, nor shall I initiate the suggestion that it be given.

. . . The least exception to the unconditional respect for human life would place the doctor in a position which he could not accept. It would curb the enthusiasm which is the prerequisite of progress in medical knowledge. Furthermore, it would destroy the confidence of the patients, without which there can be no Medicine.

But surely the oath is greatly misinterpreted and the historical foundations of medicine strangely misunderstood. The Hippocratic oath mainly concerned the Greek habit of administering poison to those condemned to death. Hippocrates considered it beneath the dignity of a doctor to become a paid executioner. Moreover the world in which Hippocrates practised gave a limited authority to the doctor in the matter of life and death. His duty was to cure those who wished to be cured, but he did not interfere with ancient practices. In his day and for a century or two afterwards, in all the city states except Thebes, deformed or sickly children were exposed. Aristotle, a great admirer and younger contemporary of Hippocrates, thought the custom should be made law, for he writes: 'With respect to the exposing or bringing up of children, let it be a law that nothing imperfect or maimed should be brought up.' Plato gives the same advice to the law-givers in his ideal republic. Is there any evidence that Hippocrates opposed what was a universal custom?

The Greek father could decide whether a child was to live or die, for the infant did not become 'a member of the family' till he was formally presented some days after birth. Infanticide was not eugenic, though Plato and Aristotle would have treated it as such, for the father had a right to eliminate even a healthy infant whom he did not wish to rear, and this was freely exercised in the case of girl infants whose dowry might present a problem. The unwanted infant was placed in a cradle or pot and put in the corner of the marketplace, in the temple or wrestling ground. It might be picked up and reared by a stranger, so sometimes some objects of value were wrapped up with it. But the father had the right later to claim it after it had been reared, so the infant was usually left to die.

Only at Sparta was the absolute right of the parent over his children disputed, for the state would sometimes weed out, for eugenic or military reasons, sickly infants whom the parents had spared.

All this is very shocking to Christians, if Christians have not forfeited their right to be shocked at such things by their connivance at Auschwitz and Hiroshima, but some great classical scholars have shown sympathy. Of Greek infanticide Zimmern writes:

The Athenian had a traditional horror of violence and interfered, when he could, on behalf of the helpless. If he consented to exercise his immemorial right over his own offspring, he did so with regret for the sake of the city and his other children, because it was more merciful in the long run. We have no right to cast stones either at him or his fellows.

And Bernard Bosanquet writes in his *Companion to Plato's Republic*:

The high mortality of young children today suggests that we are superior to the ancients more in theory than in practice. . . Can any race safely arrest selection? It is quite conceivable that the actual infant mortality on the ancient system might be less than ours at present.

Plato and Aristotle both had the pragmatic, society-centred religion of most modern scientists. They did not see in the eugenic infanticide, which they preached, anything incompatible with orthodoxy. After a sentence or two about infanticide Aristotle returns to the subject of childbirth and urges that for the sake of exercise and the tranquillity of mind, which is favourable to successful parturition, the pregnant woman should walk to the temple every day and offer prayers to the gods who preside over matrimony.

All this has a callous, calculating sound. In our society our leading thinkers are more humane and imaginative, but Greek society itself was less cruel and impersonal and we have discovered new forms of physical agony and lonely introverted misery of mind of which the Greeks were incapable. The gulf between Plato or Aristotle and daily life at Athens was large, but not so large as that between, say, D. H. Lawrence and daily life at Nottingham, or the Bloomsbury group and Bloomsbury (it would be easy to discover some more modern and apposite antithesis), and I do not feel perverse or paradoxical in suggesting that there has been a real deterioration.

What are the principal forces that have drawn us away from the Greeks? First there is 'science', which, looking for conformity in men, tends to impose it. It classifies all living things by their shared characteristics. It pares down those distinctions upon which personality is built and which defy classification. It achieves its best results by treating men as statistical units rather than as individual persons. Such methods are damaging to that flexibility of conduct on which Greek ethic is based.

Secondly there is professionalism, which claims exclusively for itself spheres of authority, fields of investigation and experiment, which were once open to ordinary men, parents, neighbours, friends.

Thirdly there is universal democracy, which aspires to offer to the whole multi-racial, heterogeneous world, laws which all will accept. That means boiling down into a simple code of Do's and Dont's a vast complex of interlocking moralities deriving from very varied traditions and customs.

The Greek moralist or law-giver always had in mind the small community in which public opinion could sometimes enforce the law, sometimes replace it. So occasionally Aristotle, instead of saying, 'Let there be a law that. . .', says instead, 'Let it be held in utter detestation that. . .'.

Today public opinion, manipulated by pressmen and politicians, has become so ignoble a thing that we distrust it and put our faith instead in the law. Its chief defect, its inflexibility, becomes in our sad circumstances a merit.

Finally there is Christian theology, which has shaped the law, so that even those who reject its dogma are still bound by it. Bosanquet, for example, argues that our respect for human life has been deepened by religious doctrines, even discredited ones, such as that concerning the fate of unbaptized children in the world to come.

Modern churchmen are evasive about the future world, its penalties and prizes, and tend to judge our actions in accordance with their conformity to something they call 'Natural Law'. But it seems to me that Greek custom was closer to nature than we are and that it is not 'natural' for a doctor to insist on prolonging, by drugs and inoculations, the life of a defective child against the wishes of its parents. Bosanquet is surely justified in writing of the 'immemorial right which a parent has over his own offspring'.

In regard to infanticide I ought to add that the Greek practice had been inherited from primitive times. It can be traced among such primitive peoples as the anthropologists have investigated and it is usually linked with religion or food. The Aruntas of Australia suckle their infant children for several years and a new child whom the mother thinks she will be unable to rear is killed at birth. It is thought that the child's spirit goes back whence it came and can be born again. Twins are thought to be unnatural and are immediately killed.

Among the Todas of South India twins are also regarded with dismay and one of them is killed. New-born female babies are somtimes laid in the mud for buffaloes to trample on. These practices are most prevalent among the priestly caste in the Nilgiri hills where Western influence is weakest. Margaret Mead describes them as 'the desperate expedients to which a simple people have to resort to fit their survival rate to their social structure. These practices are dying out but so are the Todas'. She tells much the same story about the South Seas and the far north, where the Eskimoes practise female infanticide. And there is much in our own social history which is seldom remembered and is never written. An Irish friend of mine, herself the mother of a loved and cherished defective child, remembers as a girl being told how in her country neighbourhood a malformed infant was usually put at the end of the bed and left there unfed and untended till God, in his good time, should take it. I have never heard of this elsewhere or read of it but I believe it to be true.

No sensible person, of course, considers that primitive people can give us directives as to how to behave. We are not qualified to learn much from them or they from us. Yet there is a tendency to argue from 'the natural law' which we are supposed to have inherited from the remote past. There is no such thing. The most that a traditionalist might claim is that in all times, lands, peoples, we can trace, however faintly, one constant passion, the distaste for cruelty, injustice, waste. It is sometimes a minority sentiment but, when held with tenacity, it invariably prevails.

Surely today any deeply concerned parent, grandparent, or friend would agree that we have to retreat from many strongly held convictions which we have inherited from the past, and that 'desperate expedients' may have to be contemplated, if slowly and laboriously a new ethic and a new morality are to be built around our new convictions. How widely are these convictions shared? Am I just dreaming when I think that almost all those who have the same cause for sadness think as I do?

In *Le Dossier Confidentiel de L'Euthanasie*, Barrère and Lalou endorse what I have said about the attitudes of Greeks and Romans with quotations from Epicurus and Seneca. To them a man was the master of his own body and had a right to leave it when it could no longer give shelter and sustenance to his faculties. It was not till St Augustine that suicide and euthanasia became the crimes which Christians hold them to be today. And even in Christian times devout men could think differently. St Thomas More in the Second Book of *Utopia* wrote that when an Utopian was dying in incurable anguish, the priests and the magistrates exhorted him

Either to dispatche himselfe out of that payneful lyffe as out of a prison or a racke of tormente or elles suffer himselfe wyllinglye to be rydde oute of it by other. . . But they cause none suche to dye agaynste his wyll . . . He that killeth himselfe before that the pryestes and the counsel have allowed the cause of his deathe, him as unworthy they caste unburied into some stinkinge marrish.

And Francis Bacon had similar ideas.

As for the present state of the law in various countries I must depend as others have done on R. Raymond Charles's *Peut On Admettre L'Euthanasie?* The laws of Spain, Holland, Hungary, Italy, Poland, Norway, Denmark, Brazil treat with leniency those who kill from pity with the consent of their victim. Peru and Uraguay go further for they permit the judge to grant exemption from all penalty where no selfish motive can be discovered. In Europe the Penal Code of Czechoslovakia arrives more cautiously at the same conclusion.

In the USA and USSR the law has advanced and retreated. In 1906 the State Parliament of Ohio passed the first reading of a law permitting a man who was dying painfully to summon a commission of four to judge his right to end his life. A few months later Iowa voted for a law of still greater latitude, for it embraced defective children and idiots. However, when Congress had to pronounce at Washington, its verdict was wholly hostile.

In the USSR a law of 1922, which abolished the penalty for

homicide whose motive was pity, was repealed a few months later because of evidence that it was being abused.

Sometimes the law seems to nourish itself on its own vitals, developing without relation to what happens around it. In Nazi Germany in 1944, when the slaughter at Auschwitz was at its peak, a law was passed which prescribed the full legal penalties for those who from pity kill the incurable and the mentally deficient.

How then does it happen that in France and Britain, countries with long humanist traditions, no special exemption for those who kill from pity is embodied in the law? Is it perhaps that in these sophisticated countries there is an awareness that in human relationships there are zones in which a man may make his own terms with the Source of Law, whether he deems this to be God or the Natural Order, and that such a man needs no intermediary. Certainly in France, at least, euthanasia trials, despite the law, have usually ended with an acquittal or token punishment for those whose integrity is manifest.

IV. CHRISTIANITY AND KILLING

Was there ever before so much mental confusion about the killing of men by men?

Where does human life begin? There is the widest dispute. When does it end? Even that is not so clear as it once was. Granted that a man may kill in self-defence, is he also obliged to? And, if so, how many others is he obliged to defend by killing as well as himself? His family, his friends, his neighbours, his fellow citizens, his nation? And has he to kill on behalf of the friends of his friends and on behalf of the nations, who are allies of his nation? And should he practise preventative killing? Should he in this way defend himself or his friends or his nation when they think they are threatened? Or might be threatened? And has he to kill people in order to bring about justice in the world, in the way that his elected representatives think best?

Wherever his duty may lie, what actually happens is always the same. The individual, till a man rushes at him with knife or gun, can kill nobody, not even himself. The state can force him to kill anybody, though his whole soul rebels against the killing, and the Churches, because for their survival they have made their own pacts with the state, can give him no support in his rebellion. On the contrary they will support the state against him and often bring to bear all their supernatural sanctions against the individual, so it seems to him that he will be damned in the next world as well as in this if he does not kill those whom he neither fears nor dislikes.

Their clergy are kindly sensible men, anxious to preserve the venerable institutions which they serve and whose future is precarious. Therefore almost without exception they have interpreted the commandment THOU SHALT NOT KILL in the way that is most pleasing to secular authority. They have given their blessing to those that kill from fear and hatred, and they have condemned as sinners those who kill from love.

When I was thinking of this, the *New York Times* came in and I read of a seventeen-year-old boy in Detroit who had tried to kill himself with a stick of dynamite rather than go out to kill people of whom he knew nothing in Vietnam. In the adjoining paragraph I read how 500 Rabbis, American and Canadian, assembled in Toronto, had by a majority vote censured the Vietnamese war and insinuated that its roots were largely commercial. Later on I read how other denominations had also debated the war, and, except for the Orthodox of America, had also by a majority censured it. In fact there can never again be a war whose 'justice' is uncontested by religious men. It is a measure of their helplessness, their cowardice or their confusion of thought that they still continue to sanction war. They will still censure a bewildered boy for killing himself rather than become a killer. Should we censure them? I think not. They are caught, as we are, in a trap from which it is very hard to escape.

Yet the Churches still consider themselves to be the unflinching champions of the rights of the individual and the family, of the sacredness of human life; there is an ostentatious straining at gnats by those who have swallowed camels.

Even the nine Catholic authors, though they write so modestly and perceptively, sometimes appear to picture themselves as representatives of an austere tribunal from whose unbending judgment the timid layman shrinks away. Father Beirnaert SJ, for example, says that a merciful doctor will sometimes in disregard of Christian principles suppress a defective child 'because he finds the morality of the Church too severe'.

On the contrary it is not its severity that is repugnant but its extreme flexibility. The Churches make absolute judgments, but they qualify them for the powerful and only enforce them against the weak.

Father Roy, for example, says: 'The affirmation of respect for human life must therefore be absolute and univeral – that is, categorically binding all mankind – if we are not to founder in multiple disasters.'

This covers Mme Vandeput but not Hitler, for conscience obliges Father Roy to add a footnote about the right to kill in war. He makes a distinction between 'human life', which must be absolutely respected, and 'biological life', which we can destroy in self-defence, or in 'a just war'. And he says that the Church, while tolerating killing in war, has 'never given formal approval to it'.

Surely this distinction between 'human life' and 'biological life' is a dishonest one? Does a man's life become biological rather than human when he puts on a uniform? The only true distinction is that between views that it is politic to hold or 'tolerate' and those that are not. Father Roy's Church, a vast multi-racial organization which is unpopular with many, cannot afford to assert unequivocally against everybody the sacredness of life, as it was asserted in the first two centuries of Christianity. In those days there was no conscription and all that the Christian expected from the state was to escape its attention. The distortions and compromises, which we accept as inevitable, had not yet been forced upon him.

Can we still accept them? I think not. There has been a great change. Long after other historic events are forgotten the name Auschwitz will recall the most stupendous crime in history. And, linked to it enduringly is the greatest non-event, the Silence of Pius XII, more terrible now that his apologists have argued that prudence and Christian charity demanded it. For this argument shifts the guilt of impotence from one man to the whole of Christendom and justifies a billion meaner connivances.

The gospels say that a darkness fell upon the earth when Christ was crucified and when a new era began. Surely the Silence of Pius has the same symbolic quality. It was mysterious and ominous, like the silence of woods and fields that precedes a total eclipse of the sun. It must herald some great change, either the final collapse of Christianity or its rebirth in some new and unforeseen shape.

In fact, if there is a rebirth, I believe that the ancient law THOU SHALT NOT KILL will have to be interpreted with greater severity and not less. And, if it is to be qualified at all, those who kill from loving compassion will seem to us far more forgivable than those millions of conscripted killers whom the Churches forgive and even exalt.

The problem of 'unnatural death', that is to say death which is not due to accident or bodily decay, is a unitary one. The hastened death of the defective baby and the incurable adult to whom life is only useless pain is linked to the involuntary death of the criminal and the conscript soldier and allied to all other assaults which we make upon human life, to birth control, sterilization and abortion. We shall never be able to face the problem of the useless, the unwanted, the criminal, the hostile, the unendurable life with courage and understanding, so long as our laws compel the innocent to kill the innocent against his will. So long as the Churches condone it, the taint of expediency must colour everything they say. Nothing can change till the leaders of the Churches dare to say once more: 'Those that take the sword shall perish by the sword.'

This would be a lightning flash, dazzling and destructive, that would shake the world. Many venerable establishments would crumble, but the dark unvisited places, which breed ugliness, would be illuminated. All the things that we do or fail to do in the ante-chambers of life or at its exit would be seen in their proper perspective, birth control, sterilization, abortion, euthanasia. Our judgment, no longer clouded and crippled by the great betrayal, the stupendous fallacy, would be free to act. Our little K's life, a frosted bud that will never open and bear fruit, would be allowed to drop.

V. CHURCHES UNDER PRESSURE

The ideal does not become more remote when the real is closely examined. The man who intends to escape must know each stone of his prison walls as though he loved it.

The narrow territory on the verges of life and death, which is now almost all that remains of the once vast spiritual dominion of the Churches, is constantly under dispute. Let us observe how its Christian defenders behave when they are under attack. If most of my information is about Catholics, that is because in recent years they have excelled others in self-scrutiny. Let us watch how they acted when the Nazis tried to interrupt the cycle of man's life at its generation, in its prime and in its decay. We shall see that in general the Churches capitulated to the powerful and compensated themselves for their defeat by tyrannizing over the defenceless.

Maybe this is just a law of life. If you have to draw sound from an instrument whose principal chords are dumb, you must strike those that remain all the harder. As their power to enforce laws that are binding on peoples and governments declines, the Churches enforce them with special vigour in those spheres where men are solitary and amenable to persuasion. In all that concerns child-birth and sex and marrying and the death of relations, we are so much alone as to be almost grateful for public interest and hence ready to be counselled, cajoled and coerced. The warrior, defeated in the field, finds consolation in being a tyrant at home.

In Germany, which sometimes calls itself 'the Heartland of Europe', ideas which are current elsewhere are often acted out so boldly and dramatically that, like the details in an enlarged photograph, we can see universal human behaviour most clearly in a German context.

There were three stages in the attack on the sacredness of human life, and corresponding to them two great ecclesiastical and one partial triumph. The Nazi sterilization laws attacked the unborn; the euthanasia campaign was directed in the first place against life in its decay; genocide, which was an attack on life in all its stages, was little more than an extension of the 'just war' which the Nazis claimed to be waging.

It was to the question of procreation that the Nazis attended first. In May 1933 Hitler laid before the German bishops the draft of a law providing for voluntary sterilization. The Catholic bishops rejected it as a violation of the encyclical *Casti Conubii*, 1930, but the concordat with Hitler was about to be signed and the day after the signing a law for forcible sterilization of the diseased was approved. Catholic resistance was strong but, National Socialism having been accepted, the encyclical had ultimately to be set aside. Finally even in Rome compromises were made, and in 1940 the Sacred Congregation ruled that Catholic nurses in state-run hospitals might under certain circumstances assist at sterilization operations. It was argued that, if a recalcitrant nurse were dismissed, she might be replaced by an antireligious person who would withold the sacraments from those in danger of death. And, though it remained sinful for a Catholic physician to apply for the sterilization of any patient, he was allowed to report to the authorities the names of those afflicted with ills calling for sterilization.

The relationship of Church and state followed this familiar pattern of quibble and counter-quibble; when the Church was forced to some shameful capitulation, it invariably tried to make good its losses by some tiny usurpation in the domestic sphere. And thus it was that the German hierarchy forbade the marriage of sterilized persons, since 'by natural law the main purpose of marriage is procreation'. However, in the first three years of the decree 170,000 people had been sterilized and the Catholics among them made a formidable body. So even the Church was forced to retreat and to withdraw its veto.

Then followed the euthanasia campaign and a Church-State war of great significance, for in it the Church proved its power and influence and demonstrated that it was unwilling to use them except when public opinion was favourable. On 1 September 1939 Hitler decreed that all those with incurable diseases should be killed and before the end of the year establishments for the shooting and premises for the gassing of victims were opened in Wurtemberg and Hesse. As soon as rumours of this reached the clergy there were furious protests and after the campaign had lasted two years and 70,000 patients had been killed, there was an abrupt change of policy. The principal credit for this must go to Bishop Galen of Münster, who delivered a famous sermon demanding that those who had done the killing should be prosecuted for murder. He warned them that human life was sacred except in the case of self-defence or a just war, and that invalids and seriously wounded soldiers would be next on the list. Some of the Nazi leaders wanted Galen hanged but they dared not do so, so great was his popularity in Münster and in all Westphalia. Instead, the campaign of euthanasia was called off.

This great Church triumph was significant in several ways. It showed that in our frailty we are strengthened by being able to appeal, beyond our conscience, to infallible dogma. In other words it is easier for us to say: 'That is forbidden by the Encyclical *Casti Conubii*, 1930,' than to protest: 'That revolts me to the bottom of my soul!' But the disadvantage is that if we wait for the august and infallible Voice to proclaim the truth and the Voice is silent, we are more helpless than those who have treated their consciences as primary and not secondary sources of enlightenment. For the testing time for Christians in Germany came not when the government began to kill their crippled and defective kinsmen. It came when the Nazis began to kill their innocent and helpless neighbours the Jews. When the Voice was silent and the priest and the Levite passed by, it was inevitable that the ordinary man should consider it no concern of his and that the cold and cruel heart should be sanctified.

At that time the ecclesiastical opposition to euthanasia, successful as it was, showed that the bishops knew about gas-chambers before the Jews did. They knew that they were built for the elimination of the 'unproductive' and that Jews were officially declared 'unproductive' and that many clergy had endorsed this view. They knew that they had been deported to the east. . . The bishops were not mentally deficient. . . and they had heard rumours.

If the purpose of religion is to arouse our conscience and to sharpen our sensibilities to the perception of evil, the Churches had failed disastrously. What they offered was not a stimulant but a drug. In the matter of euthanasia we must turn aside and listen to the voice of our own conscience.

There is abundant evidence that the bishops' minds had been befogged by the theory of the just war and the image that it had printed indelibly on their imaginations of the conscript soldier as a knight errant and even, in the fight against Bolshevism, as a soldier of Christ. In a fog of crusading holiness Auschwitz was hard to distinguish from an air raid, one of those sad events which it is necessary to endure and to inflict if, in our imperfect world, justice is to prevail. In order to preserve morale one must not say too much about specific cruelties and injustices of the war, in fact, better say nothing at all. So that Guenter Lewy in his magnificent book *The Catholic Church and Nazi Germany* writes: 'While thousands of anti-Nazis were beaten to pulp in the concentration camps, the Church talked of supporting the moral renewal brought about by the Hitler government.' And Gordon Zahn in *German Catholics and Hitler's Wars* declares that after exhaustive research he could only find a record of four German Catholics who had openly refused military service. He attributes the 'near unanimity of support' for the war from German Catholics to 'the external pressure exerted by leading Church officials' and the spiritual influence that their words and examples were bound to have on their flock.

For years after the true character of the war had revealed itself the clergy went on proclaiming it a just war and denouncing those brave men who refused to serve. For example, when the Austrian peasant Jägestätter chose to be beheaded rather than to take part in what he deemed an unjust war, his bishop reprimanded him severely for his disloyalty. They were all of them deceiving themselves in the interests of ecclesiastical survival.

Years later the President of Western Germany, Lübke, said in a memorial address: 'No one who was not completely blinded or wholly naive could be completely free of the pressing awareness that this war was not a just war.'

That is to say that much innocent blood was shed, often by innocent men, because of the Church's failure to follow its own teaching. Lewy believes that had the leaders of German Catholicism opposed Hitler from the start, they would have made the home front so unreliable that he 'might not have dared going to war and literally millions of lives would have been saved'. But once a war has started it is not easy to see how the Church, with its intricate relationship with the government of every state, would be able to oppose it. When nations are engaged in combat it is already too late to ask where justice lies and to urge soldiers to desert.

I hope I have shown how vacillating the Christian approach to those problems has been. The encyclical about sterilization was only scrupulously observed so long as observance was not likely to injure the faithful seriously and damage the prestige and authority of the Church and alienate its disciples. The euthanasia of the innocent was only vigorously denounced when it concerned people of the same race as the denouncing ecclesiastics. The problem of the 'just' or 'unjust' war was never seriously considered. I believe that there is not a bishop in Germany or in all Europe and America who would now dare publicly to assert that Hitler's war was a just one. Yet when they were already in full possession of all the facts, thousands of bishops, and not only in Germany, asserted this.

Public and Private Killing

I see only one path through this moral chaos. The Church sometimes claims to be a higher court attending to those spiritual needs of mankind which governments, concerned for its material welfare, must ignore. If that is so, could she not insist that a man is the master of his own life and that he cannot be obliged to offer it or preserve it against his will. The community may try to educate him in the use of this right but cannot deprive him of it. If he should abuse it, no doubt we might suffer 'multiple disasters', but not so many as we suffer through denying that that right exists.

In the matter of killing in self-defence, which the Church tolerates and often commands, this new code of ethics might work more justly and effectively than the old one. Science allied to bureaucracy concentrates power in the hands of the few; a genius in a laboratory conceives an idea and shares it with a governing minority. As a result great cities crumble, army corps collapse, empires capitulate. The only antidote to the captive genius and his captors is the free man's passionate conviction. He normally operates single handed and is trusted by neither Church nor state. All the honours, all the blessings, go to the conscript armies. These armies are composed of a few men who identify themselves with the aims of the government and are prepared to kill for them, a few more who are convinced that it is their duty to suppress all private judgment and to kill as they are ordered, and finally vast hordes of ignorant or innocent or deeply reluctant conscripts. If there is often or ever a clear-cut antithesis of good and evil, the last place to look for it would be in the opposition of rival armies. This is an old story which we have come to accept as inevitable. What we should not accept, what is obscene and intolerable, is that the Churches should bless this arrangement and continue to preach as Father Roy does that 'respect for human life must be absolute and universal and that it must be categorically binding on all mankind'.

Only a Quaker or one of the other pacifist sects can talk like that without the grossest hypocrisy.

Yet if the Quakers are wrong and we have to kill in defence

of innocence and justice, how best can it be done? In scientific warfare the innocent and the just who are conscripted and forced to use modern weapons will be as indiscriminatingly murderous as their fellows and must be resisted with the same mechanical ruthlessness. There is only one way in which death can be dealt out selectively and that is by assassination, a form of private enterprise on which the Church has always frowned. Those who took part in the July 20 attack on Hitler are now recognized as great heroes, who, had they succeeded, would have ended the war and preserved the unity of Germany. Yet at the time they received nothing but discouragement from even those of the Church leaders who had opposed the Nazis. Cardinal Faulhaber, for example, when questioned by the Gestapo after the plot had failed, is said to have expressed the most vigorous condemnation of the attempt and to have affirmed his loyalty to Hitler.

Yet it is obvious that assassination, when a man chooses his victim of his own free will and risking his life takes upon himself the complete responsibility for his acts, can have a nobility that must always be lacking in the mass slaughter of conscripts by conscripts. And after the event the successful assassin will certainly get the blessing of the Church. It has been said that Bishop Preising, who had been informed in advance of the July 20 plot, was to have replaced the pro-Nazi Orsenigo as Papal Nuncio to the government of assassins. Whether or not this is true it is certain that Archbishop Stepinac cordially welcomed the government of Pavelitch, whose members had been involved in the assassination of King Alexander. All the Croatian bishops extolled Pavelitch who was himself received in audience by Pope Pius XII.

If the Church were to accept assassination as a form of resistance, which, however deplorable, was preferable to conscript warfare, it might be able to judge it by some subtler criterion than success. In that case it would surely condemn Pavelitch and Stepinac and praise Stauffenberg and Preising.

But could the Church ever show greater indulgence to the assassin than to the soldier? Not as she now is. Being herself a social organization, she is always disposed in a time of crisis to ingratiate herself with the great political aggregations to which she is affiliated. Though she often claims to be the defender of the individual conscience, she usually concedes that when mankind organizes itself into powerful national groupings, it can legitimately dodge the impact of those 'absolute and universal laws' which are 'categorically binding' on the individual. In the matter of killing the Churches will therefore line up with the worst of governments till it is defeated, rather than with the best of assassins before he succeeds.

I have written sympathetically of assassins without recalling any particular one of whom one could unreservedly approve. The German heroes of July 20 seem to have plotted to destroy Hitler principally because he was losing the war. Bonhoeffer, who excites interest and was executed for his complicity, does not seem to have been deeply implicated. Pavelitch was a bloodthirsty fanatic. Perhaps I have most sympathy for Princip and Chubrilovitch, the assassins of Sarajevo, who, as many think (not I), precipitated the First World War. Why are assassins mad or simple or discredited people, or else like Princip have a fatal illness? I think it is because public opinion is conditioned to abhor what they do and only the most desperate conviction and courage will induce a man to risk a healthy life for it. He knows that a conscript who mindlessly kills a hundred other equally harmless conscripts will be criticized by nobody, while a brave and resolute man who rids the world of a tyrant is staking his honour and his reputation as well as his life.

How trivial my problem seems compared to his, yet I have linked them together because law and religion have already done so. I too ask more than orthodoxy could ever concede. I am claiming much more than the right over my own life, which in the long run no one can permanently withhold from me. I believe that love can give us the right of life and death over those who are helpless and dependent on us. And that when circumstances are desperate we must snatch it, as did those parents who flung their children from the trains transporting them to Auschwitz. It is a right that can never be confirmed by any legislature, for the essence of law is impartiality and detachment, and those who are detached cannot judge the depth of love and the urgency of despair.

*   *   *

VI. THE NORMALITY OF LOVE AND THE LAW

It is not healthy to live alone for long periods with dreams which you cannot realize, for it is certain that little K's parents can never claim their rights and it is improbable that I will. But you can obtain relief from a particular problem by generalizing it, observing its impact upon others and preparing for its solution by posterity. So I took the subway downtown to East 57th Street, New York, where the Euthanasia Society of America has its headquarters, and there I came to my senses. The secretary told me that there is no likelihood that in our lifetime euthanasia for defective children will be legalized. 'You see,' she said, 'religion is very powerful in America. Even to work for legalization might be unwise. We have to approach our objective step by step, and the first step concerns the elderly and hopelessly diseased who wish to die.' She showed me an article in *Harper's Magazine* of October 1960, 'The Patient's Right to Die' by Joseph Fletcher, who has a chair in Ethics and Moral Theology at Cambridge, Mass.

This article is very illuminating but confirms what the secretary said. It is the problem of the old who wish to die which occupies the mind of these reformers. He tells the familiar story well. He describes how we have altered the whole pattern of life and death; men live far longer than they used to do and die painfully and slowly as their faculties decay. 'The classical death-bed scene with its loving partings and solemn last words is practically a thing of the past. In its stead is a sedated, comatose, betubed object, manipulated and subconscious, if not sub-human.'

The doctor, who from worthy motives refuses to prolong this indecency, must first be protected by the law; the next to be championed is the doctor who deliberately curtails it. The case of little K is something quite other; it cannot even be considered.

Evidently modern medicine has caused us to invert the thinking of the Greeks for whom old people, whose lives were never artificially prolonged, presented no problem, since if they were not reasonably healthy they soon died. Not even Aristotle or Plato, who favoured the killing of defective children, required that old people should be helped into the tomb.

Reading Mr Fletcher I have come to think that in fact the Greeks understood better than we do the nature of the affections. We stress the 'sacredness of life' but a Greek would consider that life becomes sacred but is not born so. The reverence which we feel for the young is woven out of memories and hopes and gathers in complexity as they grow older. But where there are no memories and no hopes the Greeks would only see 'biological life', to use a phrase of Father Roy in a way which he would greatly dislike.

'Biological life' is something that we spare and cherish from biological instinct, and instinct will perhaps only slowly develop into love. Where there are no hopes, we may come to feel resentment or even hatred towards the life which instinct bids us cherish.

There is indeed in general estimation nothing sacred about the instincts. We defer to them perhaps even less than we should do, inhibiting all those that are incompatible with social order. The sexual and philoprogenitive instincts, the instinct of self-preservation and many others, are subordinated to the needs of the state. Even the maternal instinct submits to control.

Joseph Fletcher talks of a new 'morality of love', which he also calls 'the morality of human freedom and dignity'. He does not define it, but he seems to think that it is something that the law could be brought to tolerate. Could it? To me, this morality of love will always be apart from, and sometimes in conflict with, the law. For as the law extends its scope wider and wider over men of all creeds and races, it will concern itself less with the intimate relations of men and more with their public communications. Its goal will be to avoid social collisions. The only support that the morality of love could offer to a man in conflict with the law would be the assurance that he was doing right.

A pamphlet which I was given by the Euthanasia Society, combined with Fletcher's plans for a graduated reform of the law, made me wonder whether I even wanted the legislation of what he calls 'the morality of love'. Attached to the pamphlet is a specimen application form which the seeker after death would have to send to 'the authorities' (in this case not GOD but some medical – legal committee). Can death safely be made something you apply for like a widow's pension, a traveller's visa, a set of false teeth, filling in details about your age, your illness, the degree of your pain? Is it some tenderness of guts that makes me squeamish? I should like to ask permission to die from those I love, for they alone can judge whether it is time for me to go. I would prefer that old laws should be generously applied than that new ones should be made. Otherwise in a bureaucracy one application form begets another. It might happen that when the Society had won its cause, the application form for dying would breed as its legitimate heir an application form for living. Even if this did not happen, the pressure on useless people to make them feel unwanted is intensifying. There used always to be room for an old grandfather by the chimney corner but now there is a waiting list for every bed in the hospital.

Father Roy was talking sense when he said that 'this principle, the suppression of abnormal children, first announced as a right, is in danger of being insensibly transformed into a duty', and that 'war is being prepared against the feeble and the abnormal'.

This danger is a real one and if infanticide were left to the medical services it might become a branch of eugenics and under government control. This would be an outrage upon the 'morality of love, of freedom and dignity'. For what we have to assert is that a man has a right over his own life and a shared right, in certain cases, over the lives of those that are dear to him. We cannot define these rights but love, which is not transitory, has duties and powers and will define them according as we acknowledge its authority. I believe that it would define them unmistakably for those that love little K.

Because of this, it might be better to take a life in defiance of the laws of the state and to be called a murderer than to arrange a legal death, if by so doing we allowed it to appear that the state had any right over the lives of the innocent. Though we might come to claim that even an adult belongs to those that love him, we could never admit that he belonged to such random collectivities as the state, the people, the nation, the race.

In another respect I feel myself in sympathy with the nine Catholic writers. Fletcher links artificial insemination with birth control, sterilization and abortion as 'a medically discovered way of fulfilling and protecting human values and hopes in spite of nature's failures or foolishnesses'.

Now artificial insemination seems to me to belong to a different category from these others. It is a prim suburban device for replenishing the nursery without the illicit pleasures of adultery or the illegal obligations of polygamy. It is anti-social and anti-historical, and an affront to those who believe in the ties of kinship and are ready to be bound by them. It undermines the solicitude that a man must feel for his offspring. The most care-free adulterer cannot free himself from concern for the child he has begotten, even though it may be hard for him to express it. A 'donor' on the other hand releases his child into the unknown and will never think of him again.

And artificial insemination is only the first of the scientific marvels by which the family is liable to be transformed. It is now possible for a woman, through the transplantation of fer-tilized ova, to bear children unrelated to her own family as well as to her husband's.

Would Fletcher consider such devices as ways, like artificial insemination, of 'protecting human values and hopes'. I think that they violate them and that though they may be legal, they should 'be held in utter detestation'.

How can artificial insemination be integrated into 'a morality of love', since to love the real father of one's child instead of his assumed father would bring fresh complications to an already complicated situation? If Fletcher does not see how fraudulent and furtive such arrangements are, he has not understood the true nature of family love, how it develops out of ties of blood, out of shared memories and associations, responsibilities. He does not see what a huge part the sense of continuity plays in the love we bear for our children and their children. I think of my little K as carrying with her till she dies the rudiments of tastes, qualities, talents, features, prejudices, which I and her father and mother have seen in those akin to us or observed in ourselves. Because of this sense of continuity she is called, like many others of my family, after an ancestress who lived cen-turies ago and of whom we know nothing but without whom we should none of us exist. Because of her affliction she will never be able to co-ordinate her inheritance or develop it. She is starting on a long and hopeless journey in more or less the same direction as we and ours are travelling and have travelled. She may be travelling it alone when we, who brought her into the world, are no longer there to shield and love her. Is this conviction that her destinies and ours are interwoven a neces-sary part of family love or something that can be detached from it and quite irrelevant? I can only say that it is not irrelevant for me and mine. And sometimes when I have been thinking up arguments for the legalization of infanticide, I pull myself up with the reflection: 'What business is it of theirs anyway, the doctors, the police, the judge, the jury, the hangman?' Little K is ours, irrevocably ours, in virtue of our deep involvement and I abandon myself to a vision of the future that is more like a Chinese puzzle than a dream, for even as I construct it I see all its intricate improbabilities. Yet there is no other way, at present, in which 'human values and hopes' can be protected.

VII. ORDER AND CHAOS

There is very small chance that any widespread change of opinion about these things will occur during peaceful times. Not till something desperate happens will parents of defective children dare to articulate the knowledge which they have found in their hearts, or look to others to endorse it. The average man is unconcerned. Since death and decay await us all, he might take a remote interest in euthanasia for the old and sick but he will be more likely to dodge the law when his time comes than to try to change it in advance. I cannot see that even for the elderly or diseased who wish to die, there is any likelihood of a change in the legal or religious position till the graver problem of the conscript killer has been faced. A reconsideration of this by Church or state might cause a revolution in the structure of society, as Christianity did in its first centuries. In the rebuilding of a new order, a man might recover the rights which he once abdicated to the state.

Certainly the desire for a revolution, a rebirth, is there but no one knows in which direction to look for it or how to prepare for its coming.

The state seems to wish to renounce its right to kill or to expose its citizens to be killed for causes they do not approve. Capital punishment has gone and the rights of the conscientious objector are acknowledged though not widely acclaimed.

Can it go further without laying itself open to internal decay and external assault?

In the Church too there are signs that under pressure of

science and public opinion some of its most sacred tabus are being relaxed. If birth control is permitted, a very ancient and fundamental belief about the human soul will have been abandoned. At the other end of life, science has pushed back the frontiers so far that most people can outlive their faculties. This means that the preservation of life, which was once a sacred duty, no longer appears so.

Therefore Pius XII has said that, when life is ebbing hopelessly, doctors need not try to reanimate their patient but 'may permit him, already virtually dead, to pass on in peace'. And Dr Lang, the Archbishop of Canterbury, wrote that 'cases arise in which some means of shortening life may be justified'. There are clergymen on the committees of euthanasia societies.

Yet in these directions Church and state, with their survival at stake, must move so slowly and cautiously that frequently their leaders have to appear as the enemies of the causes in which they believe. A great prelate may find it impossible to exhibit in public the rebellious wisdom and gentleness of his nature. Whatever his private views might be, he could not give public comfort to the conscript who felt no hate and refused to kill, or to the men and women who killed because they wished to spare suffering to those they loved. That is the price he pays to the people for the platform from which he is permitted to address his message *urbi et orbi* or to his nation.

The pyramidal structure of a great state or a great Church imposes prudence. By his exalted position at the apex a prince of religion is exposed to pressure which obscurer men can dodge, and, as with a general who capitulates, his surrender forces submission on men still capable of resistance. Pius XII, for well-known reasons, lagged very far behind the most enlightened of his bishops in his defence of the innocent. The bishops on their part, crippled by the weight of bonds and bargains by which their relations with the state were regulated, passed on to their priests the responsibility of protesting. The priests passed it on to the laymen. And, equally fearful of damaging the Church, the laymen passed it on to those outside the Church. Was there in all Germany a Christian who resisted Hitler as promptly, unreservedly, heroically, as the non-Christian Ossietzky? But the clerics were justified in their prudence. The pyramid still stands, a massive monument to the advantages of discretion.

But even now its security would be endangered by any serious squabble with the state. So it is unlikely that leading churchmen will ever support aggressively the rights of conscience or question unbecomingly the justice of any war in which their government is engaged. Until something happens to interrupt the easy tenor of events, this prudence is obligatory. For if the government were to grant to each citizen the right to decide who his enemy was and whether he should be killed (a right which many savages enjoy), not only would armies be in danger of disintegration but so would states and Churches. There would be chaos of a kind.

But what kind? We have been conditioned to think that even war is better than chaos or disorder. Though we do not, like many great Victorians, actually value war (Ruskin said it was 'the foundation of all the arts, all the high virtues and faculties of man'), many see it as the mother of invention, of better aircraft and nuclear discovery. And a huge number of respectable people find in it great enjoyment and liberation of spirit. In contrast few social opportunities and interesting assignations are to be offered by the disorder that results when some conflict of principle, normally inhibited, flares up into violent civil discord. And everybody condemns it. Yet the free human spirit is less enslaved by the worst kinds of social disorder than by the best kind of war. The most dreadful crimes of the century have been committed by orderly people subordinating themselves to the commonweal. When the Czechs unburied the corpses of the thousands who had been massacred at Theresienstadt, they were able to give each victim an individual tombstone, for a number had been attached to his or her big toe which corresponded to a name and an address in a carefully kept register. It was not brutal people who did this, but hundreds of selfless and dedicated morticians and stenographers. The massacres which were conducted chaotically as in the Balkan countries were not nearly so comprehensive. The killers often tired or felt queasy or amorous or compassionate or accepted bribes. Nature was able to assert itself. And nature is not evil till we make it so.

In fact fruitful ideas are often nourished by what the Organization Man calls disorder. They grow like ferns in the interstices of crumbling walls. You cannot say, as some do, that the ferns are pulling down the wall, for unless it was already collapsing the ferns would not have a foothold there.

Today, in the huge discrepancies between official belief and private behaviour, almost any revolutionary idea could comfortably take root and slowly dislodge a stone or two from the established certainties. Half of Europe is officially dedicated to the belief, which shows no sign of being fulfilled, that the state will one day 'wither away', its mission accomplished. Would it matter if the other half also came to think of states and governments as provisional, as methods of collective administration concerned with the problems that arise, when men meet each other impersonally in large numbers, with traffic, that is to say, rather than with ethic? Such a view might be more congenial to us than it is to the Russians who preach it. Things would move slowly but by degrees problems of morality and ethic, of punishment and penance, might be released, finger by finger, from the palsied and uncertain grasp of the Church and the state, and settled quietly by men who knew each other.

Maybe the right to kill is the last that the state will relinquish, but the pattern of society is changing rapidly. Consider Charles Whitman, the psychopath, who killed his mother and his wife and then climbed to the top of a tower in the University of Texas and killed and injured forty passers-by before he was himself killed by the police. Friends, relations, neighbours, all knew what he was like and might have foreseen and forestalled what happened. Do we not need dreams, ideas and plans that will strengthen the authority of those who are fond of us, or at least interested in us, and weaken the power of the remote, indifferent people who are normally appointed to judge us?

This is fantasy, of course. But the world of Auschwitz was a fantastic one, built upon evil dreams, which no one except the dreamers thought could be realized. The ordinary familiar methods failed to disperse them. We might do better with what is extraordinary and unheard of.

VIII. THE SMALL COMMUNITY

So it appears that for me and mine the situation is hopeless for many years to come. Legalism becomes increasingly more powerful than love, and religion sanctions it. The secret ways of ending life are carefully guarded by the specialist. Only a doctor can defy the law and terminate an unwanted life without being detected. Frequently, of course, he will refrain from 'respirating' a malformed infant. But in this he cannot be said to be animated by love but by certain scientific classifications.

Even in that kindly book about the Liège trial, the nine religious writers print an appendix in which the retarded are divided into four grades according to their IQ percentages. Little K belongs, I believe, because she has only two-thirds of a brain, to the lowest group of the four, and Hitler's doctors would have given her a high priority for the gas chamber. But by these physiological groupings we distort the problem and make it likely that a categorical 'No' will one day lead to a categorical 'Yes'. Science has, in fact, by reducing the significance of the individual human life, disintegrated love and impaired the rights which a man has over his own life and his child's. Almost everybody today would agree that the doctor, the judge, the clergyman and the geneticist should have greater authority over the life and death of a baby than those who begot him and bore him.

The nine French authors, dreaming of fresh fields opening up for the compassionate heart, the dedicated volunteer, have exiled themselves from reality, as I do when I speculate how I can end little K's life, which can bring only suffering to her parents and to herself. Measuring our convictions, we may be ready to believe that present reality will change more easily than they will. In the meantime I see that I cannot follow my conscience without causing complications for everybody and in particular for those I wish to help, and so I put all my proudest hopes into reverse. Because I cannot take life I become anti-life, and I pray that little K will have a sort of vegetable apathy and that she will never be so conscious of her inadequacies as to suffer for them.

But how can one wish that anyone one loves should be as stupid and helpless as possible? That is a sin of course far worse than the act which I accept as right but cannot perform, yet I am driven to it by a society which refuses to recognize the rights of love.

Moreover, I am forced to admit that till the whole structure of society changes, there are excellent reasons for this refusal. In an acquisitive society, where property is accumulated and inherited and men advertise themselves by their offspring, where labour has to be mobile and families move from place to place, it would be very easy for prudence to pass itself off as love, and for respectable people to engage in a covert war against all physical and mental non-conformity. It would be very difficult to establish that kind of community in which the fraud would be detected and 'held in utter detestation'. In an open society love is easy to simulate. One cannot trust it, and even when one can, one could not allow our social institutions to be shaped by such a trust. As democracy widens its scope and we reach towards a universal government with uniform laws, it is less and less safe to judge a man's acts by the purity of his motives. We have to be impartial, which means impersonal. In a mass society news of our actions reaches far beyond the small circle which they directly affect, so we must be punished not for what we do but also for things that are done by those unknown people who imitate us. That is to say that if we do what we know to be right, it may be something that society is forced to condemn.

Will this always be so? Can there ever be a society in which the rights of love are recognized and even the law bends before them? If so, it will necessarily be a small society. It will differ I think from the kind of society in which Aristotle preached and Hippocrates practised, because Artistotle thought it was a matter of law, not of love, that defective children should be killed. One may suspect that such laws, where they were enforced, were very loosely administered. The city-state grew up as an aggregate of many families and was itself a vastly inflated family, and its laws must have been flexible enough. Despite Aristotle, natural affection probably played a larger part in their application than eugenics. It was not the state but the parents themselves who exposed their infants on the mountain sides. All the same, good citizenship and not love was the criterion by which behaviour was judged, and if Aristotle had his way the state would have usurped the rights of the parents and made the exposure of defective children the concern of the city not of the family.

But even if we wished to, we could not recreate the city-states. Where else can we look? In our loose and inchoate society are there any traces of a submerged or nascent community in which the rule of love is observed and to whose collective judgment we could refer? There are many; but they crystallize round some specific problem and evaporate as soon as it is solved. And of course there are our families, more permanent in their mutual dependence but seldom acting as a unit. If they had the confidence and assumed the authority, it seems to me that my family and D's could judge more wisely about what concerns them intimately than any government could. And, if we considered, too, the judgment of those friends to whom we are bound as closely as by ties of blood, we should have a community as capable of deciding its own affairs as, say, Megara or Sicyon ever claimed to be.

In such a community the weight of the decision would bear most heavily on those that love most, but concern would travel outward from the centre, the focus of agony, to the periphery, and authority to endorse or dissent would be proportionate to love. If such a community were to coalesce out of chaos, I would trust it to decide wisely about little K or to form a loving background for such a decision.

But it has not coalesced and there is as yet no sign that it will. And, even if it did coalesce, how could it ever acquire legal status? This question can be illuminated by another question. How would it be possible to withold legal status from the offspring of scientific marriages, the children of sperm-filled capsules and transplanted ovaries? The answer to these questions is that the law in both cases is helpless. These matters are outside the law, and men and women must decide for themselves.

Before there is any change we shall have to live through this period of remote and impersonal control and, in the meantime, for the sake of future freedom, a greater burden than ever before will fall upon the man who refuses to conform. Politically, socially, domestically, the individual may have to make in solitude great and tragic decisions and carry them through in the teeth of a hostile and mechanical officialdom. Ossietzky and Stauffenberg, Sinyavsky, Daniels and Djilas are well-known names, but they owe their deserved celebrity, at least in part, to the publicity services of their country's enemies. In other spheres thousands of men and women will have to fling themselves fruitlessly against the barriers before they collapse. Their names will be known only to a very few, and by the time they are due to be honoured they will be forgotten.

Joseph Fletcher says that we are at the end of the theological era and that those who do not believe in personal survival after death do not fear it as much as those that do. Certainly this is true of me. As it approaches, I seldom look forward but often backward, thinking of the things I have never done, the faculties that are likely to decay before they have been used.

When I do look forward, I see a faint line becoming fainter as I draw closer to it. Beyond it I will live for a certain period in the thoughts of those I love or have influenced. This measured immortality belongs to almost everybody, but for little K the dividing-line is dim and blurred. The emptiness beyond can scarcely be more empty than that through which she is passing now. Maybe in ten or twenty years, as little K climbing very slowly has reached the highest rung she will ever reach, she will meet me there descending much more rapidly. If that were so, she would be the companion that I would choose above all others to travel back with me into nothingness.

[1967]